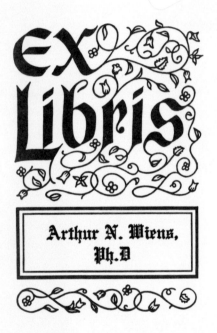

Ex Libris

Arthur N. Wiens,
Ph.D

Mind and Body:
The Psychology of
Physical Illness

Mind and Body:
The Psychology of
Physical Illness

Stephen A. Green, M.D.

1400 K Street, N.W.
Washington, DC 20005

Cover design by Sam Haltom/Another Color Inc.
Text design by Richard E. Farkas
Typeset by Donnelley/ROCAPPI
Printed by RR Donnelley & Sons

Library of Congress Cataloging in Publication Data

Green, Stephen A., 1945–
    Mind and body.

    Bibliography: p.
    Includes index.
    1. Sick—Psychology.   2. Sick—Interviews.
3. Medicine, Psychosomatic.   4. Mind and body.
5. Medicine and psychology.   I. Title.   [DNLM:
1. Disease—psychology.   2. Chronic Disease—
psychology.   3. Physician-Patient Relations.   4. Sick
Role.   WM 178 G798m]
R726.5.G74   1985   616'.001'9   85–13496
ISBN 0-88048-043-2

For Madeleine, Jessica, and Julia

Contents

Foreword

THE SCHISM BETWEEN mind and body, psyche and soma, has long been identified, studied, and even celebrated. Terms such as "psychogenic," "psychosomatic," or even "it's all in his head" abound in our vocabulary. The relationship between the mind and the rest of the body is one of fascination and importance to us for medical and psychological reasons as well as vocational and economic ones. A great deal has been written on these subjects, and no student of the healing arts can escape some exposure to discussions of the impact of mentation and attitude on physical illness.

Yet when major or chronic illness strikes an individual and calls forth a large and growing array of biomedical interventions, what place does our collective wisdom about the mind's influence on the body play in the treatment strategy? Amid dialysis treatments and the cardiac care units, bone marrow transplants and cancer chemotherapy, transplant surgery and cyclosporin therapy, who is custodian of the time-honored wisdom we possess about the effect of physical illness on the mind and, in turn, the mind on the body?

These are difficult questions and ones that do not have simple or uniform answers. In some cases, the clinicians treating seriously ill patients are exquisitely sensitive to the psychological ramifications of the conditions they are handling. In other cases, psychiatrists, psychologists, or social workers are crucial members of the medical team dealing with acute and chronic illness. Often, though, physicians and patients together labor to achieve cures or remissions without benefit of either a specialized or generalized appreciation of the psychodynamics underlying and complicating the sickness itself. The lessons of medical and nursing school are easily forgotten amid the demanding technicalities of fluid and electrolyte balance or the choice of the proper oncolytic agents to assure maximum survival time.

In this book, Stephen A. Green has set about a systematic inventory of the common issues and coping mechanisms that seriously and chronically ill patients invoke on their own. His use of extensive, personal case reporting brings his commentary to life. He then addresses the strategies available to clinicians to bridge the mind-body gap. This is not a simple task, and Dr. Green's solutions are not cookbook in nature. Rather, he provides stimulus for the clinical architects who wish to build bridges between the mind and body that will benefit both physicians and patients and make the experience—the predictably tough experience—of major illness more humane and less punishing for all involved. This is a good book and a useful one for all those who are willing to recognize the potential gulf between mind and body but are not content to leave that gulf unspanned.

Fitzhugh Mullan, M.D.

Preface

I ENTERED MEDICAL SCHOOL already committed to a future in internal medicine. Though apprehensive about the anticipated rigors of training, I hoped that responsible work would provide me with the knowledge required to pursue my intended life task: curing the sick. My preconceptions concerning the study and practice of medicine were idealistic and supremely naive.

My enthusiasm persevered during two oppressive years of wrestling with the basic sciences. Ironically, it began to falter in the early weeks of clinical clerkships, the stage of training I had longed for because it finally permitted intimate interaction with patients. My excitement was cruelly deflated by a growing realization that regardless of the well-meaning efforts of physicians, a startlingly small number of patients were ever cured. Many improved, some died; however, most continued to suffer from persisting, progressive illnesses which were at best stabilized despite all the medical interventions attending inpatient hospitalization. As the third year of my training progressed, I was badly shaken by the absurdly obvious realization that most illness is forever—regardless of the patient's motivation to get well or the physician's efforts to effect a cure. Although the lesson was new to me, it apparently has been part of the rites of passage for generations of medical students. Recalling his training in the 1930s, Lewis Thomas writes, "It gradually dawned on us that we didn't know much that was really useful, that we could do nothing to change the course of the great majority of the diseases we were so busy analyzing, that medicine, for all its facade as a learned profession, was in real life a profoundly ignorant occupation" (1983).

Nothing had prepared me for this discovery. Basic science teaching had an insidious cause-and-effect orientation. The unstated philosophy was simple: comprehensive understanding of an illness— its etiology, pathogenesis, and treatment recommendations—provided the practitioner with the requisite knowledge to cure the patient. Prior to my clinical experience, I had been too ignorant to question this underlying belief system; however, as my patient work progressed, I felt a growing resentment for having been deceived. My anger was heightened by the discovery that this conventional wisdom persisted into the clinical setting. Conversations concerning the chronic nature of illness, and the helplessness of physicians in their attempts to relieve persisting, progressive symptoms, were nonexistent. The consequences of this silence infuriated me. I witnessed repeated variations on a common scenario. Most patients initially received sympathetic and encouraging support from medical personnel—often perfunctory, but genuinely motivated. However, if the patient stagnated clinically, a remarkable transformation occurred. He or she was progressively depersonalized by caretakers who came to regard the patient more as an intellectual challenge and less as a human being. Laboratory tests and hospital charts received meticulous attention, sometimes considerably more than the individual lying in bed. Relevant articles sparked increased interest in the "case," but not in the patient. One indelible episode of my medical clerkship involved a woman who had a hypertensive encephalopathy. During the last minutes of her life, with relatives huddled around her bedside, the attending physician attempted to elicit what he presumably considered to be necessary medical data. He was completely oblivious to the priority of the communication that should have occurred between the patient and her family during her fleeting seconds of lucidity. The contrast between physician-as-technician versus physician-as-humanist was never more clear to me. This poor woman had lost her identity and consequently her dignity in the morass of the medical world. She had been objectified, defined by her particular pathology. Members of her treatment team, myself included, could recite relevant physical findings and laboratory data from memory; we knew little about the woman as a human being. That encounter marked a transition: I had become a demoralized student, increasingly disillusioned by a medical world whose atmosphere was one of institutionalized intellectual curiosity and emotional reserve. Although I recognized and respected many physicians who approached their patients with genuine empathy and humane concern, I observed that they were the exceptions.

Several weeks later I attended a case conference presented by a consultation-liaison psychiatrist. He interviewed a man who, having been admitted because of progressive weakness and fatigue, was found to have miliary tuberculosis. Although the patient responded rapidly to treatment, he seemed neither relieved nor grateful. He had become increasingly argumentative with the ward staff, prompting a psychiatric consultation. During this meeting the patient related his history intelligently but with an oppressive sadness. When questioned about his mood he became somewhat suspicious; few physicians had expressed interest in his emotional state, and he was wary of the interviewer's motivations. After gentle but persistent prodding, he responded to the question. He reported that he had recently emigrated from the South and felt isolated and frightened in a metropolis as imposing as New York City. As his strength began to falter he was unable to work; he became frightened about his ability to provide for himself and therefore sought medical attention. In spite of his subsequent improvement he was pessimistic about the future, anticipating frequent relapses and progressive debility. He feared that his disease would get worse and prove resistant to treatment and that he would die young. This fear was aggravated by a strong sense of shame about his morbid preoccupations. Additionally, he was resentful of his physicians, whom he perceived as emotionally unavailable whenever he attempted to discuss concerns about his future health. The interviewer suggested that separation from the support of family and friends would heighten anyone's concern about his or her ability to be self-sufficient. Moreover, this might cause one to want increased attention from medical personnel in an effort to substitute for the missing support of the home environment. At this point the patient began to sob. After several minutes he composed himself, made no apologies for his tears, and proceeded to talk about himself in an animated fashion. He continued, essentially uninterrupted, for the remainder of the interview. As he spoke his spirits lifted; his relief was palpable.

This was another indelible experience of medical school; in tandem with the first episode, it began my transformation from future internist to future psychiatrist. The patient's medical treatment, though successful, had seriously neglected his emotional needs. Despite physical improvement, his overall ability to function remained significantly impaired. His discussion with the psychiatrist not only addressed these concerns but helped alleviate his worry. I had witnessed an intimate interaction between patient and physician in which mutual honesty enabled the patient to gain necessary perspective concerning his illness. A physician had helped a patient merely by talking with him, or more precisely, by carefully listening to him and communicating back an empathic and accurate understanding of his plight. The patient felt less isolated and consequently less handicapped by the powerful emotions he had been unable to contend with by himself. Experiencing enhanced support, he was finally able to explore the feelings precipitated by illness and was no longer frightened that they would overwhelm him.

Reflecting on these two patients, and on later experiences, I wrote the following in an evaluation of my medical internship:

> There is an inherent failure of medical education: from the first day of medical school we are taught that the patient is a compartmentalized organism, not a human being. . . . One too easily forgets that he has feelings—fears and desires—and that his physical pathology affects those feelings and is in some part a reflection of those feelings. . . . The effect of this on the individual, and the entire system of health care, is enormously detrimental.

Unfortunately, I believe this statement to be as true today as it was fourteen years ago. Despite the efforts of many schools to provide more integrated curricula, learning to attend to patients' emotional needs is frequently lost in a highly specialized and technical medical world. As I developed professionally I continued to be disturbed by the institutionalized mind-body dichotomy of medical training. Eventually, when I was teaching a fourth-year course entitled "Psychiatry and General Medical Practice" at the Georgetown University Medical School, I found myself in a position where I could attempt to alter this philosophy. This book is an outgrowth of that experience.

In the following pages I have attempted to demonstrate that all medical illness produces emotional responses which are, in fact, an integral part of the disease process. If there is one point I wanted to make, it is this: medical personnel who ignore these psychological reactions provide suboptimal, if not detrimental, treatment. Normal and abnormal illness responses are defined and discussed, utilizing verbatim patient interviews. Of course, identifying characteristics have been altered in order to preserve anonymity and protect confidentiality.

I have relied heavily on clinical material in an attempt to illustrate as accurately as possible the existential experience of being ill. I felt this could best be accomplished by allowing patients to describe the illness states in their own words—by what they do and do not say. I subscribe to Dr. Balint's belief that editing case histories entails the risk of "weeding out most of the remnants of the emotional recesses in the mind of the reporter . . . thereby giving disproportionate emphasis to intellectual processes" (1957). Additionally, verbatim transcripts of the physician-patient interaction provide insight into the willingness of individuals to openly relate painful, distressing feelings when they sense they have a welcome ear. Following an introductory description of the interrelationship between the grief process and medical illness, five chapters review the most common illness responses, discussing each patient interview in terms of how and why the individual reacted as he had. Chapter 8 summarizes those factors that delineate the biopsychosocial medical model. The closing chapter addresses therapeutic techniques that can be utilized to help patients work through the feelings precipitated by illness. Taken as a whole, the book is intended to provide a framework for understanding and responding to the fears, needs, and wishes of individuals who become physically ill. As such it should be of general benefit to those who work intimately with patients: medical students, house officers, and nonpsychiatric practitioners, as well as related health care personnel. The book is also intended to provide specific assistance to the psychiatrist dealing with patients in the common clinical contexts: as an expert consultant to colleagues in other medical specialties, as a member of a consultation-liaison team, and as a therapist contending with the impact of physical illness on the ongoing psychotherapeutic process.

A final word—of gratitude—to those whose energy and empathy have been central to my development as a physician. My interest in psychiatry began when I was a student of Dr. Vernon Sharp, and it was solidified during my medical internship by the friendship and guidance of Dr. Don R. Lipsitt. The instruction I received during my residency training from faculty and colleagues—particularly from Drs. Elvin Semrad, Steven Sharfstein, and Sheldon Roth—has been invaluable. Those who taught me best share one common characteristic: a basic respect for patients as human beings, not merely impersonal victims of some pathologic process.

1

Biopsychosocial Medicine

IN MOST RESPECTS a bout of flu and a heart attack are vastly different experiences. The former is more of an annoyance when compared with the severity of symptoms and the threat to life accompanying heart disease. However, in one way they are identical occurrences: each produces obvious, often predictable, physical and emotional changes in the patient. Any illness, major or minor, alters an individual's homeostasis, his psychobiologic balance. The body no longer functions in an anticipated, routine fashion. This is most readily perceived by the patient in the form of physical symptoms. Pain or impaired vision, for example, can easily be observed; however, significant emotional reactions also accompany illness, and they frequently go undetected or are ignored by patient and physician. Feelings such as anger, depression, or anxiety are experienced to varying degrees and for varying lengths of time by all patients. Such emotional responses occur throughout the course of illness, from the onset to the recuperative phase. They may be mild, such as the irritability and helplessness experienced by the bedridden flu patient; they may be severe, such as the upheaval precipitated by terminal illness, as described by Kübler-Ross in her early study of death and dying (1969). The intensity of the emotional response is usually proportional to the severity of the illness; however, illness is a subjective experience, and there are many exceptions to this generalization. This is because a myriad of psychological and social factors, such as cultural influences, past medical history, the patient's personality type, or his stage in the life cycle, impact differently on an individual's physical condition to form a unique understanding of illness in his own mind. Two patients with identical symptom complexes may have dramatically different perceptions of the same illness. A relatively benign disease is readily managed by most people but may have a devastating emotional effect on others, depending on their life circumstances, past and present. That emotional effect, in turn, can adversely affect an individual's physical status, establishing a negative feedback system with a resulting psychobiologic deterioration. Correct medical treatment therefore requires an understanding of what an illness means to a particular individual at a particular time in his life. This means the physician must acknowledge the psychological and social forces that affect the patient in addition to understanding his physiologic pathology. In current terminology this is the humanistic approach to medicine. It demands attention to a patient's mind, as well as to his body, because of their inseparable interrelationship. It requires treating patients as individual human beings with unique fears, wishes, and needs rather than merely defining them by their specific organic pathology.

Unfortunately, emotional responses to illness frequently go unnoticed or are perceived by patients (and often their physicians) as abnormal occurrences which should be minimized or even ignored. In general, individuals readily recognize the impact of a disease on their bodies but are less able or less willing to recognize its impact on their minds. My experience with Eric, a twenty-year-old college student whom I met several months after he was told he had diabetes, illustrates this point in more clinical terms. Originally brought to the hospital in a coma by his roommate, he was diagnosed, treated acutely, placed on a regular regimen of insulin and a controlled diet, and discharged from the hospital within ten days. At that time he was free of noticeable symptoms, and shortly thereafter he returned to his regular classes. He felt physically well during the next two months, and his blood sugar level was in the normal range. During the same period of time, however, his roommate felt that Eric was uncharacteristically irritable and more withdrawn. He became increasingly aloof from friends, broke off with his steady girlfriend, and began failing several courses. During a routine visit with his physician, Eric reported some of these changes. He attributed them to his diabetes and, despite a feeling of physical well-being, complained that he was not receiving correct treatment. When questioned about this he also related that he had been sleeping poorly, primarily because of some disturbing dreams in which he saw himself dying in various circumstances: in battle, in an automobile wreck, or as a result of a sports injury. He mentioned that he had found himself crying "for no reason at all" on several occasions and that this frightened him. When his physician asked why he had not been told about these symptoms, Eric was surprised, as he did not classify his "outbursts" as symptoms. He admitted being ashamed of his recent behavior and became increasingly determined to hide his supposed weakness from friends and relatives. He felt that being a diabetic was hard enough—he did not want people to know he was also an "emotional basket case." He could not comprehend the drastic changes that had occurred in him during a mere six months. He had previously been a personable, gregarious young man, an honor student, and a varsity athlete who was seriously contemplating marriage. Now he described himself as "a wreck, a nothing." His only explanation was, "the diabetes is doing this to me," and he angrily demanded that the physician try some other treatment, despite the fact that the results of all his tests were normal. He precipitately decided to stop using insulin because "it wasn't helping anyway," and this resulted in a progressive increase in his blood sugar level that culminated in readmission to the hospital.

Eric was correct in attributing his recent behavior change to his diabetes, but the change was not due to the physical manifestations of the disease. Rather, the emotional impact of his illness, his growing comprehension that he was in some way different because of the diabetes, caused his sleep disturbance and distressing dreams, his episodic crying, and his diminished concentration on school work. Eric was, quite simply, depressed. When I asked him if he realized that, he replied, "Sure I'm depressed. I don't want to be sick all my life." When I asked him to elaborate on his statement he became more animated, speaking rapidly and punctuating his speech with frequent jabs of his hand. He told me he wanted to get married, but he was not sure his girlfriend "wants me the way I am," and he was afraid to discuss it with her. He wanted to go to graduate school but imagined that he would be unable to meet the academic demands. He even wondered if "any school would accept a diabetic." He told me of his love of sports. He had toyed with the idea of trying out for a professional team but now felt he would have to give up athletics altogether "because I'm so sick." He felt pitied by his colleagues, which infuriated him and caused him to drift away from friends and increasingly into his own world. He was afraid he would be denied a driver's license, because "I could black out at any time." He was also angry with his physicians because "they've been treating diabetes for so long and you'd think they'd have a cure by now." As I listened to Eric, it became increasingly evident why he felt frightened, angry, and depressed about his illness. He had legitimate concerns about his ability to lead the full life that a twenty-year-old envisions for himself. But he also had unrealistic fears about his illness; for example, a diabetic uncle had never lost his driver's license, despite a stormy thirty-year course with the disease. Eric was currently regressed, functioning far below his usual level of competence. At this point his social, academic, and athletic skills were impaired. However, he was far from the "nothing," the cripple he perceived himself to be. His whole self-image was distorted, impairing his ability to be objective about his illness and interfering with his relationship with his physician, the foundation of any successful medical treatment.

During his rehospitalization I visited Eric regularly. Initially we talked about school and the Boston Red Sox. One day, however, he asked me to "give a lecture" about diabetes. He was full of questions about the disease, questions reflecting his current fears. During our conversation (which rarely focused on the physical aspects of diabetes) he began to understand that his recent behavior was an acceptable response to the onset of illness, particularly a chronic illness. It was expected that he would be fearful of the effects of diabetes on his body and, consequently, his daily functioning. It was anticipated that he would be depressed by realizations concerning the course of the disease. It was expected that he would feel angry with friends who were not afflicted by illness and with physicians who could not restore him to his prediabetic existence. All of these emotions are normal feelings that surface when an individual becomes ill. Eric slowly understood this and permitted himself to share his burden of dealing with these feelings by openly discussing them. His so-called outbursts soon disappeared. The understanding and support provided by his physicians allowed him to put his emotions into perspective. He became increasingly able to deal appropriately with his frustration and sadness; his clinical depression remitted, and he resumed his insulin therapy. When he left the hospital he felt "strong now, strong enough to tackle my diabetes."

The feelings experienced by Eric when he learned he was diabetic—the fear, frustration, sadness, anger, helplessness, dependency, worthlessness, self-doubt—are experienced by anyone who becomes ill. These feelings are usually present to a lesser degree with minor illnesses, but they are still present. The abnormal aspect of Eric's response to diabetes was his determined attempt to hide from himself and others the presence of these feelings. Because of his particular predilection for isolating himself from people when he was under stress—a personality trait frequently seen in late adolescence—he had no outlet for a growing reservoir of negative feelings. Consequently, they began to overwhelm him. He tried to keep them to himself, communicating them in behavior, such as (angrily) withdrawing from friends, discontinuing his insulin, and demanding alternative treatment from physicians. Only when he began to ventilate and confront his fears, wishes, and needs concerning his illness did he begin realistically to assess the impact of diabetes on his life. He gradually regained control over his feelings and again felt competent, confident, and strong enough to tackle his illness aggressively as if he were facing an opponent on the football field.

As Eric's case illustrates, the disturbing emotions accompanying illness frequently go unrecognized or unacknowledged by patient and physician until they complicate medical treatment. Generally, it is only in severe illness or injury that a patient's emotional response is automatically considered an integral part of the disease. Such traumas as the residual paralysis following a stroke or the amputation of a limb so drastically affect the body that they precipitate intense emotional responses in patients. If ignored, these feelings interfere with comprehensive medical treatment. For example, angered by his debilitated, helpless state, a patient may become uncooperative and refuse treatment, such as an important diagnostic procedure or physical rehabilitative therapy. (Eric resumed insulin therapy only after his feelings of anger were dealt with correctly.) Similarly, a patient's depressed feelings may become so pronounced that he may give up and become negligent or unconcerned about his health. From this emotional perspective he becomes more dependent on those around him and is less likely to assist in his own care, and his eventual return to work or social functioning becomes that much more difficult. These situations may be extreme in degree, but they highlight a universal truth in the practice of medicine: patients' emotions affect response to treatment and, consequently, the course of illness. Another way of stating this is that all medicine is both psychosomatic and somatopsychic; that is, the interaction of physiologic and psychological processes insures that any pathology affecting the soma (body) also affects the psyche (mind) and vice versa. If this is not understood by the physician and patient, the patient will not receive optimal care; he may even suffer unnecessarily.

Consider this proposition in terms of heart disease, one of the most pervasive health problems affecting Americans. Emergency treatment of a heart attack is directed toward physical symptoms, such as relieving pain, controlling an abnormal heart rhythm, or minimizing complications caused by the decreased flow of blood throughout the body. At this stage of illness, the patient is forced to be passive, a consequence of his weakened malfunctioning heart as well as the prescribed regimen of bed rest and sedation. He can do little more than place his life in the hands of others; however, although he is physically immobilized, his mind is racing as he contemplates the future. He asks himself if he will die. He wonders if survival will bring pronounced physical limitations. He thinks about the potential effect heart disease will have on his work, his family life, his sexual functioning—in short, his daily life. He considers the cost of illness, both in terms of medical expenses and lost income. He wonders if his physicians are competent. He has scores of such questions and concerns, and as he ponders them he becomes flooded with emotions. He is fearful of dying, depressed at the prospect of potential handicap, angry that his illness has interrupted his life, and self-recriminating about his apparent neglect of his health. These are all normal feelings, and they are as legitimate and important in overall treatment as are clear-cut physical symptoms, such as anginal pain, or objective diagnostic data, such as an electrocardiogram. Indeed, they are part of his disease because of the continual feedback, or reactive sequences, between soma and psyche. Myocardial ischemia causes physical symptoms that precipitate the emotional response noted above. The emotions, in turn, aggravate the physical pathology. Excessive anxiety, with its accompanying adrenergic response, may precipitate or enhance cardiac irritability. Depression can retard the body's normal immunologic response (Amkraut and Solomon 1974) and, consequently, the body's ability to combat an active disease process.

Additionally, depression may so undermine the resolve to improve that the patient insidiously succumbs to his disease by just giving up, along the model of Engel (1968). To repeat, the mind and body are integrally connected, and if the emotional response to physical illness is not dealt with, the patient's *psychological and physical* well-being suffers. Dealing with emotional responses to illness requires the clinician's disciplined adherence to humanistic medicine, especially as the medical world continues to evolve into a progressively depersonalized environment of technology and specialization that is decreasingly attentive to patients' emotions.

Proper medical treatment requires an understanding of what an illness means to a particular individual at a particular time in his life. This is not a difficult task; it merely requires listening to patients and understanding what they communicate in words and by their silence. This book is designed as a framework for achieving such an understanding.

2

The Grief Process and Illness

IT IS PART of the human condition to suffer losses. The death of a loved one or losses of self-esteem that accompany disappointments, such as professional setbacks or rejection in love, are experienced by all. In the vocabulary of psychiatry, the normal response to these losses is a grief reaction, a limited period of mourning during which the person adjusts to the particular loss experienced. Grieving occurs in well-delineated stages of denial, anger, depression, and acceptance or resolution. Predictable emotional, and often physiologic, changes accompany each phase. Ideally, at the end of the grief process the individual stabilizes at a level of functioning that is optimal given his particular loss. To view this overall process in clinical terms, consider the response to the universal experience of a death in the family.

Upon first learning that a loved one has died, the initial reaction is denial. The bereaved gather to comfort one another, and their shared sorrow triggers an outpouring of emotion characterized by such statements as "Oh no, it can't be" and "I saw him this morning and he looked fine." A more marked example of denial is the shocked disbelief that some mourners demonstrate. Numbed by the news, they seem incapable of reacting or unable to understand. They think, or hope, that some terrible mistake has occurred, and they ask the physician if he is certain the person is dead. Intellectually they know the tragedy is real, but they are not willing or able to accept it emotionally. This phase of grieving is usually brief, lasting a matter of hours. The reality of the loss sinks in, and the bereaved experience a growing comprehension that a loved one is gone forever. Some degree of denial usually persists for several days; those grieving become preoccupied with the image of the deceased, and although they know he is dead, they may anticipate his return from work or imagine they see him walking on the street.

Denial gives way to a period of anger. At this point the bereaved begin to appreciate the full intensity and range of emotions that are partially concealed during the initial shock. They feel irritable, resentful, argumentative, and even rageful toward people around them. This period basically reflects an attempt to make sense out of death, to find someone or something to blame for their anguish. Consequently, angry feelings are focused in many directions. Those grieving feel a generalized, global anger and condemn the injustice, the unfairness of life. Feelings of anger may be directed more specifically, for example, at the physician for presumed negligence or insensitivity to the needs of the deceased. The bereaved may be angry with themselves, self-critical of real or imagined failure to be sufficiently loving and supportive to the deceased during his life or period of illness. Hostility is also commonly felt toward the dead person, fostered by a sense of abandonment. The loneliness of mourning invites fleeting accusations toward the deceased because he left the family to suffer the pain of his passing. Although longer than the period of denial, this stage is also relatively short, usually lasting from several days to several weeks.

As the initial emotional turmoil accompanying death begins to wane, the bereaved become increasingly sensitive to the impact of their loss. A growing sadness evolves, which characterizes the depression phase of the grief reaction. This stage, with pronounced emotional and physical components, most readily comes to mind when recalling a period of grieving. The most characteristic emotional change is a pervasive sadness, with episodes of crying that occur either spontaneously or are precipitated by memories of the deceased. (Less commonly, shifts in mood may produce manic, hyperactive behavior or heightened anxiety.) Mourners usually feel empty, isolated, despairing, and helpless, thinking it impossible to carry on with their lives alone. They experience a generalized social withdrawal, lacking interest in any activities apart from family matters. They are bored and increasingly disinterested in social activities or professional responsibilities. Preoccupied with the memory of the deceased, they spend a great deal of time reminiscing, recalling shared experiences both good and bad. Obvious physical changes accompany this phase of grief, including difficulty in sleeping, disinterest in eating, gastrointestinal symptoms, impaired concentration, forgetfulness, decreased libido, and increased lethargy and fatigue. Existing physical illnesses may become aggravated—an ulcer may act up or anginal chest pain may occur more frequently—or new symptoms, often vague aches and pains, may arise. These physical symptoms are a representation of our feeling state; for example, a generalized withdrawal from daily life is reflected in decreased appetite or diminished libido. More than any other part of the grief process, the depression stage is a time when the energies of the bereaved person are most clearly directed toward himself. He spends enormous amounts of time and emotional energy acknowledging and experiencing a new psychological equilibrium that prepares him to continue life without the love and support of the deceased.

The grieving process reaches a conclusion in the acceptance or resolution stage. At this point the intensity of feelings about the deceased progressively diminish. The bereaved person places those feelings—both positive and negative—in some perspective. He better understands the good and bad aspects of his attachment to the deceased and ultimately reaches an emotional resolution of that relationship. This does not mean he forgets the person; that is neither possible nor desirable. In simple terms, he comes to the harsh conclusion that life must continue despite his tragic loss. As this emotional readjustment occurs, it is reflected behaviorally. The bereaved person begins to emerge from a shell of grief and finds himself with a renewed interest in life. He becomes more energetic, resuming previous activities and rekindling friendships. In essence he redirects toward other people and interests the emotional energy he previously shared with the deceased. Daily behavior becomes more routine and more normal, as does physiologic functioning. The physical symptoms that characterized the depression stage diminish and eventually disappear. At the end of the grieving process the bereaved person accepts the fact that life is forever different because a beloved person is gone. However, he also recognizes his strength and ability to carry on and even enjoy future happiness.

Normal grief, then, is a comprehensive psychophysiologic response to loss. Grieving enables human beings to appreciate a loss emotionally as well as intellectually. Rather than just dispassionately programming a death into our brains via a process akin to filing data into a computer, we react with our whole being. Our minds and bodies are affected as we readjust to a world that is missing someone very dear to us. This process of re-equilibrating is normal; it is not merely anticipated, it is required. Failure to adapt to such losses is restricting, if not harmful. People unable to accept the death of a loved one can spend the rest of their lives stagnating, reminiscing, and living in the past, speculating on what might have been as everyday life slips by. Some individuals are so totally nonaccepting of such losses that they retreat into a world of despair and themselves die shortly after their beloved. Normal grief, then, affords us the opportunity to examine and place into perspective a wide range of feelings following a painful loss. This allows us to carry on our lives without an excessive or debilitating emotional burden.

Impaired health is another type of loss shared universally by human beings. It may be experienced concretely, as with a pronounced illness that causes permanent changes in physical status. Blindness or the amputation of a limb are readily recognizable physical deficits. They require the patient to acknowledge loss of health in a literal sense; he is lacking functionally or anatomically and consequently is forced to suffer obvious restrictions of his independence. Even when illness is minor, causing no visible or lasting changes in one's physical status, it often precipitates feelings of loss. This is because sickness has a symbolic, as well as real, impact on individuals. In the most general sense, the symbolic meaning of all illness forces the patient to abandon his childhood notion of omnipotence—a tremendous loss. He is reminded of his own mortality, forced to give up the infantile belief that he will forever be well and the fantasy that he will live indefinitely. This simple but staggering truth frequently crosses every person's mind when he or someone close to him is ill. After having weathered the flu or a fractured wrist, one feels more vulnerable, more a victim of physical ailments which are often unexplainable and unpredictable in their onset, course, and response to treatment. This is usually not a persistent, conscious feeling that affects one's life on a day-to-day

basis. However, such concerns are incorporated into our consciousness as we mature, and our recognition of them is clearly enhanced
by an episode of illness.

Illness also has specific symbolic meanings for patients. Each of us
experiences the state of ill health idiosyncratically and, consequently, assesses the losses brought about by illness from a highly
subjective viewpoint. The onset of anginal pain in an active,
competitive, athletic young man is viewed as a significant threat to
his social, occupational, and recreational life. The potential losses he
could suffer are staggering for him to imagine. However, this same
symptom might be viewed with a calm bordering on indifference by
an elderly, sedentary man who lost both parents to gastrointestinal
cancer. He may stoically accept cardiovascular symptoms as a fact
of later life, especially if they only minimally affect his daily
activities. On the other hand, an episode of cholecystitis, or even
constipation, may greatly distress him. Each of these symptoms
could be perceived as the first signal of his mortality. Illness, then,
has a highly personal meaning that derives from the interplay
between the patient's physical pathology, his intrapsychic life, and
the supports and stresses of his social context. These factors combine
to form standards by which a patient evaluates illness. They are
subjective criteria for an extremely personalized measurement of the
losses he experiences because of his particular pathology.

Whether impaired health is experienced in the literal sense as a
result of clear limitations in physical functioning, or in the more
abstract symbolic sense, it precipitates the same psychological
response: illness is accompanied by a natural grieving process, which
is analogous to the grief reaction caused by the death of a loved one,
during which the patient mourns his previous state of health. Illness
forces the individual to acknowledge and confront his new level of
physical functioning. The subsequent working through of feelings
attendant on this realization permits an acceptance of the illness.
This is reflected in the reestablishment of an emotional equilibrium,
as well as the implementation of requisite therapeutic changes in the
patient's life-style. And just as incomplete grieving of the loss of a
loved one can progress to emotional illness, nonacceptance of
physical illness by an individual can result in suboptimal medical
care. The reluctance of ulcer or heart patients to admit to themselves that they are not as healthy as they used to be may promote
dietary indiscretions which can precipitate bouts of crippling
abdominal pain or congestive heart failure. Such patients actually

aggravate their medical problems because of an inability to put into perspective all the feelings precipitated by the illness.

The following interview illustrates the normal grief process that accompanies physical illness. Gary L., a fifty-year-old nurse, suffered from persistent kidney infections for more than a decade. At the time of our meeting he was hospitalized for evaluation of his declining renal function; however, as he revealed in the opening statement, uncontrollable hypertension was currently his overriding concern. Although we had not met prior to the interview, he agreed to be seen on teaching rounds after being informed that I was a psychiatrist interested in discussing his medical history, including the progression of his illness, his response to treatment, and his general outlook about being sick. Gary L. was spontaneous and thorough in articulating his emotional status during the various stages of his illness.

Doctor (D): How are you doing?

Gary L. (P): Well, my blood pressure is going up instead of coming down. It was 162/102 this morning. It had been lower than that. The last time I really made a check it was 142/80, sometimes up to 90.

D: In the past few days it's gone up?

P: I can't honestly say that, because I haven't taken it in quite some time. I haven't been taking it since I first saw Dr. D., which was a couple of months ago.

D: Why are you in the hospital now? We can start from there.

P: I'm in for evaluation of a kidney problem.

D: What's the problem?

P: That's what I'm trying to find out. I have had a history of infections. When they first started, somehow I think I never really got over them. It just got worse, and finally I was hospitalized for kidney stones, and the stones in my ureters were removed. There was one in the left kidney at that time. Since that time, in a matter of ten years, I've developed another one.

D: How do you know?

P: Because I've been followed and had x-rays.

D: Do you have any symptoms?

P: No. I've had cystoscopy and retrograde IVPs [intravenous pyelograms] done also—until I became allergic to the iodine during the IVP, so they had to resort to a flat plate.

D: This all began ten years ago?

P: About twelve years ago.

D: How old are you now?

P: Fifty.

D: How did it begin? What happened?

P: The blood pressure or the kidney?

D: In general.

P: I just had a series of infections and was hospitalized. It just kept getting worse, and I went to several different doctors and finally was hospitalized. And at that time I had had several bouts of really severe pain—side pain—to the point that I was taken to the emergency room twice, and they x-rayed me and didn't see anything. But when I was admitted and they did the cystoscopy and retrogrades, they found the stones in both ureters.

D: And you were operated on?

P: Yes.

D: That gave you relief?

P: Well, they were able to remove the stones in both of the ureters and felt that considering there was damage to both of the kidneys, they felt it was better to just leave the stones in the kidney alone because they felt the stones wouldn't be causing any problems.

D: The pain went away?

P: Yes. But I was on medications for a long time.

D: What medications?

P: I was on Keflex at that time for quite a long time. Then I was on Mendelamine for years until that didn't seem to be doing the job anymore.

D: You started getting more infections?

P: Yes.

D: How long were you without symptoms and the urine was not infected?

P: It was never really not infected. But I was symptom free for a couple of years.

D: What happened after those two years?

P: I developed a really bad infection. I was in bed for about one week to ten days. And after that I still stayed on the Mendelamine. He tried to change me and I didn't respond to the medication, so he put me back on the Mendelamine. And I stayed on that, and it was at that time that I really started having problems with my blood pressure. I didn't have any problem, really, but I just by chance had it checked where I was working and it was 180/90 at that time. So then I was put on different medications—diuretics—while they tried to lower the blood pressure. But it just kept going up until finally it was checked one day and it was 240/120. And then I went into the hospital for evaluation.

D: Who checked it? Your doctor or someone at work?

P: It was one of the nurses, then I was checked by the doctor.

D: Had you been followed by a doctor for the high blood pressure?

P: Yes.

D: And how often would you see your doctor?

P: Not very often, because I felt fine.

D: You had no symptoms?

P: Well I had headaches, but I didn't feel it was associated with the blood pressure.

D: You've had headaches during your lifetime?

P: Yes, tension headaches. I've also had migraines. I have one today.

D: How often do you get them?

P: I haven't gotten them for years until this one developed. I'm sure it was related to the medication.

D: So for nine or ten years you've had some headaches, but you didn't think they were connected to your hypertension. Any other symptoms? Shortness of breath, dizziness, anything?

P: No.

D: Then you went back into the hospital?

P: I saw a different doctor at that time. He put me back into the hospital and did an evaluation of the blood pressure, and at that time I was put on medication. And then I was followed every couple of months.

Despite a headache and obvious fatigue, Gary L. was personable and cooperative as he related his medical history. During this initial part of the interview he talked of his kidney disease—renal stones and repeated infections—which had been persistent and progressive for twelve years. He had had multiple diagnostic procedures, including specialized x-rays (intravenous pyelograms) which eventually caused an allergic reaction to the radiologic dye. Various antiobiotics had been prescribed, none of which effectively eradicated his chronic infection. With the exception of one successful surgical procedure, medical treatment neither cured nor significantly impeded his illness. At the time of the interview, he was hospitalized for evaluation of pronounced hypertension, most likely an insidious consequence of his kidney problems.

Despite some obvious concern about a persistently elevated blood pressure, Gary L. seemed determined, even positive, as he related his gloomy saga. He displayed some irritation, primarily when discussing the chronic nature of his problems and the inability of his physicians to cure him, but this seemed a reasonable, understandable emotion. His major annoyance stemmed from the fact that he was stuck in the hospital; he was inconvenienced—as he had been many times before by diagnostic studies and hospitalizations—and anxious to be discharged so that he could proceed with his everyday life.

The interview continues with Mr. L.'s description of the first acutely life-threatening consequence of his illness. While discussing his heart attack, he clearly describes the stages of the grief process that accompanies medical illness.

D: Is that what's been going on over the past nine years?

P: Well, apparently the blood pressure wasn't controlled too well because I had a slight heart attack about five or six years ago.

D: Could you tell me something about that?

P: You want to know what happened?

D: Yes. The circumstances.

P: I had been working. It was early in the morning. I was getting the medicines ready. I developed a pain which I thought was indigestion. And it was really bad. I kept waiting for it to pass and it didn't. But I had all those patients to get the medicines out, so I tried to do that, and finally the pain was so bad that I couldn't so I called and did get my relief. Then I went over to see the doctor in the next building. He checked me and said he thought it was just a chest inflammation and sent me home to bed and I went to bed. I was feeling bad. The pain would come and go. The next day it was still really bad so I called him up and he told me I was being neurotic. So I let that go. I was changing jobs at the time and I was at the new job, going through a couple of weeks of orientation which meant that I wasn't doing anything but sitting. Then one day, near the end of orientation, we had to work on the units and I had to push one of the patients up to the infirmary in a wheelchair and there was an incline and it started all over again. At that time I went back to the doctor who had been checking me for my blood pressure, and he listened to what I told him and did an electrocardiogram.

D: What happened then?

P: Then he said he'd make arrangements to put me in the hospital. I was really unnerved and he gave me Valium, and even that didn't help much and it got so bad that that night the pain was really severe. There was another doctor on call—a doctor I had worked with in the hospital—and he said he thought I was having another heart attack and I had better get into the hospital right away. But I told him . . .

D: You mean you weren't in the hospital.

P: No. I was at home waiting to be admitted. So he wanted me to go into the hospital that night. The doctor I was seeing was not on the staff there, and I told the covering doctor that my doctor was getting a bed for me. He said I think you're crazy and gave me some medication for pain and it was pretty bad all night. But when it got to be 7:30 in the morning and I thought he'd be up, I had my wife call him and then I went right to the hospital.

D: Why did you wait overnight?

P: Oh, because I didn't want to wake him up.

D: What do you think of that now?

P: I was lucky.

D: The only reason you didn't call him was because you didn't want to wake him up?

P: Yes. That's right.

D: You *were* lucky. You went into the hospital and then what happened?

P: I was put in ICU for seven days.

D: Were they just observing you? Did you have any complications of the heart attack?

P: Apparently I was having arrhythmias. And I was being medicated, getting oxygen. I was having a lot of pain. Then after seven days they felt I was well enough to be transferred out of the ICU. And also I was going crazy in that room with no windows and nothing but monitors to look at.

D: What do you mean you were going crazy?

P: I was just getting more and more depressed. It's a very depressing experience to be in one of those. Particularly if you're well enough that you know what's going on.

D: How often did your wife come in and visit?

P: They let her come in quite a lot.

D: You went out to the wards afterwards. How long were you in the hospital totally?

P: A month.

D: Then you came home to recuperate?

P: Yes. I stayed home one month and then went back to work.

D: Was that what the doctor ordered?

P: He agreed that I could go back.

D: How did the month on the ward go? Anything exceptional about that?

P: I was awfully depressed, terribly depressed.

D: What thoughts were going through your mind?

P: Well, I felt I was pretty young to have something like that. I don't know, I just didn't seem to handle it very well.

D: You were pretty young you say . . . remind me when this was.

P: Six or seven years ago.

D: Any other things that went through your mind while you were in the hospital?

P: Yes. I had just started a new job, and I was afraid they wouldn't hold it for me and that I . . . the second thing that I was afraid of was that I wouldn't be able to handle it. I figured I'd recover, but I just felt working where I was that I had to be able to carry my own weight.

D: You were afraid you wouldn't be as active as you'd have to be?

P: Yes. I work with older people.

D: Did you go back to that job?

P: Yes! (*obviously proud*)

D: Are you still there?

P: No. I was there three years. I chose to leave.

D: So you were depressed about being able to keep up with the pace required. Anything else?

P: No. I don't think so.

D: When did you get over that? The depression.

P: Probably when I got out of the hospital. When I was at home I was all right after a while. I felt OK.

D: There was something about being a patient in the hospital that got you down?

P: Yes. It does every time.

D: What kind of things get you down?

P: Uhm. It's very hard to be on the other side.

D: What makes it hard?

P: Probably because you know just enough to keep you worried. Not enough, but just about enough.

D: So that you think in your mind what things could be going on.

P: Well, I know enough to realize some of the things. I think I get mostly upset when I realize that there's really nothing I can do about it.

D: Feeling helpless about it?

P: Yes.

D: It's been that way for a number of years. Yet you've been carrying on. Right?

P: Yeah. Right.

D: Are you the type of person that likes to be in charge of things and keep functioning.

P: I like to keep functioning. I don't know if I like to take charge. But I really like to keep going.

D: Actually, I mean to take charge of yourself.

P: Oh yes. Definitely. I've always been that way. Very much so.

D: So it's the helpless feeling that gets you depressed. You feel depressed when you're in the hospital.

P: Yes.

D: Do you feel depressed outside the hospital?

P: I don't feel depressed when I'm outside of the *bed* (*emphasized*). The hospital itself doesn't bother me.

D: You mean just walking around you feel all right.

P: I mean when I am a patient I feel depressed. When I am working it's different . . . I like to keep functioning.

Gary L. vividly described the range of emotions he experienced after his heart attack. His initial denial, the first stage of the grieving process, was pronounced. Remember that he is a trained nurse, attuned to signs and symptoms of medical problems. When he developed chest pain he accepted the diagnosis of chest inflammation, even though he knew heart disease was a common consequence of hypertension and that chest pain was a cardinal symptom of a heart attack. When the pain persisted overnight he accepted the doctor's insensitive—and inaccurate—assessment that he was being neurotic, even though he had never dramatized or exaggerated any previous medical problems. Finally, when his clinical condition deteriorated, the night before his scheduled admission to a hospital, he refused to call his doctor because "I didn't want to wake him." This behavior, which seems irrational in retrospect, merely reflected his wish to ignore or minimize the obvious indications of illness. It reflected his denial.

During this part of the interview, Gary L. did not spontaneously report the feelings of anger that surface when denial breaks down. However, when one of the students questioned him about his hospital stay, Mr. L. clearly revealed some justified irritation. When asked what he thought of the physician who called him neurotic, he smiled grimly and said, "Oh, I don't know if I would have avoided hospitalization if I had seen another doctor. But I'm not going back to him." He added loudly, "He just wasn't responsible. He was a bad doctor."

In describing the depressed phase of the grieving process, Gary L. was most explicit. He reported some common concerns about illness that depress patients. He thought he was "pretty young" to have a heart attack and was confronted with this loss of health at an early age. He was also worried about his work: would he retain his job during a prolonged recuperation? Would he be physically able to handle it, or any other job, in the future? But aside from these anticipated concerns, Mr. L.'s feelings of helplessness greatly augmented the overall stress of his heart attack. He was an active, independent individual. Confinement to bed stripped him of his autonomy and caused him to feel "terribly depressed." His helplessness was also depressing because he was knowledgeable about medicine and, as he put it, "well enough to know what's going on," yet there was nothing he could actively do to improve his health. He had to rest passively in bed and place himself completely in the hands of his physicians and fate.

The steady remission of Gary L.'s depression as he convalesced at home was the first indication that he had progressed into the acceptance stage of his illness. But this phase of the grieving process was best revealed when he discussed his return to work. Becoming brighter and more animated as he spoke, he told me of his return to his previous job, where he remained for several years until he decided to move on. He had survived a life-threatening illness and had succeeded in putting his fears and concerns associated with that episode behind him. Neither his physical nor his emotional state prevented him from retaining active control of his professional career. As Mr. L. put it, "When I am a patient I feel depressed. When I'm working it's different—I like to keep functioning." Unfortunately, as the remainder of the interview indicates, his daily functioning has increasingly been affected by his kidney disease.

D: Would you say that you generally have not been depressed over the past few years?

P: I don't think I have been. The doctor I went to—I'd see him routinely—he'd do all the laboratory tests and would say, "Now you call me in two days and I'll give you the results." And I'd call him and he'd say, "Everything looks all right. Nothing to worry about." And that's what I heard all the time. And then when I started the job I have now, I got access to getting my own lab work done. And I could see the results. And it was at that time that the doctors at my job saw the results and wanted to know why I hadn't been doing something about it. Did I realize what the results were. And I said I guessed they were not normal, but the doctor told me everything was, that I was doing all right. They would just shake their heads.

D: They wouldn't believe it.

P: No.

D: What results, tests, are you talking about?

P: BUN, creatinine.

D: What were they?

P: I can't recall, but they were very much more than they should be. What brought me to the doctor was that I developed a kidney infection, and I was treated for that. A month later I developed another one. Then I stayed on the medicine longer, and I still got a third infection while I was on the medication.

D: I see.

P: So then they sent me to a urologist, and then I was referred to Dr. S.

D: How long have you seen Dr. S.?

P: I just saw him once, just before I was admitted.

D: This is the first time?

P: Yes.

D: What are the plans for you in the hospital now?

P: I was only supposed to be in three days, and I was to just have tests. It's gotten to be longer and longer, and my blood pressure has stayed up. I still haven't heard anything.

D: No one has told you anything.

P: They said that they didn't know anything yet. I haven't seen Dr. S. in all the time I've been here.

D: Have you asked to see him?

P: No, because they said he'd come when the tests were done.

D: Who is "they"? The house staff?

P: Yes, and some of the men who are working with him.

D: Who are they?

P: I can't remember their names. There have been so many people in and out of here.

D: So you're left in the dark here. People haven't told you anything, and you've just been waiting around.

P: Right. Well, they've been doing tests. They've been doing x-rays.

D: How do you react to this, to your being kept waiting?

P: Well, I understand that they have to have everything in. I feel I should have been told something by now. But I assume they're doing what they can.

D: Do you feel anything in particular? Any specific type of feeling about this?

P: Probably uneasy, worried.

D: You think the fact you haven't been told is because they may know something.

P: No, that never entered my head. I just felt they probably didn't have all of the information, and I'm sure they will tell me when they know.

D: So you're uneasy because you don't have the data now.

P: I think what's really bothering me is that my blood pressure is up. It's one thing to have it up and not know what it is, but it's another to have it taken six times each day and know what it is and that it's not coming down but it's going up.

D: It's steadily been going up?

P: No, the highest it has been is 180/102, I guess.

D: And before you came in here . . .

P: I don't know. When I would go for my checks it would be 155/80 or

90. Ninety is what it's been mostly, recently. But . . . I've been in here for my blood pressure to go down. It's irritating just lying here, with the blood pressure going up, going the wrong way.

D: Yes?

P: It's no one's fault; it's just happening. I get annoyed, and then that passes and I'm depressed. I'm in the hospital, in bed in the hospital, not getting better, and that depresses me—I told you that already.

After recuperating from his heart attack, Gary L. returned to work and felt well for approximately five years. He thought his medical problems had stabilized, and he had no clinical symptoms of infection or hypertension; however, his kidney disease was actually progressing insidiously. He implied that the physician he went to for routine checkups withheld from him the fact that his kidneys were failing. This may have been the case, or possibly his clinical condition declined rapidly and was first discovered when he changed jobs. In any event, when he did learn of the abnormal results of his blood tests, denial was the first response. He refrained from seeking medical treatment until he had tangible symptoms, namely, those of infection.

Hospitalization was required because of a succession of kidney infections, the last one occurring while he was receiving antibiotics. Mr. L.'s angry feelings, characteristic of the next phase of grieving, were obvious and were directed primarily at physicians. He was angry at previous physicians for not curing him, for incorrectly treating him, or for not providing him with a true and accurate assessment of his condition. He was angry at his current physician for not yet seeing him in the hospital, prolonging his hospital stay beyond the promised three days, withholding the test results from him, and not preventing his blood pressure from rising. His anger, though reflected in the text, was evidenced more by his manner during this part of the interview. He spoke loudly, in clipped, curt sentences, and was sarcastic and somewhat challenging.

As our meeting ended, Gary L. talked of becoming depressed in the hospital, indicating his progression toward the third stage of the grieving process. We know nothing of the acceptance stage, because the final treatment had not yet been formulated, and the options were diverse, ranging from controlling his blood pressure with medications to surgical removal of his kidney. If neither approach was successful, he faced the prospect of renal dialysis. Mr. L. could hardly be expected to resolve his feelings about his current uncontrolled hypertension when he did not know what he would be required to accept in the form of continued treatment. However, given his medical history of the past twelve years, particularly his response to a heart attack at the young age of forty-four, one has reason to be optimistic about the ultimate adjustment to his illness. He is an assertive, striving man, who has kept fighting in order to preserve his independence and ability to function in as normal a fashion as possible.

In relating his feelings about chronic illness, Gary L. vividly described the grieving process, with its shifting emotional stages, that accompanied his heart attack and his current hospitalization for high blood pressure. These individual bouts with illness precipitated a wide range of intense feelings: anxiety about his persistently elevated blood pressure, anger at his physicians, depression caused by his passivity while in the hospital, pride that he continued to function effectively despite his illness. And with the passage of time he was able to put these emotions into perspective. In effect, he was able to say to himself: "The physical damage to my kidneys has had a tremendous impact on my life, forcing me to experience a lot of emotions. Fortunately, I've been able to become accepting of those feelings. I understand the implications of my illness and realize that I have no choice but to continue living my life and not dwell on the negative." This is the purpose of the grieving process; it allows one to adjust emotionally to losses. In the case of medical illness, these are changes in one's physical status, which affect the extent and degree of independent functioning, and changes in one's perception of one's own mortality.

What if someone is unable to accommodate emotionally to illness? Earlier in this chapter when discussing the normal reaction to the death of a loved one, I mentioned that some people simply cannot accept such losses. They may spend the remainder of their lives stagnating, withdrawing from society, and reminiscing about the past, rather than continuing to enjoy the richness of life. Or they may spend the rest of their days angrily complaining about the unfairness of life. They become handicapped by their emotions as unresolved feelings interfere with daily experiences. It is as if the individual's view of life is obscured by a veil of emotions he has not come to terms with. In this same fashion, unresolved feelings about physical illness can readily evolve into an emotional burden that adversely affects the patients' overall health by either directly interfering with specific medical treatment or indirectly fostering the patient's general neglect of his physical well-being. In either circumstance the patient's daily functioning is inhibited, with ramifications that affect his family life, social relationships, and professional work. Recall the case of Eric, whose angry feelings predominated his response to illness. He was so enraged at being stricken with diabetes that he eventually disregarded his physician's orders and had to be rehospitalized. Only by gradually becoming aware of the existence and appropriateness of his emotions, particularly feelings of anger and depression, was he able to assess accurately the impact of diabetes on his life and continue to work collaboratively with his physicians.

The following segment of an interview offers a more detailed example of an abnormal psychological response to medical illness. Emily B. is a seventy-one-year-old woman with an eleven-year history of hypertension. She was admitted to the hospital for her second episode of congestive heart failure within six weeks. Her cardiac status had previously been well controlled by a regimen of antihypertensive medication, diuretics, and digoxin. Her physicians were puzzled by her present condition; a relatively mild cardiac impairment did not adequately explain the recent deterioration in her physical condition. While talking about previous hospitalizations, Mrs. B. revealed the most significant aspect of her medical history, the episode that affected all of her subsequent health care.

P: I had the amputation in 1971.
D: Why did you need that?
P: Phlebitis.
D: How did you get that?
P: I don't know.
D: How did you notice it? What was happening?
P: Well, I was having pains in the leg, and I was already a patient here for the high blood pressure. Every week or two I was here. And, uh, I noticed that I was getting pain in my foot and my leg. I told the doctors about it, and they gave me pills from time to time. I think they were thinking about the blood pressure and the heart more than they were paying attention to my leg. When they came to the realization that there was something wrong with my leg, they had to take it off right away. It had gone too far.
D: So it wasn't all that sudden, but it was a surprise.
P: It was a surprise because I did not expect ever that the leg would be off. And I was telling them all the time about the pain and discomfort that I was having with the leg. I really don't think that I hollered

loud enough. But I was doing the best I could, I thought. It just slipped by them. And then, coming to the clinic, I wouldn't see the same doctor all the time. And the last time I came to the clinic about the leg, my doctor wasn't in. And then another doctor, a surgeon, said, "You are so-and-so's patient, and I can't take you down to the x-ray today. He was going to take you to the x-ray department, but I won't take you. I'll wait until next week, and he can take you down." So then when he told me that, I must have been back home one or two nights, and I called the doctor and said my foot was getting dead on the side and was killing me. And he said, "Come right away, come right away. I think you have phlebitis." That was the first time that they said that. And I came into the emergency room and was here in the hospital . . . he admitted me right away. Then about two days later the leg was gone. Didn't have time to make x-rays or do anything about it. And that is one of the things that has been on my mind ever since. I mean I haven't been able to rest good thinking about this.

D: What do you mean by that?

P: Uh. It worries me that the leg is off and had to go so quickly . . . without . . . I felt . . . the proper care. I think before my leg was amputated this way I should have had x-rays and somebody paying attention, special attention, to the leg.

D: Do you think they neglected you?

P: I do.

D: And had they not done that, you feel you wouldn't have needed the amputation?

P: I might not have needed the amputation. I'm not sure.

D: There's no way to be sure.

P: No. I might not have needed it had I got the proper treatment in time. But they were just taking the blood pressure and checking the heart and giving me new pills.

D: Even though you had told them your leg was bothering you?

P: Yes.

During the next part of the interview, Emily B. related her cardiac history at length. She detailed the limitations of her current life, attributing them to her disease. Many complaints sounded like depressive symptomatology, so I pursued that area with her.

D: How has your appetite been?

P: Well, recently it hasn't been so good.

D: Why is that?

P: Well, I started off to try and diet by cutting down—I didn't take any pills or anything. I just denied myself certain things, like sweets and the pies. And I just got to the point where I didn't want to eat. I just refused.

D: When did you start doing this?

P: Almost four years ago.

D: Do you sleep well at night?

P: Sometimes. And there are times when I stay awake all night.

D: Why is that?

P: I don't know. I don't have any pain or anything, but I just can't fall asleep.

D: You think thoughts while you're up all night?

P: Yes.

D: What kind of thoughts?

P: Well, this leg is one of the things. I have always been able to carry my own load and when I have to stop and ask somebody to do this and do that, they, I . . . I can't even get up out of bed to go to the bathroom, you know . . . and it worries me, it really does.

D: What kind of thoughts do you have when you say it worries you?

P: Well, I think that now here I am. I used to be able to get up and go and take a trip and do my own work and everything. Now I can't take a trip unless somebody goes with me. My friends and family say, "You can go; use a wheelchair. Wherever you go they'll provide a wheelchair for you." But I can't have my husband push me around in a wheelchair everywhere, because he won't enjoy himself either.

D: Has he said that?

P: He hasn't said it, but he doesn't care to go places. Now I will take an airplane ride, but he will not go. I have been on a boat, but not since the amputation. I haven't really been anywhere since the amputation. Only to New York and South Carolina.

D: And it's because you feel you can't get around?

P: That's right. And I don't want to say, "Why is it me?" I know all of us belong to God. It could happen to me as well as to anybody else. So many times I might . . . but I can't express it. Then you have to hold it in, keep your mouth shut about it.

D: You don't express that to anybody?

P: No.

D: Not even your husband?

P: No. (*softly*) And that is one of the things I hold back. There are many things I hold back and don't say. It's just not right.

D: Why isn't it right?

P: Because it could happen to me as well as to anyone else. When I look around and see people with no legs at all, then I feel grateful that I have one. And this is the thing that kind of helps me go along with the situation. Knowing that I'm not the only one. So I just go on and do the best I can.

D: What you're saying is that you feel it's been unfair.

P: I do.

D: And for some reason you want to keep that a secret.

P: Yes.

D: I don't know why. I don't understand.

P: Well, I don't know. I just don't say it.

D: Well, it has been unfair. It is unfair.

P: I feel it's unfair, and I blame the hospital. I blame the hospital. Of course sometimes I feel the doctors did the best they could, and yet I also feel they didn't do the best they could.

D: So you just keep everything you told me to yourself.

P: And I keep it to myself. And this is the first time I've come out and opened up and talked about how I feel in nine years.

Mrs. B. has been a different person since her surgery. She has markedly limited all housework, despite a lifelong wish to maintain a "clean, pretty house." She has abandoned her hobby of quilting, which had previously brought her great satisfaction. Except for infrequent visits to family in New York, she has stopped traveling, a former passion of hers. Although she continued to drive for several months after her surgery, she decided to stop after being involved in a minor traffic accident, which she recognizes was the fault of the other driver. Most important, she completely discontinued her daily routine of visiting neighborhood friends. Her social contacts have become solely dependent on friends calling on her, and over the years these visits have become increasingly infrequent. Physiologic changes accompanied these self-imposed limitations on Mrs. B.'s daily life. Her diminished appetite of approximately four years in duration has resulted in a progressive weight loss. She has chronic insomnia, accompanied by obsessional ruminations about her amputation, contributing to her chronic fatigue.

Lamenting, "I just can't do what I used to," Emily B. is unaware that changes in her level of functioning and capacity to enjoy life are not solely the result of a disfiguring physical handicap. She suffers from an additional handicap, namely, her obvious difficulty resolving the powerful and painful emotions stirred in her when her leg was amputated. These emotions were patently obvious during the interview. Her anger at physicians is blatant, although she tries to minimize it. She perceives her physicians as ignorant and as "thinking about the blood pressure and the heart, more than they were paying attention to my leg." To her they were insensitive and condescending, ignoring her complaints about phlebitic pain because she did not "holler loud enough." She felt they were neglectful, if not negligent, postponing an important radiologic study and sending her home with severely compromised circulatory functioning. In sum, she felt she had been treated "without the proper care." Whether or not these perceptions were justified could only be substantiated by discussion with her physicians and detailed review of her medical record. However, she was convinced she was correct, although she never overtly verbalized her strong feelings prior to our meeting. She suppressed her resentment, keeping it even from her husband, and the consequence of her silence was tragic. Her overwhelming unexpressed anger toward physicians festered, daily strengthening her conviction that she was a helpless victim. She felt this so strongly that she began to live her life accordingly. She progressively withdrew from the world around her and spent more time in her private world, ruminating about her fate night and day. Trying to answer the unanswerable questions such as "Why me?" she insidiously, but steadily, abandoned her previously pleasurable activities. She was not physically incapable of cleaning house, quilting, or driving; rather, she chose not to do these things. She was on a sitdown strike, angrily demonstrating to the world what her incompetent physicians had done to her. Her suffering was largely self-imposed, a self-destructive acting out of her anger. This could have been minimized, or avoided, had she expressed her feelings, especially to her physicians. After our meeting I wondered if Emily B.'s resentment of physicians had reached the point where she was angrily rejecting their current treatment. She had mentioned that her low-salt diet and cardiac medications were not necessary "all the time," and I suspected her recent hospitalizations were necessitated by her inattention to a prescribed medical regimen. I think Mrs. B. took secret pleasure in observing her physicians' inability to discern the true cause of her recent symptoms.

An abnormal psychological response to illness occurs when a patient is unable effectively to grieve the losses incurred by ill health. For a myriad of reasons he cannot recognize, feel, or come to terms with some or all of the emotions precipitated by illness. He may completely deny his feelings or, more commonly, experience one emotion to the relative exclusion of all others. In effect, the patient gets stuck in a particular stage of the grief process, becomes

consciously or unconsciously preoccupied with the feelings characteristic of that phase, and thereby prevents himself from achieving
some emotional resolution regarding his loss of health. Emily B.
strikingly illustrates this phenomenon. Her pervasive, but muted,
anger fostered a generalized regression, with social isolation, depressive symptomatology, and probable noncompliance with her medical
treatment. This is a staggering price to pay for an inability to deal
effectively with the angry feelings fomented by her illness.

The most frequent abnormal psychological reactions to illness are
the denial response, the anxiety response, the anger response, the
depression response, and the dependency response. Again, each of
these emotional conditions characterizes a phase of normal grief.
One factor that makes an abnormal response to illness is the
patient's preoccupation with one of these affective states to the
extent that he interprets his illness predominantly from the perspective of that emotion. Another is his denial of all feelings attendant on
the loss of health. Why people react to sickness in these different
manners is a complex question; the answer lies in the patient's
understanding of his particular illness at a particular time in his life.

Individuals perceive, evaluate, and defend against loss in a highly
subjective fashion, a personal reaction that can facilitate or hinder
the necessary grief process that accompanies illness. Chapters 3
through 7 will investigate the abnormal illness responses that occur
when grieving is ineffective, utilizing case histories of individuals
with a variety of medical illnesses: thrombophlebitis, sarcoidosis,
renal failure, subacute bacterial endocarditis, acute myocardial
infarction, chronic cardiovascular disease, and pancreatitis. These
particular patients were selected because of the clarity with which
they demonstrate a given illness response. I emphasize that they
should be studied as illustrative examples of medical treatment in
which attention to the mind and body was so dichotomous that the
patient's overall functioning was markedly diminished. Most clinical
situations are not so extreme. Well-intentioned physicians tend
effectively to the emotional lives of their patients, either by conscious effort or intuitive skill, and consequently, the next five
chapters should not be construed as representative of general
medical care. However, many practitioners do lack an appreciation
of the feelings that are precipitated by medical illness and that affect
its course. They are handicapped in their ability to help patients deal
with unresolved emotions accompanying illness, a situation detrimental to each member of the physician-patient relationship, be-

cause they confine their attention exclusively to physical pathology. The following chapters are presented to better acquaint those clinicians with the specifics of each illness response. With that knowledge, and with an appreciation of basic psychotherapeutic techniques discussed in Chapter 9, the physician should be better able to treat his patient as a total person by tending to his mind and body.

3

Denial of Illness

DENIAL IS THE REFUSAL to perceive or accept external reality. It is a common ego mechanism which, like all such mechanisms, operates unconsciously. Consequently, it permits us to ignore certain events and emotions without any awareness of doing so. Denial is considered a basic, elementary psychological mechanism because of its absoluteness. It does not modify distressing thoughts or affects; it negates them. It can be thought of in terms of a child's attempt to deal with worldly fears. The excited six-year-old repeatedly declaring, "I'm not scared," while staring at caged lions in the zoo clearly illustrates denial. While another child may openly express fear through words or tears, the little boy who declares he is "not scared" is genuinely unafraid. By exercising denial he can enjoy the adventure of observing enormous beasts stalking back and forth, while simultaneously preventing any frightening thoughts from intruding on his pleasure. This is quite an achievement; without actively marshalling mental energy the negative feelings are neutralized, permitting enhanced enjoyment of positive emotions. Denial, then, serves a defensive and adaptive function. It permits us to adjust to stressful situations by defending against distracting feelings, thereby preventing those emotions from overwhelming us or handicapping our routine functioning.

We exercise denial daily to cope with the normal stresses of life or with more specific threats to our well-being. One common example of adaptive denial concerns operating an automobile. The dangers of driving are obvious: 50,000 Americans die in traffic accidents annually, and many more are injured. If the average driver were constantly to remind himself of these statistics, he would never get into his car. A brief trip to the supermarket would be seen as a treacherous journey. Obviously Americans are not inhibited by such fears, as every rush-hour commuter well knows. We either never think about being in an accident, or we dismiss the possibility by reassuring ourselves of our caution and driving skills. Of course, we also try to control our fears by taking sensible precautions, such as using seat belts and driving at a safe speed. However, most of our anxiety is automatically defused, outside our consciousness, by the adaptive exercise of denial. Were this not the case, our fears would immobilize us, and we would never get behind the wheel of a car.

Denial is used when more focused stresses occur in our lives. Nuclear weaponry, for example, is discussed as an option in military conflict. Despite the horrifying implications of that threat, national polls demonstrate that the majority of Americans doubt the inevitability of nuclear confrontation. They base their beliefs on the contention that neither superpower would risk global annihilation. Only history will testify to mankind's ability to preserve and better itself; however, inherent in the belief that nuclear war will not occur because it is unthinkable is a great deal of adaptive denial. If we had to deal continually with the anxiety of imminent nuclear war, we would be so drained of emotional energy that effective daily functioning would become impossible. Every news bulletin would become an exercise in fear, as each world event would be interpreted as another inexorable step toward the brink. Our preoccupation with impending doom could become so intense that daily life would continue absent any joy, because of an overriding terror and foreboding.

Without the ability to deny powerful thoughts and emotions deriving from hundreds of day-to-day situations, we would be incapable of leading normal lives. However, denial can be excessive. When it is too defensive it becomes maladaptive and detrimental, as it prevents us from accepting and assessing the realities of life. Examples of this behavior include sitting for an examination without studying, driving while impaired or disoriented by alcohol, or, to return to the discussion of our nuclear age, failing to mount any political challenge to the arms race. Depending on the situation, the consequences of such denial can be grave.

Medical illness is a common stressor to which people frequently react with excessive denial. The fact of being sick, possibly seriously ill, is too frightening to many. Consequently, their reaction to illness becomes a nonresponse. Fear of being overwhelmed by the powerful emotions that accompany illness causes them to simply deny the reality of ill health. Working a routine shift in a busy emergency room will convince most physicians of the ubiquity and intensity of denial as an illness response. A common example involves the individual with several days of precordial pain who is finally cajoled by his family into coming to the hospital. Despite knowledge of common cardiac symptoms, this patient dismisses questions about his reluctance to seek medical attention by calmly reporting to his physician, "I thought it was indigestion." Such statements, coming from a diaphoretic, semicyanotic individual in obvious pain, offer perspective on the power of denial. Other common clinical situations include the individual with hematemesis who delayed medical assessment because the fresh blood in his vomitus was simply due to "something I ate." Another example is the elderly individual with slurred speech and a mild hemiparesis who discounts the presence of a cerebrovascular accident by convincing himself his symptoms are due to fatigue. These clinical examples do not represent the normal emotional response accompanying the onset of illness, that is, the first stage of grieving. They illustrate denial that is excessively defensive, reflecting the patients' difficulty in accepting the realities implied by their acute symptoms. And this degree of nonadaptive denial is not necessarily confined to the early stage of illness, but can be manifested during any phase of a disease process. It can occur even before an individual becomes sick, for example, in the neglect of long-term preventive measures such as important immunizations. It may be present during the prodromal phase, during the acute course (even if hospitalization is required), and into convalescence and aftercare. It is even seen in dying patients who adamantly declare their good health in response to attempts by family members and friends to say a final goodbye. In all these circumstances denial is invoked as a defense against the reality of illness—which does not have to be terminal, debilitating, or even serious—by those who find the state of being sick too distressing.

The following interview illustrates the presence of denial during the progression of a previously diagnosed illness to a more serious, chronic state. Jeffrey W. is a twenty-one-year-old with renal failure secondary to an episode of glomerulonephritis at the age of five years. He is currently hospitalized because of increasingly frequent and severe symptoms. As the interview indicates, his symptoms have necessitated a new medical regimen with drastic implications for his daily functioning and long-term well-being. Despite a long-standing awareness of his medical condition, he exhibits considerable denial about his current symptomatology, his treatment plan, and his view of the future. The interview took place in Jeff's hospital room, which seemed more like a movie set of a young bachelor's pad—a bachelor who was still struggling with the fear, as well as adventure, of emerging manhood. The macho decor included framed pictures of two girlfriends adorning his nightstand, along with copies of *Playboy, Penthouse,* and *Guns and Ammo,* a tennis trophy, and an old photograph of a young man being congratulated for a tennis victory. (I later learned that the man was his father, celebrating his success in a national tournament.) Jeffrey's manner matched the mood of his room, a tentative bravado.

D: Why are you in the hospital?
P: OK, well, I have a kidney disease. OK? And I've had it since the age of five. I've been seeing Dr. T. since then, and my progress since then has been that nothing really has happened. My health has been pretty good, and I've been in the hospital several times for them to check me out. They took a couple of biopsies of my kidneys. Just to find out what I had. They never did tell me, pinpoint exactly what I had. They know now, but they never told me. So I've played tennis. I've been very active and everything like that. I've never been on a diet, I've always eaten regular kind of food. Just lately, in fact just two months ago, I started feeling sick, and I started getting colds awful fast, getting dizzy, and things like that. It just kept on coming. I've seen the doctors several times, and finally they thought to put me in the hospital a couple of weeks ago and told me my kidneys are not working effectively anymore. And they're putting me on dialysis right now (*very softly*).
D: This started when you were five years old?
P: Yes. They noticed then that my urine was dark.
D: How old are you now?
P: I'm twenty-one right now.

D: So it's been sixteen years now. And you say you've pretty much been all right?

P: Yes.

D: Have you been in the hospital?

P: Yes. I've been in the hospital—two years ago the last time. Different times for different things. They did a biopsy on me last time I was here. They took a section of my left kidney.

D: Now things have changed for you recently?

P: Yes.

D: What's been the main difference in how you feel now?

P: You mean on the machine now, or before I came into the hospital?

D: Before you came in.

P: Well. I'm very tired. See, I worked at a job. I would go to my job and start working, and I would all of a sudden really feel tired. Like I would start at 10:00 in the morning, and by noon I'd feel tired, drowsy, confused a lot, and in fact, my boss noticed it a lot, noticed I was tired. I just couldn't do anything very much. I went home a lot of times sick—headaches and dizziness.

D: How long had that been happening?

P: Just around a couple of days before I called Dr. T.

D: Before that, had you been feeling tired?

P: Before that I felt healthy as could be. I just moved out into my own apartment two months ago, living on my own. I felt healthy. In fact, I jogged everyday . . . but my blood pressure was going up.

D: Did they tell you why your blood pressure was up?

P: According to Dr. T., it was because of my kidneys. They weren't functioning.

D: He told you that when he gave you the medicine?

P: What's that?

D: He told you that when he gave you the medicine?

P: Yes.

D: And when was that?

P: That started a couple of months ago. The high blood pressure.

D: So a lot of things started a couple of months ago.

P: Yes. A couple of months ago a lot of things happened. It's changed my way of living (*laughs for several seconds, then pauses*).

D: That was March?

P: Yes.

D: Do you remember that day?

P: No.

D: When were you twenty-one?

P: January.

D: When were you admitted to the hospital this time?

P: I came in on Monday (*ten days previously*).

D: The reason was to begin dialysis?

D: No. My reason for coming was because that's when I was dizzy at work and wasn't feeling good. See, that had been going on. I've been sick, I've had a cold for two months. In fact, I made an appointment with Dr. T., and he felt my headaches and being sick was because of my blood pressure being too high and causing my body not to function right. And that's what he thought. It might have been that too, but it kept on going on even though I was taking the pills. I kept feeling sick. My head—I kept getting splitting headaches, dizziness, tiredness, so I called him again, and this time he put me in the hospital. So I came in on Monday. They took several tests, and they found out the reason why. My nitrogen or ammonia in my blood wasn't very good. It was causing me to be dizzy, and my kidneys weren't functioning.

D: When did they start dialysis?

P: They started dialysis on Wednesday (*eight days previously*).

D: So when you came into the hospital you didn't know you were going to be on dialysis.

P: No. I thought it was my blood pressure.

D: When were you told about dialysis?

P: They told me on Tuesday. They came and told me my kidneys had gone pretty far and that I would have to go on dialysis. You know.

D: What were your thoughts about that?

P: Dr. T. always told me that my kidneys would eventually stop functioning correctly all the way. But they were trying to see how long they could keep it functioning so I wouldn't have to . . . so he always told me . . . we always figured it would be about thirty or forty years old. I'd be pretty old by then. I never thought it would start this young. I was kind of surprised.

Throughout the interview Jeffrey recounted his medical history in an indifferent, if not dispassionate, manner. He attempted to negate the seriousness of his current symptoms by proclaiming that since age five his health "has been pretty good . . . since then nothing has really happened." He cited his level of activity, his physical conditioning, and his unrestricted diet as proof of his fitness. Furthermore, he tried to minimize significant symptoms by attributing them to "a cold," despite a concurrent two-month trial of antihypertensive medication prescribed in an attempt to control his headaches and fatigue. Finally, he tolerated his uncomfortable, distressing symptoms until he became too dizzy to function at work; only then did he recontact his physician. He was immediately hospitalized, and after further evaluation he was placed on hemodialysis. Jeffrey professed surprise at this change in his treatment; however, as his last statement suggests, dialysis was not only a possibility, it was the probable next therapeutic step. He attempted to deny this reality by accepting it as a possibility only of later life, yet he had never been given a time frame for his anticipated renal failure. All he definitely knew was that "my kidneys would eventually stop functioning correctly all the way."

Of those factors responsible for Jeffrey's denial response, two stand out: the nature of this illness and his stage in the life cycle. Progressive renal failure can remain an insidious process for many years. Although Jeffrey intellectually understood the implications of his ailment, he was able to deny his emotional response until his symptoms became tangible and actively interfered with his functioning. This progression occurred during his adolescence, a period of psychosexual maturation when one struggles to carve out an independent identity and become increasingly free from parental control. This developmental stage is normally accompanied by an enhanced sense of omnipotence, basically a defensive posture in which one attempts to feel greater autonomy by simply declaring absolute independence. Dependent wishes are often hidden behind a facade of narcissism characterized by contempt and disregard for any support or guidance by elders. This can be a dangerous situation during the normal adolescent passage; just consider some risks of greater autonomy, such as experimentation with alcohol or sexuality. Medical illness can make the adolescent passage even more treacherous by posing an additional threat to emerging independence and, consequently, provoking an even more extreme omnipotent stance. This can result in frightening negligence of medical realities. The dietary indiscretions or careless use of insulin by the teenage diabetic are classic examples of this phenomenon. Fortunately, Jeffrey's disregard of his progressive renal failure, obvious throughout the interview, had never really reached life-threatening proportions. Despite his vigorous life style and his attempt to move away from the support of home during an intensification of physical symptoms, he ultimately appreciated his physical decline and, consequently, sought necessary treatment. Although denial had interfered with his ability to grieve effectively for the loss of his kidneys, it only transiently interfered with his treatment, ultimately yielding to the reality of his symptoms.

Jeffrey W.'s behavior is characteristic of countless medical patients whose initial unconscious rejection of illness persists much longer than anticipated for normal grieving. Such individuals use a variety of psychological maneuvers to deny their illness. Displacing attention onto another part of the body is one such technique. I treated a woman who was quite knowledgeable about multiple sclerosis, as her mother had died of the disease. Yet when she experienced her first episode of optic neuritis, she sought evaluation for a congenital port-wine nevus. Patients also rationalize their feelings in an attempt to deny concerns. For example, some people "welcome" unexplained weight loss because they consider themselves obese. Others may simply interrupt their medical evaluation by refusing diagnostic procedures or even leaving the hospital against medical advice. They convince themselves of the correctness of such decisions without recognizing their true motivation—denying the reality of illness by preventing collection of necessary medical data. As these examples demonstrate, excessive denial protects patients from bearing the painful emotions associated with illness, but it protects at the price of placing them in peril. Usually such denial dissipates as signs and symptoms of disease intensify, which, hopefully, occurs before the chance for successful therapy has been significantly jeopardized. The next two cases of pathologic denial illustrate its effects at different stages of the disease process—during the acute phase and over the thirty-year course of an illness—and demonstrate the varying degrees to which denial may interfere with medical treatment.

Thomas H., a forty-six-year-old architect, has thrombophlebitis complicated by pulmonary emboli. With correct treatment, this illness usually remits; however, it is potentially fatal if neglected. The interview readily demonstrates how Mr. H. effectively denies the significance of alarming signs and painful symptoms, despite an intellectual appreciation of their presence.

D: I understand you came into the hospital on Sunday.
P: Right.
D: And what brought you in then?
P: I had severe pains in my chest and back and was very short of breath.
D: All of a sudden?
P: No. It had been going on . . . well . . . all of a sudden in the sense that it became acute. I'd actually been having problems for about a week and a half. Do you want me to trace those for you?
D: If you would please.

P: It started about . . . I lost track of time . . . I came into the hospital last Friday (*six days previously*) . . . so go back a week and a half before that. On a Tuesday or Wednesday I started developing what I thought was a cold in my shoulder. It wasn't much painful, it was like if I touched a spot here, there was a little bit of pain, and it seemed to shoot a little bit, you know, spread when I touched it. But it was sort of something that bothered you a little bit but not that much. And then I felt for a couple of days a pain here (points to his upper back), but it was the type of pain you felt if you turned the wrong way in bed. You shift to another position because you kind of felt pressure or something . . . nothing severe, and it lasted for a couple of days. Then on Friday I went down to South Carolina for a meeting, and that night in the hotel room I developed a pain—not a constant pain—in the back here, and I found that I couldn't really lie down in the bed. Whenever I turned to get myself into a frontal position it would be an extreme discomfort, and as a result I spent most of the night sitting up, or standing actually. So I assumed that I had a cold here (*points to his shoulder*) and that the cold had moved throughout the back. I thought it was all muscular, but the next day, as long as I was up and around, I felt a little bit of discomfort. If I wasn't trying to lie down—that's where the real discomfort was—I got through the day. I got on an airplane and came back. But that night at home I had equally as difficult a problem: not being able to sleep. I couldn't lie down. Finally, I'd get down and find a position, and I'd get a couple of hours' sleep maybe. Then I'd turn the wrong way, and I'd feel this back here and I'd wake up and I'd have to get out of bed. I missed the football game on Sunday because I thought it was a cold, and I wasn't going to sit out there in the cold. You know I had to be sick to do that, in other words. Sunday was pretty much a repeat of Saturday. During the day it wasn't too bad, at night some discomfort, or a lot of discomfort. I stayed home from work on Monday. I could have gone to work on Monday, but then I figured, Hell, I don't want this cold to go on and on. I figured that maybe the more rest I got the better off I'd be. So I stayed home Monday, but Monday afternoon, for example, I went out food shopping. You know, I drove around. And Monday night, in fact, I was more comfortable. It didn't bother me as much, and I think I slept Monday night without pain or any big problems.

D: That was the first time you had a good night's sleep?

P: Yeah. Needless to say, by then I was pretty tired, too. Now this is the question the doctors keep asking me, and I can't remember whether it was Monday afternoon or Tuesday afternoon . . . I kind of think it was Tuesday afternoon . . . when I first developed a pain in the calf of my right leg. And it was not anywhere as severe as the pain in my back, and it seemed to me to be a different pain. I'm not very good at describing pain—I could drive some doctors crazy last Sunday describing the pain—really this is the first time I've been in the hospital. I really haven't had that much pain in my life, I guess. They kept saying to me, "Describe the pain." Well, how do you describe a pain? (*Patient pauses.*) You know, it just hurts. But this one was more like a cramp. It hurt the most with your initial movement from having been in a restful position. Like when you get up in the morning, that hurt first. Walking to the bathroom, standing there shaving was stressful. But as time went on, by the time you got into the car to drive to work, you hardly noticed it. Say at work you'd be sitting at the desk for a period of time, with the first five or six steps after you got up you felt it. But you seem to walk it off. This was tender to the touch; if anybody pressed on it I could feel that it hurt. Whereas the back was never particularly sensitive to touch; it just hurt, and was related to movement and breathing. Throughout this thing I guess I did have some shortness of breath, but I never noticed it that much. Unfortunately I smoke a lot.

D: How much?

P: About two packs a day.

D: Do you do physical activities like running or playing tennis?

P: Play tennis some. At any rate that was Tuesday. I had no problems, say, Tuesday night sleeping, because this did not bother me at night. Wednesday the leg pain was still there, and I'm really not sure why but I called the doctor. I guess I still had some feeling in my back, but it was no worse than it had been. I did call the doctor, and my doctor, the internist, wasn't in. I told the nurses what the problem was, and they said one of the other doctors could get back to me. I did get a call back in the afternoon, not from the doctor but from one of the nurses. She was sort of the intermediary, and she wanted to know what the symptoms were. I explained and she said, "If you put you toe back or up like that (*gestures*) does it hurt in the back of the calf?" And I said yes. And she said, "Hold on for a few minutes." Then she came back and said, "The doctor says to take two aspirin every four hours for twenty-four hours, and if it's not better to come and see us." On Thursday it really wasn't any better, but it wasn't worse so I didn't call back. Thursday night I started again to get pains in my chest. I had trouble sleeping Thursday. It was shifted up to the front, so Friday I stayed home. On Friday morning I called the doctor's office and said there had been no improvement. In fact, it had gotten worse, at least in the chest area. They told me to come in at 4:00, which I did. I drove in.

D: Was it painful driving?

P: No. Never have I had a great problem with the leg. See, I thought my leg was part of the cold that I had. Well, I got into the doctor's office, and Dr. B., who has been my internist over the years, still wasn't there. I had to see someone else. He immediately focused on my leg, and I thought, "Why in the hell is he doing that? That's not what really hurts as much." So it was late in the day, and he said he wanted to get some x-rays before the x-ray place closes down. So they hurried me downstairs and took chest x-rays, and then I went back up again, and Dr. D. came in, felt my leg, and told me that I've got phlebitis.

D: Did you know what it was?

P: I had an idea what it was. OK, I figured, I've got phlebitis in my leg, and I knew it could be problematic. They gave me medicine for phlebitis. The x-rays showed apparently the chest is all right. And they sent me home. They said, "Go home, stay in bed all weekend, and take this medicine."

D: Did you know what that was?

P: No.

D: Was it a pill?

P: Yes. It wasn't strong. I mean it was not something . . . I remember Dr. D. saying it was a surface situation, and he didn't think it was necessary to go to one of the more difficult drugs. So I went home. On Friday night I was just . . . they said I had to stay in bed and keep the leg elevated . . . hell I just could not stay in bed. I just could not get myself comfortable. And the pain was more severe now then it's ever been.

D: Where was the pain in your chest?

P: Up here (*points to his shoulder*), through here, and in the back. It was the *whole* right side. So finally, the only way I could get myself comfortable was to sit straight back with my leg propped up on another chair. I could sit there, and that's what I did all Friday night. I never got to sleep at all. So Saturday I continued to stay in the same position, and mid-afternoon I called Dr. D. and said, "Look, you're taking care of my leg and I'm doing what you told me to do, but the problem is my chest hurts so much. I can't get comfortable in bed—I've got to sit up." Well, he had never been part of that conversation. He had come in to look at my leg, and I guess he was aware that I had some problems with my chest, but he had not been involved in the discussion I had gone through with some other doctors. So he got frustrated with me, asking "Where's the pain? What kind of pain is it? How long have you had the pain?" et cetera, et cetera. And I kept describing it as a muscular pain, which I in fact thought it was. And he said, "Do you have any shortness of breath?" I said some, but that was not my problem; my problem was the pain.

So he said he'd try a muscular relaxant. He gave me something. I took that Saturday afternoon, along with three of the biggest martinis you ever saw in your life. And I did get some sleep until about 1:00 A.M. But then once I got awake Sunday morning I was back in a mode of having to sit up straight with the leg up and stayed in that position throughout the morning. I noticed Sunday morning that even the slightest walking from here over to a chair would give me shortness of breath, and it would take me about five minutes to kind of recover and get back to normal breathing patterns. About noon I found that just sitting in a chair I would lose my breath. I wasn't doing anything and still having shortness of breath. Plus, and this probably scared me more than anything else—no one seems to give a damn about it really—I coughed up some blood. Then I called Dr. B. and explained what it was, and he put me here, and I was over here in the hospital in half an hour.

D: Were you frightened during this?

P: No. Though I don't know why coughing up blood scared the hell out of me. But that did frighten me. I never connected the two, the leg with . . . the idea never crossed my mind that I had blood clots in my chest. I had attributed this all to muscular problems.

D: Have you ever heard of that, that you can get phlebitis and get blood clots going through your chest?

P: Yes, I guess I had.

D: Nixon had that.

P: Yes I heard of it then. But I never put the two together. And I guess the other thing was, even when I was here for a couple of days, it seemed to me that the pattern of that is that you get the leg first. The leg starts hurting, and they treat that and they worry about that breaking off and going to the lung. But if you go back to my case the first pains were in the chest, and the leg pains were minor compared to the chest.

The degree of self-deception permitted us by our unconscious is quite extraordinary. Listening to Mr. H., I marvelled at his ability to protect himself from emotional distress. He began the interview with a measured calmness so pronounced that I felt he was discussing someone else's medical history. He proceeded, with the same emotional neutrality, to deliver a five-minute monologue, obsessionally describing a week and a half of significant discomfort which interfered with all aspects of his life. I wondered if he had actually experienced what he was reporting. Could anyone recount such a physically painful and distressing period so dispassionately? In fact, Mr. H. could because of his extreme powers of denial.

Why Thomas H. responded to illness with denial is not clear, as the interview did not address the psychodynamics of his illness responses. Certainly the fact that this was his first serious illness and first hospitalization played a part; however, there is obviously much more. What is striking about the interview is the pervasiveness of denial, which was so pronounced as to be obvious even to the psychologically unsophisticated. Mr. H. uses many different maneuvers to ignore the presence of illness. First, he continually minimizes his symptoms. His severe thoracic pain was described as "something that bothered you a little but not much . . . not a constant pain." Yet it prevented him from sleeping and required him to spend several nights sitting up in a chair, even standing, to obtain relief. Because of discomfort and fatigue he stayed home from work one day—a very rare occurrence—but he went out food shopping in an attempt to convince himself he was all right. The following day he developed calf pain, which he also minimized—both to himself ("I seemed to walk it off") and to his physicians—by being vague as to its onset, quality, and intensity.

When Thomas H. finally sought medical attention, he was still able to maintain a high level of denial by completely abdicating to his physicians the responsibility for recognizing and accurately assessing his physical impairment. His logic was simple: I am sick only if my doctor finds something wrong. Of course, this logic is invalid if the patient distracts his doctor from pertinent signs and symptoms, and Mr. H. was repeatedly guilty of such transgressions. On one occasion he was told to come in for an appointment if he wasn't feeling better. He didn't comply because "it wasn't any better, but it wasn't worse." Later, when he did submit to a physical examination, he was puzzled when the doctor only "focused on my leg"; however, he neglected to mention his chest pain. He was informed he had phlebitis, given medication, and instructed to elevate his leg during bed rest. But because his chest pain became increasingly severe, he could not remain in bed and spent another sleepless night in a chair. He eventually contacted his doctor who was already concerned about the possibility of pulmonary emboli, having ordered a chest x-ray the previous day. However, Mr. H. minimized his shortness of breath by stressing his muscular pain. This again distracted his physician from the real problem, which finally became apparent when his patient developed hemoptysis.

It seems incredible that Thomas H. was unaware of the significance of his symptoms, especially given his appreciation of Richard

Nixon's much publicized experience with phlebitis. He denied any connection between his physical condition and that of the ex-president by rationalizing that leg pain always precedes chest pain in thrombophlebitis. Even if his powers of denial were that effective, one would presume his recognition of *some* serious illness. No cold could debilitate him so, yet during his ten days of symptoms he convinced himself that this was the case. He concealed his true medical status from his doctors because he first concealed it from himself; and during our meeting he was still denying the full truth. In relating his history, he sounded more mechanical than human. He seemed devoid of emotion, speaking primarily from his head, not his heart. This is the hallmark of obsessional personality types, who use characteristic ego mechanisms to achieve a logical understanding of the world to the detriment of their affective experience. Mr. H.'s predominant defensive maneuvers included intellectualization, rationalization, and reaction formation (primarily against dependency). When threatened, he automatically utilized these psychological mechanisms to inhibit his emotional response; this, in turn, minimized or neutralized the impact of the stressor. Thomas H., like many, is less concerned about events until he *feels* something. He presents a textbook illustration of defensive denial during acute illness and of the inherent threat that denial poses. He is the type of patient who must be taken very seriously whenever he contacts a physician; no matter how trivial the complaint, its significance can be extreme.

It may be difficult to imagine a more pronounced degree of denial; however, the following case illustrates just that situation. The patient, a forty-eight-year-old accountant, has maintained a level of denial consonant with Thomas H.'s throughout the thirty-year course of his illness. He is the type of patient whose chronic illness is paralleled by an illness response of chronic denial, an astounding and frightening achievement. At the time of the interview, William R. was hospitalized for treatment of malignant hypertension, a consequence of progressive renal failure. He was born with a kidney malformation which has predisposed him to repeated infections since his early life. As our meeting demonstrates, he has always ignored evidence of its impact.

D: What brings you to the hospital?

P: I have been on a bunch of hypertensive medications this year, none of which have been very effective. I shouldn't say they haven't been effective. Either they've been ineffective or the side effects have been horrible. And my kidney function has been degrading throughout the year. I'm trying to get to Dr. A., to try to get some captopril from Stanford, which I was hoping would hold my blood pressure down. The situation has been fairly critical for the past month while I've been waiting for my appointment. So anyway, I thought I was going to make it to my appointment before things got really critical, but last Friday my serum creatinine hit 13, and at that point my nephrologist said, "Come on into the hospital and forget about Stanford."

D: You were going to the Stanford clinic for a new type of medication they're using there?

P: Yes. The conventional hypertensive medications to date generally either deal with your central nervous system diuretics, whereas captopril acts on the angiotensin hormones, so it's an entirely different approach from the other medications available. That's what makes me feel that there's some hope that it may work where the others have not been very successful.

D: How long have you had this problem with hypertension?

P: I don't know how long I've had it. I've . . . we've been treating it for almost twelve years now. I've had the kidney problem certainly for at least thirty years. And several times in the past my doctors have mentioned to me that my blood pressure is up, but they never told me how much it was up. Perhaps if I had seen more doctors I would have started treating my blood pressure earlier than twelve years ago.

D: What kind of kidney problems did you have?

P: Bilateral hydronephrosis.

D: That started thirty years ago?

P: Yes. Probably I've had a tendency for a certain amount of this all my life, because I have had polyuria ever since I can remember. But anyway, the episode of kidney disease that I had was when I was about fourteen—I got a very severe kidney infection at this time. I was essentially in a coma for about a week with a fever of 104 degrees.

D: Can you tell me about being in a coma?

P: Well, there was nothing to it. I slept basically twenty-three hours a day. I'd wake up just enough to urinate, get something to drink, and go back to sleep. Probably the first episode lasted two weeks instead of one week. After this first episode, for the rest of that year I had maybe five more episodes of the similar coma, with a lot of milky urine and a fever of 104. It would last a week, and then it would clear itself up. I was taking penicillin for it. Whether the penicillin was effective for it or not I don't know. From the data we have today, probably not; sulfa would have been a much better drug. I had perhaps five of these things that year, and they generally tapered off over the next five years. Perhaps I had one five years after that, and I haven't had another episode similar to that since then.

D: Were those comas felt to be due to infection?

P: Yes.

D: Were you arousable during those periods of sleep?

P: You could get me up, but if no one was there to keep me awake I was asleep.

D: Were you in the intensive care unit?

P: No. No. I was just at home.

D: You were never in the hospital during one of those episodes?

P: No.

D: Could you tell me how your disease progressed after that?

P: By the time I got to be twenty, the kidney disease was giving me less trouble than it was before. Sometimes, for a period of a week or sometimes for up to several months, my urine would become milky and then would clear up again. I was being treated by a urologist in Charlottesville. Meanwhile I was at school approximately 250 miles away. I didn't get to him very often. If I did have some bout of infection, he'd treat me with some . . . let's see . . . aureomycin, streptomycin, and a few other things he gave me. They seemed to keep my kidney infection from running away. About two years out of undergraduate school, these milky-urine episodes seemed to disappear, and I was thinking perhaps I don't have to worry about the kidney problems. I would say that part of the reason for not pursuing it is that when you're a student you don't have medical insurance, and once you get into this thing it can be quite expensive. It didn't seem to be a critical situation at the time.

D: At the time, did your doctor know what the problem was?

P: Oh yes. It had been diagnosed as hydronephrosis when I was in my teens. So I knew what it was; it just didn't seem severe enough to bother with my chasing down.

D: What do you mean by "chasing down?"

P: Well, as I said, I had some symptoms—milky urine. But I didn't go into coma anymore, so it seemed that I had other things to do so . . . if this gets worse then I'll worry about it.

D: The only symptoms you were having at that time were the milky urine and the burning?

P: No, I didn't have any burning. You see, twice, for several days, I had a severe pain in my back, and I had a fair amount of urine for two or three days. But at the time I was so far away from my urologist that I hardly had time to get to him before the whole thing was over.

D: Did you have these episodes without seeking medical help at all?

P: Yes. Usually it would go away by itself. I don't know. At the time when you're tied up with so many other things—after you've been through one of these episodes and nothing bad happens—the next time you say, "Oh I'm going through the same thing again." Let's see, after that I got into graduate school, and there I started some symptoms which didn't seem specifically kidney disease, but I'm sure they were. I would have periods when I would have difficulty concentrating. I felt that I had a lot of pressure in my head. I wasn't having my blood pressure checked at the time. Through my experience now, I interpret that as extreme bouts with high blood pressure. And, I had times when I would go several weeks, sometimes even a month or two, where I would be very lethargic, and I'd be sleeping fourteen, sixteen hours a day. And all the time I'd be awake I would be very tired. These would come and go. I should say, since they always left eventually, I didn't worry about them too much.

D: When did these episodes take place?

P: This was quite a bit of the time throughout graduate school (*pause*) I guess by ages twenty-three to twenty-eight, I'd say.

D: How long would these periods last for?

P: Oh, I'd say a couple, three weeks . . . two months at the most.

D: What did you feel was causing that?

P: I didn't know what was causing it. I just felt tired, so I got more sleep than I would the rest of the time.

D: Were you able to carry on with your school work then?

P: Yeah, I was able to carry on, but marginally. These things pretty well disappeared by the time I got out of graduate school. Probably the primary reason . . . was a regimen of vitamins and mineral supplements. I couldn't sleep on a regular basis when I was in graduate school, so I started an exercise program which seemed to help a lot. I did find that helped to control my blood pressure. I also started TM. I also started taking Serpasil for the hypertension. I could see as we started on each one of these things, I could see my condition improve. So it seemed that while there's no way to cure the kidney problem—which seemed to be the basis for all the other problems I was having—there did seem to be a number of measures that I could take to improve things. I did feel quite good for a few years, starting, let's say, twelve years ago. I really haven't had much poor health. I've had periods when my blood pressure has spiked up, but I haven't had any awful periods of prolonged hypertension.

Like the previous patient, William R. obsessionally recounted his medical history in an intellectualized, distant fashion, leaving me with the feeling that he was discussing someone else. In response to my opening question, he delivered a minilecture about antihypertensive pharmacotherapy. Given his subdued, didactic manner, I was completely surprised by the subsequent description of how extensive and intense his kidney disease has been. However, in contrast to the previous patient, William's long-standing and extreme denial suggested an impaired ability to test reality adequately; he responded to the stress of illness with massive denial. Despite several episodes of pyelonephritis in his early life, episodes that were characterized by pyuria, high fever, and coma, he was never hospitalized. Despite the persistence of these episodes into college and graduate school, he was only loosely followed by a physician who was located in another city. He did not seek comprehensive, ongoing medical care because his infections "would usually go away by themselves" and because of his lack of medical insurance. The latter excuse became as flimsy as the first when I learned that both his parents were well-to-do physicians. William did not feel his illness was "severe enough to bother with any chasing down," which translates to mean that he coped with a significant health problem by an equally significant degree of denial. As the remainder of the interview demonstrates, this attitude persisted even when he was suffering side effects of antihypertensive medication.

D: You've been taking propranolol recently?
P: No. I took propranolol and captopril for I guess about . . . propranolol I only took for a very short time . . . it was about two weeks or so. Then I started the captopril, and I felt almost as bad on that. I stayed on it for six weeks or so. At the end of six weeks, when I had the blood chemistry checked, I found that I was apparently losing kidney function at a very rapid rate while I was on this. I felt it was a good idea to go off it. I was very much relieved because I was dying to stop taking it, so I stopped that. The next thing I tried was Ismelin. This, it turned out, was as close as I could see to being effective. Before I started the Ismelin for maybe eighteen hours each day it was 180/130. The other six hours or so I was in postural hypotension; pressures as low as 100/60. So I had these tremendous crashes. Every morning I'd wake up, and I'd be in shock for the first hour. I'd have to sit down for a couple of minutes or I'd pass out. But, aside from these short episodes—like right after I got out of bed—my blood pressure wasn't changed. If I exerted myself, or first thing in the morning, my blood pressure dropped drastically. So anyway, meanwhile, I decided the Ismelin was totally ineffective for controlling blood pressure; the side effects were intolerable, and my kidney function was going to hell anyway. So I decided to discon-

tinue taking it. Whether that was a mistake or not I don't know because this was approximately two months ago. After this my blood pressure started to rise until it reached the point where I was sitting and it was like 210/150 in steady state. There was nothing that could bring it down right now. Before this, after I would jog or after I'd meditate, my blood pressure would always come down. But here I've reached the point where it was completely refractory. It sat there at 210/150. At the time Dr. A. was out of town, and I was seeing his associate, Dr. R. And he didn't recommend anything else for me. At the time I was still holding out for the captopril. Dr. A. had paperwork in for it. But anyway, when I got to 210/150 for about a week, I felt I had to do something, so I tried Lasix. I was very pleased because this brought my blood pressure down by twenty points. And I thought this would buy a little time to wait for the captopril. But it turned out this effect was only good for about two weeks, and my kidneys were failing. Three months ago my serum creatinine was about 6, and right now it's 18.

William R. shares several characteristics with the two previous patients. During his adolescence he used magical, omnipotent thinking in an attempt to deny his illness, a defense reminiscent of Jeffrey W. And as with Thomas H., obsessional defenses were prominent in early adulthood; however, by no means did they constitute the basic defensive style. Mr. R.'s massive denial, unique among these three patients, is best understood in light of his family history. His father, a medical researcher who did extensive experimentation with radiation, died of renal carcinoma. The patient attributes the malignancy to his father's work, stating, "He was a researcher before the days that people realized that radiation would be bad for you. . . . He had a fair amount of exposure to his midsection, and about twenty-five years ago he had a cancer of one kidney, which he had removed." William R.'s father eventually died of this tumor, which had unfortunately extended beyond the retroperitoneum prior to nephrectomy.

The circumstances of his father's terminal illness left Mr. R. resentful, demeaning, and distrustful of the medical profession. He believed that his father developed a carcinoma because of the profession's ignorance about radiation. He considered his father's surgeons inept, implying that had they been more technically skilled, his father would have survived the malignancy. And he felt that once surgery had failed to arrest the tumor, the profession had absolutely nothing to offer. There are parallels with his own illness.

He had already suffered adverse effects from prescribed medications, attributing the inconvenience to his physicians' ignorance concerning the effects of drugs. And he felt that the profession failed him in the same fashion that it had failed his father: it offered no hope for a cure. Add to this the fact that the two of them had illnesses involving the same organ system, and it is not surprising that William R. felt destined to repeat his father's fate. Whether or not this fear was conscious, he dealt with his hopelessness by denying it completely. He essentially conducted his life as if he were bothered by repeated colds rather than debilitated by progressive renal failure.

The denial response greatly complicates the task of the treating physician. His efforts toward accurate diagnosis and comprehensive treatment are impeded by the patient's unconscious rejection of signs and symptoms of disease. This can occur during any stage of illness, producing a dangerous, if not life-threatening, clinical situation. Unbeknownst to the patient, his self-destructive desire to keep unpleasant feelings out of consciousness begins to control him. He is unable to work through the feelings precipitated by illness because he simply is unaware of those emotions. As the case histories illustrate, this is an effective defense, but it is also a primitive one. The patient invokes excessive denial because he has limited psychological reserves for dealing with stressors. Consequently, the physician's aggressive confrontation of the patient's denial may enhance his helplessness and terror. At the worst this will lead to significant physical and emotional regression; at best, the patient will flee the therapeutic relationship in response to an assault on his major psychological defense. The denial response requires the physician to evaluate his patient thoughtfully and to implement the requisite treatment plan cautiously.

4

The Anxious Patient

Anxiety is at best uncomfortable; in the extreme, it is a tortured feeling. However, although it is generally an unpleasant emotional state, most people respond to the stresses of daily life with periodic episodes of anxiety. A job interview or important school examination provokes feelings of uncertainty and nervousness, often augmented by such physical sensations as sweaty palms, churning stomach, or dry mouth. This is an anticipated, common reaction. Under such circumstances, anxiety serves the useful, adaptive function of preparing the individual for stress. It alerts him to be on guard, to be poised, attentive, and observant in the interview situation or to concentrate and carefully read all instructions and questions on the test. This normal, adaptive form of anxiety is called signal anxiety. It helps individuals to anticipate and subsequently cope with stress. It is therefore a feeling that is essential for survival.

Anxiety becomes pathologic when it is more intense, or greater in duration than warranted by a particular precipitating stress. In this circumstance, the feeling no longer serves the purpose of alerting the individual; rather, anxiety restricts his functioning because of its severe symptoms. The anxious individual is tense, uneasy, fearful, and agitated. He perceives his environment as dangerous; and a feeling of dread, a nagging apprehension that something bad is about to occur, impairs his functioning. He may become so preoccupied with his surroundings, so vigilant, that he cannot concentrate or even sit still. He may become so sensitized to external stimuli that a noise such as a ringing telephone can literally make him jump. Physical distress is an integral part of this emotional state. Common symptoms include heart palpitations; rapid breathing, often with shortness of breath and a choking sensation; dry mouth; indigestion, with possible nausea, vomiting, or diarrhea; and a generalized weakness. Some individuals develop specific bodily aches when anxious; tension headaches, for example, can result from marked, sustained contraction of the muscles in the back of the neck and head. Symptoms accompanying a heightened anxiety state—symptoms such as dizziness, incontinence of urine or feces, or fainting— reflect the individual's general feeling of losing control. When anxiety is this pronounced, the affected individual feels helpless and miserable and is usually a burden to those around him.

All people feel anxious during the course of a physical illness. Anxiety is often pronounced at the onset of illness. The appearance of a symptom, whether it is as ominous as a progressive and unexplained weight loss or as bothersome as persisting headaches, warns the patient because it basically means that his body is not functioning correctly. He wonders what is wrong and speculates on the seriousness of the underlying process. He wonders whether his illness is curable or the start of a chronic, debilitating course. He wonders what the diagnostic workup and ultimate treatment will entail. If the illness is significant and the patient survives the acute stage, he begins to consider the ongoing treatment. Will he require short- or long-term restrictions on his life, such as a special diet or decreased physical activity. He wonders whether his professional life will be affected and what impact his illness will have on the relationships within his family. Will he be forced to become increasingly dependent on his wife? And if so, how will he feel about it, and how will his wife and children feel about it? He wonders how his social relationships will be affected. Will his friends take the time to visit during his hospitalization and convalescence, or will they avoid the depressing and threatening experience of seeing a peer who is ill? He wonders about the financial considerations of his illness. Will his wife have to work? Will he be able to provide adequately for his children? All this worry, this anxiety, is a normal anticipated adjunct of disease. In fact, it is often an adaptive feeling, spurring the patient to seek medical attention. The signal anxiety accompanying the onset of chest pain or the discovery of a breast lump alerts the patient and prompts him or her to do something about it. Similarly, the recurrence of a symptom, such as night sweats in a tuberculosis patient, worries him; his subsequent anxiety that his disease is progressing urges him to seek further medical care. If the patient does not feel anxious in these situations, he is denying normal concerns about illness which could aggravate his physical problem. The diabetic who is indifferent to his increased fluid intake or weight loss, which are cardinal symptoms of poorly controlled blood sugar level, is inviting the risk of diabetic coma. The recognition and acknowledgment of normal anxiety accompanying physical illness ultimately results in better medical treatment and, one hopes, an improved prognosis.

Illness can also precipitate pathologic anxiety. In this instance the patient becomes overly concerned about his physical activity, and the subsequent anxiety is much more severe or lasts much longer than is usually warranted by his particular disease. This is an abnormal response to illness; other emotions are overshadowed by anxiety and assume a secondary, possibly negligible, role in the patient's psychological adjustment to sickness. The net result is that the individual becomes hypersensitive to all aspects of medical treatment. He becomes hypervigilant, preoccupied with any alteration of body function. A new ache takes on tremendous significance in his mind, regardless of how trivial or transient it may be. Consequently the patient's ability to provide an accurate medical history is impaired. He may be so apprehensive that every diagnostic test, every change in medication or diet, every treatment, or every visit to the physician is experienced as dangerous. Eventually the patient feels chronically anxious. He then has the burden of coping with this unpleasant emotional state in addition to fighting his physical problems. This is not only distressing to the patient, it also clouds his medical picture. Because anxiety is accompanied by distinct physical symptoms, it may become increasingly difficult to differentiate symptoms with a physical origin from those deriving from anxiety. In addition, the anxious individual seeks reassurance in order to stem his worry. Continued requests for support may aggravate relatives, friends, and even the health professionals treating him. The result is that every phase of medical treatment from diagnosis to convalescence becomes that much more difficult.

The patient and those around him suffer from his excessive anxiety; this can detract from his treatment and his ultimate return to normal functioning.

The following case is an excellent example of the anxiety response to illness and illustrates the detrimental effects of anxiety on the patient. Laura L. is a thirty-year-old married woman and the mother of a nine-year-old son. She is employed full-time as a computer programmer. Eight years ago, after being examined in a hospital emergency room for flulike symptoms, she was diagnosed as having sarcoidosis. This chronic disease has similarities to tuberculosis, although it may be relatively benign. The basic pathology is an inflammation that may involve any tissue of the body. Clinical manifestations depend on which organs are involved, the most common being lymph nodes, lungs, liver, spleen, skin, eyes, joints, and salivary glands. Common symptoms include swollen lymph glands, difficulty breathing (with or without a cough), arthritic pains throughout the body, skin lesions with possible scarring, enlargement of the liver, spleen, or salivary glands, and inflammation of the eyes with possible visual impairment. In addition, the sarcoid patient may experience nonspecific constitutional manifestations such as fever, fatigue, weight loss, weakness, and generalized malaise. Unlike tuberculosis, which is caused by a specific bacterium, the cause of sarcoidosis is unknown. The clinical course of sarcoidosis also varies greatly from one patient to another. Manifestations range from incidental x-ray findings with no associated symptoms to severe incapacity and death. Some patients undergo a complete spontaneous remission with no evidence of residual disease; some have persistent physical abnormalities with little or no disability; and some unfortunates experience progressive, unremitting deterioration.

Ignorance about the cause of sarcoidosis, coupled with its unpredictable clinical course, makes it a somewhat mysterious illness. Consequently, when a patient is diagnosed as having sarcoidosis, he is usually told he has a chronic illness with an erratic course that may be characterized by acute flare-ups interspersed with periods of remission or quiescence of the disease. In other words, his doctor assures him that medical treatment will be complete and adequate, although he will not know precisely what therapy will be required until the disease demonstrates its involvement with one or more organs—if it declares itself at all. This element of the unknown makes sarcoidosis a difficult disease to cope with emotionally. An individual in remission may totally deny any concerns about possible progression. Laura L., on the other hand, became so worried about the potential danger of sarcoidosis that her mental preoccupation with the disease became a major aspect of her life; her chronic worry infringed on her family life and interfered with her work. As the interview begins Laura recounts one of her many visits to the emergency room for nonspecific pains, this time in her arm. As she relates her story, it becomes increasingly clear that she is more worried about the possible cause of the pain than she is bothered by the pain itself.

P: I came to the clinic because my arm was hurting. I couldn't see a doctor that day. They said I would see one the next day. Then I decided I'd wait till tomorrow and come back, and I made an appointment and came back the next day to see the doctor . . . and my arm was still hurting at that time.

D: Where was the pain?

P: It was going down all through my arm. This side here, all through my arm. It was an aching pain, sort of. I go through sharp pains sometimes, and this pain just ached.

D: How long did you have it before you came to the hospital?

P: Two or three days.

D: Was it getting worse?

P: It was pretty much the same.

D: You said you were concerned it might be something serious.

P: Well, to start hurting . . . if your arm aches . . . you never know. I have a disease called sarcoidosis, and they tell me I may have joint pains or any type of small pains, and I never know at what point the disease might be getting worse. I don't know that much about the disease, so whenever I start hurting over three or four days or something that has a tendency to linger on, then I want to get it checked out (*sighs*). I was just concerned.

D: How old are you?

P: Thirty.

D: When were you told you had sarcoid?

P: I think it was in 1970.

D: What happened then?

P: I had been hurting, about like I was hurting when I went to the clinic. I had been getting some pains over my side, over around in my chest and into my side, that had lasted about three or four days; and one night I decided to go to the emergency room. The doctor looked at me in the emergency room and said I had viral pneumonia and gave me some medication and said, "Go home and get into bed and rest for a couple of days." The next morning I got a call from the doctor at the emergency room who said I should consult my physician because they had taken another look at my x-rays—the x-rays I had taken that night—and I was having some problems with my lungs, and I should get them checked out. Which is what I did. I went to my doctor who recommended another doctor who said I probably had sarcoid. But the only way they could find out was to give me a test; to take some tissue out of my glands and test it to see why my glands were swollen on my lungs. Could have been a lot of different reasons. I went to the hospital, stayed for about a week, week and a half, and had the test. They ruled out everything and came up with sarcoid, which they said didn't have any cure; and they didn't know what caused it, and it would make me have joint-type pains, and it might make my eyes get bad. There was nothing they could do about it, but they could put me on some medication to keep me from having so much pain right then. But just before I went into the emergency room, I had been having pains just about every day, small pains. I mentioned to my husband that it was strange that every day something hurts on me. After that I started taking medication that the doctor had given me for sarcoid once they found out that's what it was. And then I broke out in this rash, great big bumps all over my face like chicken pox. I went back to the doctor, and he said I'd probably taken too much of the medication. So then I had to go to a specialist to clear up my skin from the medicine, 'cause it didn't disappear. So I started taking medication for that (*pause*). When I got home from the hospital I was really having a lot of chest pains. Chest pains that went back into my ribs and in my shoulders. I started going to the emergency room about every night because these were like severe pains, and I couldn't breathe correctly, and I was starting to have a lot of problems. I went back to my doctor and told him about these problems. I don't remember right now what he did, but I told him that I thought maybe it was from having gas or being constipated, so he suggested I take a mild laxative. I told him they weren't working. I still had these chest problems that would come and go, and everytime I would go to the emergency room the doctors couldn't find anything wrong with me. They would say, "It's probably gas," and gave me some medicine for gas. I'd go back home, and two or three days later I'd be back again. Because when it starts hurting in your chest and I can't breathe, I get scared and I don't know what to do. This went on for a year after I was in the hospital. I went to another doctor at a private clinic to get a physical. I explained my problems to him from having the chest pains, not digesting my food correctly. He gave me some examinations, and when he finished with them all he said I looked healthy and that I had a nervous condition. I took these medications, some tranquilizers he gave me, for a while and started getting a little better. It would come and go. I'd eat and my food wouldn't digest, and I'd start getting these severe pains in my chest and ribs. A couple of years later I went to another doctor, had a complete physical again, and he checked everything and then he told me that I have a nervous condition. Two doctors told me that. I went on for about another year or so—off and on I would still get these pains in my chest. I started taking Alka- Seltzer, which would relieve the pain faster than anything else. I moved about three years ago. I went to a physician and complained about the same problem, because it's never disappeared. It comes and goes.

D: Since 1970 you've had this chest pain on and off.

P: Yes. Since I've had my operation (*biopsy*). Yes. I've had this type pain. But before 1970 when I was in school, I had a similar problem. I used to have digestive problems (*pause*). I was living in the country and my parents didn't have much money, so unless you were really, really sick they didn't take you to the doctor. But I was having so much problems from that that my mother decided to take me, and I had a physical then—I was in the tenth grade. The doctor gave me a complete physical and told my mother I had "nervous indigestion" and gave me some medication that cleared it up. I didn't have that problem anymore until I got pregnant, and then I had indigestion for nine months, and then it disappeared. But I was doing pretty good up until I started having the problem with my arm; when I went to the emergency room is when I started having these severe chest pains. And when I moved, the doctor said it was my nerves. I tried to explain; maybe it's the food I'm eating, I know that I eat the wrong food. He said, "Forget all that, it's nothing, it's your nerves." He asked me if I had anything on my mind, was anything bothering me. I said, "No, not that I'm aware of." He checked me and said, "I don't care what you think, it's your nerves." He gave me a prescription for some tranquilizers. Just to take them for a little while. And to try to keep things from bothering me. He told me to get my mind together and to keep things from bothering me. As far as I'm concerned, nothing was bothering me.

D: Do you know what they were?

P: No. The pills helped, but now I don't have as many problems as I used to have. Every now and then, say a good six months, I get these severe pains again, and it may be because it builds back up.

D: But it's every six months now, and it isn't as often as it used to be.

P: No. When I first got out of the hospital it was every other day or every day at some point. Now it happens every six months or so.

D: You were in the hospital in 1970.

P: Yes, it was '70.

D: And you said it was a week and a half that you were there.

P: Yes.

D: First of all, the symptoms you had then, the pain, that was pretty severe?

P: It was a nagging, aching pain. Sort of little sharp pains going up in my chest, and it moved over—as far as I can remember.

D: What did they do in the hospital?

P: Took a chest x-ray. I think that was it.

D: For a week and a half!

P: Oh. You mean when I was in the hospital.

D: That's right.

P: Uh. Took some blood, another chest x-ray, and I think that's it. It was in the hospital . . . I stayed there a day or two and . . . maybe it was a week. OK? I went in the day or two before, and then I went to the operating room, and I stayed in there for about three days after, while they were testing. And then they found out what it was and released me. And I started taking the medication. But they didn't do anything while I was in there but gave me some blood tests and a chest x-ray.

D: They were diagnosing you? It wasn't treatment, they were just trying to find out what went wrong with you?

P: That's right. It wasn't any kind of treatment. They were just trying to find out why my glands were swollen on my lungs.

D: You said that they gave you some medication and that it helped you but that you developed a rash from it. Do you remember what the medicine was?

P: No.

D: How did it help?

P: Well, I stopped having as many . . . well, at that time I was having real joint pains. I can't tell whether it really helped that much or not.

D: Where were the joint pains?

P: I'd get them through my fingers and toes, you know, anywhere. I'd get sharp pains through my head, my eye, my gums, sort of all over, scattered.

D: And you say that since they operated on you to do the biopsy, you felt that you were getting the pains more often.

P: Oh yes. I was having a different type of pain. Before the operation I would have little joint pains, nothing that really bothered me that much. After the operation I was having severe pains in my chest and in my ribs, and those were the type of problems I'd been having after the operation, that I didn't have before.

D: What did you first think these new pains were? What did you think caused them?

P: I didn't know. That's why I was going to the emergency room. But after going to the emergency room so many times and they kept telling me it was gas, I thought it must be [true] because I started taking medication for gas and it helped. But then it comes back.

D: How did you feel when you started getting those new pains? What did you feel like inside, emotionally?

P: I started swelling, like my chest was swelling. I'd get really hot, and I would ache all back up in the ribs.

D: Anything up in the back of your neck?

P: Not in the back of my neck.

D: Did you feel your heart beating quickly at all?

P: Yes. Maybe, because I was scared.

D: Were you scared.

P: Yes.

D: Did you have any thoughts that it might be something serious that was troubling you then?

P: No. I didn't really think about it that way. I just started hurting and thought something was wrong with me. I figured it had to do with my lungs, but I didn't really think it was anything that serious because I had just gotten out of the hospital and they just finished checking me.

D: And they said you were fine.

P: Yeah. Except for the sarcoid. They said I'd have joint pains, but they didn't mention anything like this.

D: Your heart would beat quickly, you'd be sweating. Were you breathing quickly at those times?

P: Yes. I could actually feel my chest, like, getting larger. I'd be driving home from work, and it would start hurting, and I could actually feel myself swelling up.

D: How come you thought it was your lungs?

P: Well, because they said my glands were swollen on my lungs. So I assumed it was my lungs. But this was a different type of pain than I had had before. I had indigestion problems all my life, from remembering back, that disappeared for awhile after I took the medication in tenth grade. But I knew I had a digestive problem. I'd never had pains like that, they only occurred after I went into the hospital.

D: How would you feel when you went to the emergency room and they said it was indigestion?

P: It's amazing because by the time I would get into the emergency room—I'd be in all this pain when I got there—but by the time a doctor got around to looking at me, I'd start feeling better.

D: Do you mean the pain would be decreasing?

P: Yes. And they would give me some medication while I was in the emergency room, probably a gas medicine, a little white medication and a little cup for me to drink. They'd say it was gas, and I'd start feeling better while lying there. You know, it may have been my nerves, and after I started hurting I got tensed up and made it worse. By the time I got someone to look at me, I'd start feeling better, but it wouldn't disappear. I'd go home and take the gas medicine and not rest good for that night or that morning, and eventually it would go away, then reoccur the next day or later on that night.

D: You would tell them that a doctor told you that you had sarcoid, and they'd say it wasn't that, but it was indigestion.

P: Uh-huh.

D: That explanation would be all right for you?

P: No. It's usual that I'd go to an emergency room at night, 11:00, 12:00, 1:00 or so. I'd take the medicine, and the next day it stopped hurting, and I'd go back again. In the meantime this is when I went to the other doctors, to complain about the same thing, to find out what was wrong; and they could never find out what was wrong with me either. But I've been to about five different doctors and was supposed to have had a complete physical and check to see if there was anything that was wrong with me. But no one could find anything wrong.

D: You got a clean bill of health.

P: Yes. Except I have a bladder problem, a drooping bladder that I have to get corrected. I don't want to go into the hospital anymore, so I just forgot about it.

D: I see. With these symptoms on and off over the years, has that interfered with the way you've lived your life?

P: Yes. At certain points when I go out or my husband and I go out, we have to leave early because I start hurting. I won't feel good before I get there, so I'm miserable by the time I get where I'm going, and 99 percent of the time I can feel it coming on. I know when I'm getting sick.

D: Does anything trigger it?

P: I don't know. I just start feeling tight in the chest and sort of a slight aching around the ribs, and I know that eventually it's going to get worse. So what I do now is start taking the medication ahead of time. If I'm going out, if I don't feel totally good and I feel like something's going to happen to me, I take an Alka-Seltzer. I take a couple of them with me so I can take them while I'm there. Sometimes it helps, and sometimes I come home early. A lot of times I just won't do things because my chest is hurting for one reason or another. It's really caused a lot of problems in planning to do things.

D: Do what kind of things?

P: Go to the gym for exercise. I'm learning how to play racquetball. Or just go out with friends.

D: You work?

P: Yes.

D: Does it interfere with your work, those pains?

P: Yes, but I still work. I'll be at work feeling miserable. The day I came to the emergency room I was at work at the time. When I'm trying to work and I keep getting these pains, I just get disgusted. If it's not going away, I might as well see if there is anything else wrong other than the sarcoid. Usually when I get pains I wait around for a while because from understanding what the doctor said, I would get joint pains, or certain types of pains, up until the day I die. He said sarcoid didn't go away—it never did.

D: How did you react to that?

P: I was hoping that eventually someone would find out the cure for it.

D: Have you had chest x-rays recently? Did they show the sarcoid was the same?

P: When I came to the emergency room this time the doctor told me then he didn't see any signs of sarcoid. His explanation was that sarcoid *does* disappear. When I had an examination for physical problems, one doctor said he didn't see any signs of sarcoid, but I knew I was still having joint pains. Two months ago when the doctor checked me and another doctor looked at the x-rays, he said he didn't see any signs of the sarcoid then and that they were doing a study now, on blood and various things, to see if it was connected to sarcoid. I haven't called him back, but they do want to take some more blood to study . . . if I was having these pains . . . for sarcoid. I haven't gotten the result from that yet.

D: What you're saying is that right now, from what they tell you, you don't have sarcoid.

P: Right.

D: And the doctors are saying that that should not be the cause for the pains you're having now.

P: Right. One particular doctor told me that I should eat correctly and maybe that would help my digestive problems (*laughs*). Right after I had that test to find out if I had sarcoid the doctor told me sarcoid could make my eyes go bad. I had my eyes checked, and they were 20-20 vision at that point. The very next year my eyes were bad, and I needed glasses. From each year since then I had to have my eyes checked and my prescription changed. It gets worse each year. So I thought the sarcoid might have something to do with it, but when I go to the eye doctor he says it's just a regular nearsightedness. They don't see any problems as far as sarcoid in my eyes. So I guess my

eyes are just going bad. I can see close but not far away. And it's
getting worse. And that *worries* me (*emphatically*).

At the start of the interview Laura L. reports she came to the
clinic concerned that a persistent aching in her arm might reflect the
progression of her sarcoidosis. After several days of unremitting
pain, this seems a reasonable, responsible action, especially since it
was a similar complaint that originally signaled the onset of her
illness. However, as she continues her medical history it becomes
increasingly evident that Laura's concern about her bodily aches
and pains reflect an excessive, morbid preoccupation with her
sarcoidosis. This was first indicated immediately after discharge
from the hospital eight years previously after confirmation of her
diagnosis by biopsy. At that time she returned to the emergency
room two or three nights a week—for approximately one year—
complaining of severe chest pains. Despite repeated examinations,
her doctors would not attribute these pains to her sarcoidosis.
Rather, they recognized her heightened anxiety and told her she had
a "nervous condition" and that her pain was probably due to
gastrointestinal distress (a common anxiety symptom). Her symptoms were successfully relieved with tranquilizers and antacid
medication, further suggesting anxiety as their origin. There is other
evidence in the interview suggesting Mrs. L.'s anxiety response to
sarcoidosis. She reports the presence of chronic anxiety symptoms
during her many visits to the emergency room—rapid heart beat,
profuse sweating, rapid breathing with a choking feeling, and a
"scared" feeling. She demonstrates the pervasive nagging apprehension, the uneasiness, and doubt that accompany abnormal anxiety;
she made repeated trips to several doctors to "complain about the
same thing, to find out what was wrong," despite the fact that
approximately five physicians attributed her symptoms to "nerves."
In effect, these visits supplied her with constant reassurance against
her dreaded fantasy that the sarcoid had become more serious and
severe. And the fact that her pain vanished while she waited for a
physician to examine her suggests that the safety of the hospital
environment allayed her anxiety; as it diminished, her stomach pains
disappeared. Incredibly, we learn that the feelings and behavior
persisted despite the fact that in recent years three different
physicians "didn't see any sign of sarcoid" either on physical
examination or by x-ray. Unfortunately, Laura L.'s anxiety was so
great that she was unable to believe the doctors who informed her

she was in complete remission. Why Mrs. L. responds with such excessive anxiety in the face of reassuring evidence concerning her disease is best understood in light of the remainder of the interview. I shifted the focus to her family history, by asking about a medical illness in her family, namely poor eyesight.

D: Does that (nearsightedness) run in your family?
P: My mother. Yeah, my mother's eyes (pause).
D: Are your folks alive now?
P: My mother's alive, and three of my brothers. My father's dead. So is one of my sisters.
D: How old is your mother now?
P: She's seventy-one now.
D: Is she in good health?
P: She has a heart condition, but she gets around well.
D: What kind of heart condition? What's the problem?
P: I don't know exactly what's wrong with her heart. She, uh, got sick one day about three or four years ago and went to the hospital. They put her in the intensive care unit. They said one of her arteries had gone bad; something happened to it, and all they could do was wait to see which way the blood was going to flow, if it was going to heal itself. She pulled through it okay. All she tells me is she had a heart problem, but she didn't indicate what type.
D: Do you know what kind of symptoms she had?
P: No I don't. She has some pain, but I don't think it's coming from her heart.
D: Where does she have the pain?
P: Shoulders and hips. She says it's arthritis.
D: Have any doctors told her that?
P: Yes. She lives in California, but she told me, when I talked to her a couple of weeks ago, the doctors said she has arthritis.
D: Before the heart problem, was she a healthy woman?
P: I think she was a healthy woman, but I wasn't home much.
D: Was she ever in the hospital before for any reason?
P: No. Oh, I'm sorry. She has tuberculosis.
D: She has tuberculosis (surprised)!
P: She had tuberculosis. She stayed in the hospital with tuberculosis for nine months.
D: When was that?
P: Probably 1960 . . . '60, '61.
D: You were how old then?
P: I had just graduated from school so I guess it was '60. She went in in '60, and she stayed there for nine months.

D: Do you know what kind of symptoms she had then? Was she coughing a lot?

P: They thought she had pneumonia. She had started coughing up blood, and she went to the doctor in this rural area, and he said she had a cold and gave her some medication. I was living with my brother-in-law then because my sister had died and left three kids, so I had to move in with him to help him take care of the kids because they were small. My mother lay around the house for a couple of days and got worse, so my brother took her to the emergency room, and they said she had pneumonia and they immediately put her in the hospital. She stayed in there for a month, and then they said she had tuberculosis, and that's when they sent her to the sanatorium.

D: So the doctors were wrong initially?

P: Yes.

D: How did she do during the nine months in the sanatorium? Did she get better?

P: Oh yes. She did great. I think she's taking a medication now that she'll probably have to take for the rest of her life. But as far as tuberculosis is, as far as her lungs are, she's doing fine.

D: What did your sister die of?

P: The doctors said that she had a blood clot. She had a baby, and the baby was about a month old, and she died in her sleep one night. They said it was a blood clot.

D: Very sudden, and it must have been very tragic for the whole family.

P: Yes.

D: When was that?

P: Uh, '60, because I was in eleventh grade then.

D: So a lot happened around that time.

P: '60, '61 (*laughs*). My father went into the hospital a week after my mother went in for pneumonia. He had fluid in his left leg, and he stayed in the hospital for about a month. And I was the only one working. I had graduated, and I was working a job from 7:00 to 7:00 and going to one hospital, and then I'd leave one hospital and go to another hospital. My youngest brother was in school and so (*pause*).

D: The responsibilities all fell to you?

P: Right (*laughs*). And my sister was dead at that point. I was the only one around.

D: Your father got over his illness?

P: Yes, he did. He got out of the hospital after four weeks and was doing really well up to a couple of years ago. He had problems with kidney stones, and he had three or four operations. And he had a heart problem. Everything seems to have just happened. Finally . . . well he had kidney stones, they knew about that, but the heart problems occurred, and then later on it got a little worse and he just died. They said it was a heart attack, but it was after he had an operation for his kidney stones, and he wasn't doing well.

D: You think it was connected to the operation?

P: Yeah, because . . . I don't remember now, but my brother was reading the statement I think the doctor had written out stating the cause of death. My father died at home, and from what my brother was reading, he doesn't think it was what they said happened. I can't begin to say what it was, but he doesn't think it was from just a regular heart attack. It was from a problem occurring from him having the operation and his body not getting back all right, really not getting well.

D: Did you say this was a couple of years ago?

P: Yes, in 1976 . . .

D: How do you think, over the years, your treatment has been by the various doctors? Do you think you've been treated well? Do you think they've made some mistakes?

P: I think they've made some mistakes. I don't understand, each time I go to the doctor, it's my nerves. It may be, but from going to doctors, up until I went to the last one, I was sure there was something else wrong with me that they just didn't find. And I tried to indicate to the doctors to give me a physical . . . put me in the hospital and give me a thorough examination. But no one seems to want to do that. They say it's nothing wrong but my nerves. I would love to go into the hospital, get a thorough examination, a complete physical, check out everything, because I hurt off and on too much for something not to be wrong—unless it's like they say, it's really my nerves and it causes all types of problems. I was hurting right over here in my side, and I went to a gynecologist, and would you believe, he was telling me it was coming from my nerves, and he tried to explain to me how it could happen. I don't believe that, but what could I do besides go to another doctor?

D: Why do you think these three doctors have told you it's been your nerves? Why do you think they tell you that?

P: Because they can't find anything else wrong with me.

D: You think they are stumped, and they just use the nerves as an excuse?

P: I think that, and then I try to look at it the other way. You know nerves do cause problems. You've heard people talk all the time about people having nervous problems, and it causes all types of pains and can really make your body act in strange ways. I want to believe that, and then I sort of get upset when I go to the doctor's and he comes out and tells me that when I've been hurting. Because that's not going to help me anyway, by telling me my nerves are bad. If I'm still hurting and my nerves are bad, I'm probably not going to do any better, so I've learned to sort of accept that now.

D: Did the tranquilizers help you at all?

P: Yes I think they did. I've seen improvement since I started taking the tranquilizers. What I'd do is take a tranquilizer and sort of stay away from everything and rest for awhile. If I've been working a lot on the job, if I've been doing a lot of running around, I feel myself . . . my chest starts to get tense, it starts to get tight and I just go away, take a tranquilizer and relax. After I start feeling better, after a couple of days, then I stop taking them. I haven't taken any now for a couple of months.

D: And you haven't had any pain in your chest or shoulders?

P: No. I've had other type pains, and it may be coming from a lot of things. After the doctor told me I didn't have sarcoid, well I didn't understand that because I still had pains.

As Laura L. relates her family's medical history and details her own background, a picture emerges suggesting why she experiences an anxiety response to illness. To begin with, there is evidence that she reacts to any stress with anxiety. Her "nervous stomach," most probably an anxiety symptom, was first diagnosed during a predictably difficult period of her life. At the time she was a young adolescent, struggling with the developmental task of becoming more independent from her family. Her gastrointestinal symptoms reflected her emotional reaction to this period, signaling the potential for anxiety as a characteristic style of reacting to stress. Add to this patterned response the nature of her particular illness. Sarcoidosis is a puzzling disease; the cause of its onset, or acute exacerbations, is unknown. Its unpredictability was dramatically communicated to Laura when one of her physicians told her that "they don't have any cure for it," whereas another said that "sarcoid does disappear" and that he "didn't see any signs of it." Paradoxically, both statements were correct; sarcoidosis is a chronic illness characterized by clinical remissions and the ever-present potential to flare-up. This type of illness allows the patient the option of either gratefully accepting a remission and relaxing or anxiously anticipating a relapse. Habitually, Laura chose the latter course.

Probably the most significant factor affecting Laura L.'s response to illness was her perception of the medical treatment her family received over the years. In relating that history, she reveals a pervasive mistrust of physicians who attribute all her physical symptoms to nerves "because they can't find anything else wrong with me." Her feelings derive from the initial incorrect diagnosis of her mother's tuberculosis, the alleged mismanagement of her father's kidney stones (which she feels contributed to his demise), and the sudden death of a young, healthy sister during the postpartum period. When Laura's mother first became ill, she was told she had the flu and was sent home to rest. She showed no improvement, and subsequent physical examination revealed a pneumonia for which she was hospitalized. However, it took another month, during which time her clinical condition deteriorated, until her tuberculosis was correctly diagnosed. Although she started feeling better, medical treatment required nine months of recuperation in a sanatorium— far from the week's bed rest her physicians initially prescribed for her "flu." Coincidentally, Laura was also misdiagnosed when her sarcoidosis first appeared, and ironically, her illness was similar to her mother's, producing symptoms in the same organ system. It is reasonable to suspect that this caused Mrs. L. some apprehension as to the thoroughness and effectiveness of her treatment. It is probable that it also triggered fears as to whether she would get sicker and require prolonged medical treatment, like her mother, or even share the tragic fate of her sister and die suddenly at an early age.

Laura L.'s faith in physicians was further diminished by her father's medical treatment. Plagued by recurrent kidney stones, he required several operations. Surgery was repeatedly successful; however, he suffered a heart attack while recuperating from his last operation and subsequently died. Laura felt the operation had killed him, implying ignorance or negligence on the part of his physicians. Speaking of his death, she stated, "They said it was a heart attack, but it was after he had an operation for his last kidney stone and he wasn't doing well. . . . It was from a problem occurring from him having the operation." In other words, she feels the physicians fatally damaged her father. This is reminiscent of her feelings about the effects of the biopsy that confirmed her diagnosis of sarcoidosis. Early in the interview, when describing her recurrent chest pain, she emphatically complained that it had worsened "since I've had my operation (*biopsy*)." This procedure is benign and relatively painless, involving the surgical removal of a superficial lymph gland. To identify this procedure as the cause of her recurrent chest and shoulder pain is highly suspect. It is more likely that the biopsy, by affirming the presence of a chronic disease, provoked anxiety. Her emotional discomfort was then expressed as a common anxiety symptom (recurrent, vague aches and pains) which Laura attributed to a physical problem. And given her conviction that physicians had mistreated her family—in her mind causing them pain, suffering, and even death—she was primed to attribute some of her own suffering to the ineptitude of her physicians as evidenced, for example, by a poorly performed biopsy.

Laura L.'s abnormal concern for her health is tragic. She is crippled, a prisoner to her anxiety. Her pathologic anxiety not only brings the discomfort of annoying symptoms (gastrointestinal distress and vague pains in her chest and shoulders), it also interferes with every aspect of her life. She is distracted from her work and prevented from enjoying recreational play, such as racquetball or her exercise class. When she and her husband go out they frequently return home early because she starts "hurting." When she develops near-sightedness, a change in vision that normally occurs with aging, she becomes "terribly worried" because "a doctor once told me sarcoid could make my eyes go bad." Her sarcoidosis, in remission for approximately three years at the time of the interview, is ironically a secondary problem in her life. In effect, her emotional response to sarcoidosis has become her primary illness. And, as she indicates in the following interchange, the prospects are not hopeful that she will achieve some adaptive resolution of her feelings.

D: How do you think things will be in the future, in terms of sarcoid and the symptoms you've been having? How do you think you'll be feeling?

P: About the way I'm doing now. I think if nothing changes and they can't really find anything wrong with me—something has to be serious—I know I'll be having these digestive problems. I'll probably be taking the tranquilizers off and on continually.

5

The Angry Patient

FEELINGS OF ANGER are always associated with loss. Failing in athletic competition, misplacing the car keys, and not being selected by a particular school or club are all situations that stir up feelings that span the spectrum from mild annoyance to pronounced frustration and irritation. Life situations of even greater consequences, for example, divorce or losing a job, produce more intense and sustained hostility. Simply put, we feel angry when circumstances conspire to take from us something or someone we cherish.

Responding to the loss of health with anger is a similar universal experience. If we recall our reactions to a bout with an upper respiratory infection, it may be easier to identify with this response. It is not surprising to feel irritated when our first awareness upon waking one morning is the pain of a scratchy throat or congested sinuses. We are annoyed, anticipating several days of unpleasant symptoms. Memories of previous viral episodes may recur, especially if the illnesses were marked by particular discomfort, such as sustained high fever or a lingering bronchitic cough. It becomes hard to resist the impulse of pulling the covers back up and returning to sleep. Indeed, we frequently lose that battle, or elect to lose it.

Rather than face the day with our current level of physical distress we indulge ourselves. In addition to getting some needed rest, we also placate our feelings. At least temporarily we become insensitive to our responsibilities and feel comfortable allowing others—family members or coworkers—to do the work we neglect.

The inconvenience of an upper respiratory infection precipitates transient feelings of irritation. This is a minor, but common, situation that exemplifies the anger response to illness. It illustrates the general process of acting out the angry feelings arising secondary to illness, as opposed to working through those emotions. When individuals lose some aspect of normal functioning they may become quite angry. Obviously, circumstances dictate the degree of anger that is manifest. Torn knee cartilages may be stoically tolerated by many who rest the joint and perform the recommended exercises until the knee heals. It is doubtful a patient would be so reasonable were he the vigorous type whose overall contentment depended heavily on keeping athletically active throughout the year. Far from feeling inconvenienced and irritated he might feel handicapped, even crippled, and may repeatedly express his hostility to those around him. Similarly, should severe dietary restrictions become necessary because of peptic ulcer disease, it is naive to expect the patient not to feel anger. When dining with friends he must confine himself to bland fare while others are feasting. He may be so angry as to repeatedly decline dinner invitations; although this is a more passive expression of hostility, it demonstrates the depth of feelings, as the patient denies himself and his friends the pleasure of companionship.

In the case of profound illness it is relatively easy to see the rage of patients. I recently interviewed a young man who had had a traumatic amputation of his foot in an automobile accident. Bob was hospitalized for treatment of osteomyelitis, a subacute condition that had been present since the accident occurred, approximately one year previously. Partial loss of a limb is difficult enough to cope with, especially for a vigorous young man emerging from adolescence, eagerly anticipating the adventure and challenge of adulthood. However, life was particularly cruel to this patient, who had been a superb athlete and held a football scholarship to a major university. His shattered limb was paralleled by a shattered athletic career, which he had dreamed would provide an escape from his marginal socioeconomic existence. This young man was actually frightening in his fury. Throughout our meeting he repeatedly threatened to "get even" with the driver of the other car, who had caused the accident by running a stop sign and then fled without pausing to offer assistance. Bob talked of vengeance, almost irrationally, vowing to "make someone pay bad." He expressed bitterness towards his girlfriend, who was drifting from their relationship "because I'm a cripple," and anger towards his "useless" physicians who were unable to arrest his infection. He was frequently disdainful of me, criticizing my "stupid questions." He ended the interview by calling me "heartless" and demanding that I leave his room.

That Bob responded to the loss of his foot predominantly with anger was unquestionable. Interestingly, however, his anger was not focused exclusively on the person who caused the accident. Instead, he was angry at everybody—his physicians, his girlfriend, and even me, although we had only just met. His diffuse hostility illustrates an important aspect of the anger response: the patient's aggression is manifested in several directions—globally, toward himself, toward family and friends, and toward physicians and health care personnel—and is rarely confined to one of these areas. In this regard the illness response is reminiscent of the anger phase observed during normal grief. However, unlike grief, it is characterized by sustained, intense hostility, so pronounced it prevents the patient from recognizing and expressing his other emotions. In essence he chooses to be mad rather than sad, which inhibits the progression of normal grief, the working through of feelings attendant to the loss of health. The following describes the four component areas of the anger response.

Global anger is a diffuse, nonspecific hostility. Patients essentially rail at the gods for the unfairness of illness—an understandable reaction. The young executive aggressively climbing the ladder of corporate success must feel angry when it is he, not one of his colleagues, forced into a more sedate personal and professional life by a myocardial infarction. In such a situation the patient asks "Why me?" and becomes angry with the realization that there is no satisfactory answer. This is particularly true if he has lead a healthy life and feels he has been a giving, moral soul who deserves special consideration by the fates. But life simply is not fair. Illness is indiscriminate, and its victims respond to their poor luck with anger.

With the progression of an illness, patients also become angry with themselves. The affect may be expressed overtly, with self-deprecating, self-demeaning talk, as well as passively, via masochistic behavior. The reasons for this self-directed hostility are several.

First, some patients feel great responsibility for their ailments, believing they brought themselves to a sick bed because of excesses, such as overeating or smoking. This may be particularly true if they disregarded warnings from family or physicians about such behavior, or minimized symptoms of ill health. Patients may also become angry at themselves because of the decreased autonomy imposed by some illnesses. Individuals frequently respond to helplessness with anger, vividly demonstrated by a woman crippled with rheumatoid arthritis who screamed at me, "Now I need twenty minutes instead of twenty seconds to put on a pair of earrings." The recognition of one's mortality that is spawned by an episode of illness is another reason patients become angry with themselves. Some individuals simply hate getting older. They frequently become disgusted when something—regardless of how trivial—goes wrong with their body, reminding them they are not as strong as they used to be. Finally, should illness interfere with an individual's desire to pursue some long-cherished wish—such as travel in later life—he may become infuriated with himself for procrastinating and, consequently, forever denying himself his dream.

When struck by illness, individuals often become angry with those closest to them. They may resent family and friends, merely because they are not sick and do not have to contend with the consequences of ill health. To some degree they are perceived as alien—they are "have-nots" who simply do not understand the meaning of being sick. The woman suffering from endometriosis may appreciate her husband's soothing support but simultaneously resents it as condescending placation from someone who has no idea what she is experiencing. Patients may also resent family members if their illness alters the usual roles and prevailing equilibrium in the home. For example, the usually dependent family member may be forced into a more active, assertive position if illness prevents the predominant wage earner from continued employment. This can stir up significant resentment in a patient who, already stressed by diminished autonomy, feels threatened by the newly enhanced independence of his or her spouse. Illness may also spark angry accusations from patients who assign responsibility for their plight to various family members. Many individuals suffering from such diverse ailments as hypertension, peptic ulcer disease, or tension headaches have angrily informed me that a spouse or parent "made me sick." They may blame the family member for causing them excessive aggravation or forcing them into unhealthy habits or lifestyles.

In that same vein, patients are often angry at ancestors for passing on a defective gene, presumably condemning them to ill health. This hostility, which may be conscious or unconscious, is reflected in such statements as, "I knew I'd have a heart attack early in my life because everyone in my father's family died that way before age fifty." Even if the patient does not suffer a myocardial infarction, any symptom suggestive of heart disease (for example, hypertension) is that much more frightening to him. When a person is made to feel afraid, he usually feels angry toward those instilling the fear, in this case those who passed on to their children and grandchildren a predilection toward a specific disease. Additionally, individuals influenced by their family's medical history frequently identify with ancestors who suffered through a specific illness. Should they contract the same disease they may define it in their minds solely in terms of the symptomatology of the affected ancestor. For example, when diagnosed as having diabetes mellitus, a patient may perceive the diagnosis exclusively as a sentence of blindness or progressive amputation of the lower limbs. The patient may greatly resent his relatives for having revealed to him the devastating impact of the illness, without being aware of his idiosyncratically distorted perception of diabetes.

Finally, patients feel anger toward physicians and health care personnel. This anger, which again may be conscious or unconscious, ranges from mild irritation to extreme hostility. It may be overtly stated or communicated in a more passive fashion by a particular behavior. The reasons for it are myriad. First, by virtue of the profession, physicians are the bearers of sad tidings. In ancient times such messengers were put to death; the modern response may not be as extreme, but the sentiments are similar. No one wants to be told he is ill, particularly if the physical defect is serious or life-threatening. He responds to such news with anger, and a natural receptacle for that affect is the person who made him feel that way. Patients also resent the degree of control physicians exercise over them. After disrupting their lives by ordering individuals into the hospital, doctors subject them to multiple diagnostic procedures and therapeutic regimens which may be embarrassing, painful, debilitating, and disfiguring. They impose dietary restrictions, dictate acceptable levels of activity, condemn certain habits, and prescribe medications which may have unpleasant side effects. And this is done with the implicit—sometimes explicit—message that the patient has no choice but to accede to all these measures if he expects to improve. Patients are forced into this passive role; by its very nature the doctor-patient relationship fosters a hostile dependency, which enrages those who resent the abridgement of autonomy. Individuals may also be angry at doctors because they are stereotypically perceived as fit and healthy and, consequently, incapable of accurately empathizing with the state of ill health. These sentiments are reflected in the often heard accusation, "You don't understand what I'm going through because you don't have arthritis" (or angina, pancreatitis, or pneumonitis). Finally, some patients are angry at doctors because they have negative transference toward all authority figures. Such patients are presented with the perfect arena for venting those feelings when they come under a physician's care.

These are the four target areas for patients' hostility. As discussed in Chapter 2, everyone responds to illness with some anger and directs it toward these areas. However, unlike the anger phase in normal grief, the anger response to illness is characterized by hostility so pronounced in degree and prolonged in duration that it overshadows the expression of any other emotions accompanying illness. The patient's anger does not progressively diminish, thereby permitting the depressed feelings of grief to evolve. The anger lingers, feeds on itself, and consequently, becomes more intense with time. Recall Emily B. (Chapter 2), who required the amputation of her leg because of phlebitis. Convinced that she lost her leg because of a physician's negligence, she harbored a smoldering resentment toward doctors over the years. She acted out this anger by sullenly withdrawing from the world around her, as well as secretly sabotaging her medical treatment. Bob's tragedy more dramatically illustrates the anger response. A year after his accident he still exhibited a diffuse, treacherous rage. He had not even begun to feel the sadness associated with the loss of his limb; his predominant affect was fury, a feeling he found to be considerably more comfortable than sadness. Unfortunately, this interfered with necessary grief work and, consequently, prevented him from coming to terms with his loss so that he could proceed with his life.

The following interview offers a more detailed view of the anger response. Nellie T., a seventy-three-year-old widow, was hospitalized with a swollen and tender knee after a fall in her backyard. What she initially diagnosed as a simple effusion—she had a long history of arthritis and was all too familiar with inflamed joints—turned out to be a septic joint. She had a staphylococcal infection that was surgically drained and subsequently treated with intravenously administered antibiotics. Unfortunately, this did not contain the infection. Endocarditis developed and she was gravely ill for several weeks. Only recently, approximately three months after admission, could she realistically contemplate discharge from the hospital. She readily revealed her feelings about her accident and subsequent treatment in the following interview. As I was about to begin, Mrs. T. asked me to turn off the overhead light. I did so, and after I returned to my chair, she requested that I open the window and close the door to her closet. I again complied, and after I had sat down for a third time, she asked me for a glass of water. I offered her the nightstand pitcher, but she amended her request—she preferred that I brew her a cup of tea in a kitchen down the hall. At this point I poured her a glass of water and began the interview, well prepared for what was to follow.

D: Are you comfortable?
P: I really haven't thought about it.
D: I'd like to begin by asking you why you're in the hospital this time.
P: Why I'm in the hospital?
D: Yes.
P: I had had an operation on my left knee for arthritis. The doctor put me in the hospital for that for a week. Then, the second knee became infected—heaven knows why, though I did fall on it, but it did. Then I was rushed into the hospital in the middle of the night with an infected knee. I was operated on—it was washed out—then operated on again. I was terribly ill, and they weren't sure if they could save me, but they finally did.
D: Was that all during this hospitalization?
P: Yes. Yes, it was.
D: What was it that finally happened that made you realize you had to come to the hospital? Why did you come to the hospital?
P: I had this agonizing pain in my knee.
D: Did that frighten you?
P: I suppose so, but I don't remember now. A lot of things frighten you when you're down in bed, you know.
D: Have you been down in bed a lot lately?
P: The last couple of months.
D: Why is that?
P: Because of the infection in my knee (*loudly, staring at me*).
D: You said that you were pretty sick and that they . . .
P: I was ill, very ill, and my dear housekeeper, who's also a trained nurse, said that they barely saved my life.
D: What do you think about that?

P: How on earth should I know? I was on the other end, receiving.

D: Were you worried at the time?

P: Worried?

D: Yes.

P: No. Much further than worry.

D: How do you mean that?

P: Just what I mean. You get much beyond the point that you can worry about anything.

D: How do you get beyond that point?

P: Well that's some experience that you'll just have to have.

D: Can you tell us about your experience?

P: (Pause) Now let me think (pause). No, its hard to tell you because I think about it and float in and float out. Do you know what I mean?

D: No, I'm not sure I understand.

P: . . . and then I float in. I'll be half on the earth and half off the earth. So it's floating between the two places. Does anybody see a Kleenex around? (A large box is lying next to her bed, easily within reach. After I handed her the box, she blew her nose and returned the used Kleenex to me, which I threw in the waste basket.) Thank you very much, indeed.

D: No, I'm not sure what you mean. Could you tell us a little more about that?

P: I don't see why it's so hard for you to take it in.

D: What makes you feel that way?

P: I suppose it's partially physical . . . I would think.

D: Is there anything else?

P: (Pauses for approximately one minute) I can't think of any other expression except "floating."

D: Could . . .

P: (Patient interrupts) Please, my back is itching. Can you scratch it for me?

D: Where on your back?

P: In the middle of my back. (Interviewer scratches it.) A little further down please. It's an awful feeling when your back itches. Thank you very much.

D: Were you just floating there a minute ago, when you were quiet for a while?

P: I might have been.

D: Are you doing it right now?

P: I couldn't care about anything in the world at the moment. Nothing.

D: Why is that?

P: Because I'm detached from it all.

D: I see. Why are you detached from it all?

P: Thinking makes me terribly ill, terribly ill.

D: You've been terribly ill with your knee, which is infected. Anything else?

P: I think that's enough to kill a horse. Or at least they tell me it is.

D: What have they done besides draining the knee?

P: Every day?

D: How else have they treated you?

P: What?

D: What other type of treatment have you had?

P: I'd rather not remind myself about it.

D: Was it painful?

P: Yes. Agonizing and painful.

D: Can you tell me what it was?

P: The other treatment?

D: Yes.

P: Three quarters of an hour of pure agony which they call physical therapy. Now if that isn't enough, they add a few more things to it. I think for most people that's enough.

D: What did they do?

P: I don't want to go into details.

D: Are you getting antibiotic medication for this infection?

P: Oh Lord, yes.

D: And has it helped?

P: I assume so.

D: Are you feeling better than when you came here?

P: I don't know when I felt worse.

D: You feel worse now than when you first came into the hospital.

P: No, I meant I don't know when I felt worse than when I came in.

D: Oh, I see. So are you feeling better now?

P: Yes.

D: Much better?

P: You're asking me?

D: Yes, I'm asking you how you're feeling. (*Long pause during which patient does not reply.*) What were you thinking?

P: Nothing.

D: Are you thinking anything right now?

P: Not a thing in the world. I'm blissful, unconscious. I don't have a care in the world (*sarcastically*).

D: How has your treatment been here? How have the doctors, the nurses taken care of you? How has it been to be here?

P: Everybody's been extremely skillful, extremely kind. They've done everything in their power they could to pull me through.

D: Any complaints?

P: Good gracious, no (*sarcastically*).

D: None at all?

P: None.

D: You mentioned a minute ago that you had some agonizing treatment.

P: Yes. My father was a famous surgeon at the Yale School of Medicine. I suppose you've heard of the Yale School of Medicine.

D: I've heard of the Yale School of Medicine.

P: Yes. Well, he never submitted a patient to unnecessary pain. He always cut out the pain if possible. There was no use giving their nervous system an extra shock.

D: And you feel that has not been the case here?

P: Oh, I think it has.

D: They've tried to treat you the way your father treated patients.

P: (Long pause)

D: Is that correct, would you say?

P: Yes I would.

D: I see.

P: Thank you.

D: I don't understand why you're thanking me.

P: Because it's the courteous thing to do. There's not enough courtesy in the world today. Do you think so (sarcastically)?

D: That's a tough question. I don't know the answer to that. How long has your doctor been treating you?

P: Almost four months.

D: He was not your doctor before this illness?

P: No.

D: How did you wind up with him?

P: My nurse knew him very well.

D: Have you been sick in recent years?

P: Have I been sick in recent years?

D: That's right. Have you required extensive medical treatment or hospitalization?

P: Yes.

D: What type of medical problems have you had before this one?

P: Well, let's see. Two cesareans, a tubal pregnancy, and . . .

D: How did all that go?

P: Well, I'm still alive.

D: Still, your treatment may have gone well or not well. Can you give me an idea of how it was?

P: (Long pause)

D: Are you thinking something now?

P: No, I'm a complete blank.

D: Besides the cesareans and the tubal pregnancy, have you been in a hospital for any other reason?

P: (Long pause)

D: Do you want to continue talking, Mrs. T., or would you prefer to stop?

P: I think we've had enough, don't you?

D: Let me ask you one final question. I'd like to know what medications you're currently taking.

P: I get thousands—no, *millions* of pills. I can't tell you what they are.

D: Do you know what they're supposed to do?

P: I know what they're supposed to do. I'm not sure they're doing it. Goodbye.

D: You'd like us to leave?

P: Don't forget to write. Au revoir.

D: Is there anything you'd like to ask me before we leave?

P: Not today. Maybe tomorrow.

D: Thank you for letting us talk to you.

P: It wasn't much of a talk, was it?

D: It was somewhat informative. Thank you.

During my meeting with Nellie T. I felt I was talking to a petulant child. She seemed committed to making me suffer, presumably in an attempt to improve her own spirits. Relentlessly she tried to provoke me: she ordered me around, interrupted me, disregarded some questions, responded to others sarcastically, or purposely confused me. When not actively demeaning me—as in asking for a backscratch or using me as a receptacle for her tissues—she communicated her anger in a negativistic, passive manner. She frequently sulked in silence. When I tried to draw her out of these sullen periods she dismissed my efforts by informing me she was "detached from it all," choosing to remain aloof because thinking made her "terribly, terribly ill." Mrs. T. did not want to give me the time of day, and when she became bored with struggling she simply dismissed me—in English and French!

Mrs. T.'s anger was exclusively focused toward one target: the medical profession. She voiced no self-recriminations concerning her fall, nor did she curse the fates for her ill fortune. Rather, she relentlessly demeaned those caring for her—doctors, nurses, and physical therapists—condemning them as ineffectual, insensitive people who derived sadistic pleasure from inflicting pain. Several factors contributed to this jaundiced view. First, despite a chronic arthritic condition, Mrs. T. had lived an extremely active life. An avid traveler since her twenties, she was a true adventurer who not only explored the world's outposts, but wrote several books about her exploits. She had a wanderlust, and confinement of any kind—especially the regimented hospital routine—was her worst torture. Nellie T. was enraged at her helplessness, and she was furious about the time wasted because of her illness. Moreover, she considered her treatment to be incompetent and, consequently, the greatest obstacle to liberation from the hospital. Despite surgical and medical interventions, her infection progressed to life-threatening proportions. To her thinking, the doctors had not only confined her, they had caused her more pain and suffering, allowed her to become increasingly debilitated, and consequently, prolonged her convalescence at a stage in her life when time was particularly precious. She felt righteous indignation toward the medical community and felt fully justified in her fury.

Beyond these realities of her illness there was another strong determinant to Mrs T.'s anger response. Her father was a surgeon, according to her a "famous surgeon" at a prestigious medical center. She described his humanism and his efforts to spare patients unnecessary pain, implying a sharp contrast between his approach and her current treatment. She seemed to idealize him, and no one can compete with individuals invested with such over-determined positive regard. Consequently, all physicians disappointed her; when compared with her renowned father they were merely objects of ridicule. I certainly experienced that transference. I was in no way involved in her treatment, nor had we previously met; nevertheless, Nellie T. showered me with intense negative feelings. These sentiments could not have been intended for me personally; rather, they derived from experiences in her past that prevented an objective assessment of events in the present, specifically her view of physicians. It is enormously important for the treating physician to realize that patients can be affected by their past emotional lives. Should the physician fail to recognize the true origins of the patient's anger, the therapeutic alliance can rapidly deteriorate into an antitherapeutic tug-of-war between physician and patient. Effective medical treatment is not possible in such an atmosphere.

Surprisingly, Nellie T.'s behavior did not significantly interfere with her treatment. Despite her constant complaining and sadistic criticism of those who cared for her, she cooperated with her prescribed treatment. Although she objected to many diagnostic procedures, she never refused them. She rested in bed for weeks, despite a burning desire to travel around the hospital by wheelchair, and she struggled through physical rehabilitation while cursing the therapists. She begrudgingly allowed herself to be treated by people she considered incompetent and cruel who, for their part, responded to her desire to get well. No doubt her vitriol antagonized those who cared for her. Some may have responded by being less giving and comforting; however, they were not neglectful and, in fact, helped pull her through a life-threatening illness. The physician-patient relationship was preserved, albeit tenuously, instead of being transformed into an adversarial relationship. The following case illustrates the latter situation.

Janet R. is a sixty-seven-year-old widow with a ten-year history of cardiovascular disease. Hypertension was diagnosed when she sought medical attention for intermittent anginal pain. With treatment her symptoms were well controlled; however, when she was sixty-two she had a cerebrovascular accident, resulting in a residual left hemiparesis which clearly affected her functioning. She had to leave a factory job she had held for twenty-two years; she became dependent on medical disability payments for her livelihood and was obliged to rely on the assistance of a housekeeper. Despite her impairment, she adjusted admirably to her ill health, continuing her volunteer work for the church and traveling often to visit family and friends. Her major health complaint was her angina; its onset was unpredictable, and treatment had repeatedly failed to eradicate the pain.

Mrs. R. was rehospitalized for the first time approximately five years after her stroke. She was admitted because of a myocardial infarction which occurred when she was in another city. She recovered rapidly from the acute event, but her angina became considerably more severe. It increased in frequency and intensity, necessitating daily use of nitroglycerin. During the two years between her heart attack and our meeting, she was hospitalized three times. Each time her complaint was intractable angina. Each time she was admitted because her symptoms were felt to represent a preinfarction condition. Each time she obtained symptomatic relief only to have the pain recur at her usual level of discomfort when she returned home. Although she never suffered another heart attack, Janet R. was extremely displeased with her treatment. Throughout our meeting she made these feelings quite evident, assigning the responsibility for her continued impaired health to all those close to her—family, physicians, and even God—sparing only herself from her wrath.

D: What brings you to the hospital?
P: I don't know exactly what you want to hear, but I'll start with 1977. I was in Chicago visiting my girlfriend. She always gets up and goes to work, and she just leaves me in the day, and I just stay there until

she comes back. But that morning the pain struck me between 8:00 and 9:00. I said, "Lord, what is this?" I said, "I know you won't talk to me but I can talk to you. Lord, please remove this pain." But He didn't move the pain, and the phone rang, and it was my girlfriend on the line. She asked me how I was feeling, and I said, "I got the worst pain I ever had in my life." She asked me where it was, and I told her, "in my chest." I told her I didn't have my medicaid card; I left it home. I told her I could be constipated. So I went and had some prunes, and I felt good. The pain got less. But Sunday morning, about 1:00 in the morning, the pain started in again. My friend did all she knew she could do, and then called her girlfriend over, but she felt there was nothing she could do, so she suggested they take me to a doctor. I was gasping and she was trying to get something out of my throat, but there wasn't anything in my throat that was bothering me.

D: So you were having difficulty getting air, breathing?

P: Yes. And then I was ringing wet. So she said, "I don't like this. Why are you sweating like this?" And I told her I didn't know. She told me to go home and go straight to the hospital, and I said, "Don't you worry, I'm going." So my bus pulled out at 10:00, and I asked the ticket man what time we'd get to Washington. He said, "I'll put you in Washington at 7:00 at night." I said, "Don't say that, I'm sick." He said he was just teasing and that we'd be there by 5:30.

D: So you came back to Washington in order to use your medicaid card?

P: Right, because I didn't have anything else with me.

D: Could you describe your chest pain a little bit more fully to us? In terms of location and so forth.

P: I'm putting my hand right where it was (*middle of the chest*), and it's been here ever since. The first time it was also in my left arm.

D: It would move to your left arm?

P: Right. That's where I had a stroke. I didn't use to have pain in my arm even after my stroke. I could walk, do anything, without pain. I wouldn't have to have this nitroglycerin. But in two years since then I have had to use nitroglycerin everyday . . . if I could get them everyday. And I told the doctor, "You give me this medicine; I need it." I have a housekeeper coming in from 10:00 to 2:00. They gave me that because I had a stroke, and I can't take care of myself alone. And they gave me the medicine.

D: When did you have your stroke?

P: Seven years ago, in 1971.

D: Did you lose any functioning?

P: Oh yes.

D: Of what? Your left side?

P: Partially.

D: Did you have trouble walking after that?

P: Oh yes. I limped after that.

D: You hadn't limped before that?

P: No.

D: How about your arm?

P: This is my good arm (*lifts right arm*). But this one, when I'm laying down I can raise it up a little higher than when I'm sitting up. My hand's no good. I can't close it much farther than this.

D: Before you had that episode in 1977, you had never had chest pain?

P: Only if I had indigestion or something.

D: And that was the worst pain you ever had?

P: Oh yes.

D: How would you describe it?

P: Well, doctor, I'm trying to describe it to you the best I know how to describe a pain (*speaking louder and sounding more irritated*). It's pain that comes and stays and hurts. And if you don't take something right then you're in very big trouble. And the last two nights I had nitroglycerin pills to put under my tongue. I was sitting there watching T.V., and I put this pill under my tongue and I said, "Oh Lord, I have only one more. Now Lord, what must I do? For my sake, and your sake too, make it ease up this time."

D: You sound like you're a very religious person.

P: I'm trying to be, because that's the only way. You've got to serve God. You've got to give him all your time. You need to get on your knees and pray, to call Jesus, because he's the only one who's going to hear you. And I need him now, so I'm calling on Jesus to take me out of this hospital.

D: And you find that comforting?

P: Yes.

D: Originally in 1977, when you had the chest pain, before you got back to Washington, what did you think was going on?

P: Nothing because I wasn't drinking and I wasn't . . . doing nothing . . . just saying my prayers, asking God to get me here and he did. And my children were supposed to meet me at the bus station, but they were late and this man got off the bus and he told a cab driver, "Listen, man, I took this lady's suitcase off the bus and put it in your cab. If you don't get out and take her suitcase and put it on her porch, she'll let me know and I'll report you." The cab driver said, "Oh no, mister, don't worry, I'll put it on the porch for her." I got home, and when I got in the house the phone rang and it was my daughter. I said, "Don't say a word. Don't say my name and I won't say yours, because you know that bus was going to pull in around 5:00 or 5:30. You had nothing to do but dress your two children and come and get me."

D: Sounds like you were disappointed in her.

P: No. I wasn't disappointed (*almost shouting*), but she's just so slow in doing anything. I don't know how in the world she can dress her two children and get them to school and then get herself to work. But she makes it somehow, and I'm glad she does.

D: In 1977, just before you arrived in Washington, when you had that very nasty chest pain, did you think something medically was wrong with you?

P: No.

D: Why did you think that chest pain was occurring?

P: That's one thing I can't describe. I have thought about it, but I can't describe it. I wish I could. I really do.

D: In other words, you're not sure why you had chest pain instead of somebody else.

P: No.

D: Did you think you were healthy at that time?

P: No. I've never been healthy.

D: What are some of the other medical problems you've had?

P: I was operated on for two fibroid tumors. And I was operated on for appendicitis when I was sixteen. I stayed sick, off and on, for two years. And then I had terrible back trouble. And so since I've been up here it still hurts, from my neck down to my lower back. My feet hurt, too, now. Sometimes I can't walk around the house too good, and I can't do anything. I just sit down.

D: What did the doctor tell you the problem was? Was it arthritis?

P: He said it was bursitis. I asked him to do something for it. When I lived in Chicago my doctor there told me I'd never be cured. It lightened up a little. My doctor now gives me a pill, and I take it twice a day. When I first took them they worked pretty good, but after a while the pain became very bad again. I got no relief from the pills.

D: Retracing our steps, when you first got back to Washington you saw a doctor here, right?

P: Oh yes. I came right here. My daughter came over and brought me to the hospital, and they put me in intensive care for a week, and they kept me, and . . .

D: What did the doctor say you had?

P: He never told me what I had. They told me what they were treating me for. One doctor came in and said . . . he just came in and sat around, it wasn't like they were on rounds . . . he said, "Now you're cured," and this and that. He told me I could go home. Now, another one of them said I had a hernia. That's all I know.

D: I'm confused.

P: The doctor told me I might have a hernia. But the doctor told me I could go home, and I could come back to see him at my appointment. When I left he gave me these pills.

D: And those pills were nitroglycerin?

P: No, no. These pills are green and yellow. I take two at a time for the pain in my back and my hands.

D: Do you know the name of those pills?

P: No I don't. But I could get the name of them.

D: So at that time you weren't taking any nitroglycerin?

P: Oh yes.

D: You were taking nitroglycerin?

P: Right. I came in the hospital the first time in October. I had this severe pain all during that week. Then I called the hospital, and she sent me a prescription out and I had it refilled. So then when I got the prescription I put two under my tongue, because I didn't trust one. And I felt better, and then that Sunday night I thought it was finally gone, and I said to myself, "Thank Jesus. Thank Jesus." And about 7:00 it struck me again.

D: I see. So you had nitroglycerin before you went to Chicago.

P: Oh yes. But I didn't carry it with me.

D: You didn't take any with you?

P: No.

D: But when you did take it it did relieve you.

P: Right.

D: OK. When you got back to Washington and you had the chest pain, you took the nitroglycerin. Did it relieve you then?

P: The doctor gave me some when I got here.

D: He gave you some nitroglycerin. And that eased the pain?

P: Right. But you see, what I want to know is this. I'm taking the nitroglycerin, and I don't know where the pain is coming from. Do you know where the pain is coming from?

D: I'm not sure. I'd have to review your chart and speak with your doctors and see what their opinions are. Have they given you their opinion?

P: No.

D: They haven't?

P: That's the only thing I want the doctors to tell me. Why this pain comes and why do I have it? They should give me some relief.

D: You mean so far in the past the doctors haven't been able to tell you why you have the pain?

P: That's right. And give me no relief for it (*loudly emphasized*).

D: Have they given you any ideas as to what they thought the pain might be?

P: No.

D: They have no idea?

P: They've talked to my children. My daughter has talked to him a lot. And maybe he may tell her, but he won't tell me (*loudly*). I don't care what it is. I just want to know my condition. If God's going to take me right now, then I want to go. And I'd rather be dead. Because you hurt too much. And I don't want to go out of my mind. I want to have a clear mind in anything I do. (*practically screaming*). Because if you hurt you can't have it, you may just talk stupid . . .

D: You mentioned you have some children.

P: Yes.

D: How many children do you have?

P: I have one daughter and one son. He married and they have two babies. I wanted to take care of these babies, and I wanted a little girl, like my mother had.

D: What kind of people were your mom and dad?

P: Nice people, but my mother was mean. I had a really mean mother. You had to obey her and God. My oldest sister forgave her and I didn't. I give my sister credit. I used to get along with her, but after my daddy died, that's when I lived alone with my mother. I used to love one person, and that was my father. The day he died, I died.

D: When your father died you died?

P: Yeah. When he died I told the doctor that I didn't have anybody. He said, "Yes you do, you have Jesus." I said, "That's the only one I've got."

D: When did your father die?

P: In 1937. And my mother died in 1958. When she died I moved out after a few months and got into a house with my child and my sister. She didn't want to do anything around the house, like keeping it clean or anything. So I was the one who wound up doing the cooking and the washing and things like that. So finally I said, "I'm not going to stay if you don't work." I said, "I'm not going to wash and keep this house clean and all if you're going to do nothing."

D: Sounds like you want everybody to do their fair share.

P: Right. And they're going to do it around me. I did it around my mother. I had to do it, or else I got a chair around my neck.

D: Your mother was really demanding and forceful.

P: Right. And we had to do it or else we were out. If she saw a knife on the table and you didn't do what she wanted you to, you might have that knife land up in your heart.

D: Do you have any brothers and sisters?

P: Oh yes. I have two brothers and six sisters. In fact, I have another sister in the hospital now. She has heart trouble. She's worse off than I am. She's got too much fluid. They're trying to get the fluid out.

D: Is her problem like yours, or is it different from yours?

P: It's different from mine.

D: Now when you have your chest pain, do you notice it comes on at any particular time? Or with any particular activity you might be doing?

P: It can come on with any activity.

D: So you don't relate it to walking around?

P: Yes, even then.

D: Or if you're thinking about anything in particular? In other words, does it seem related to any particular thoughts you have?

P: No. I don't have thoughts with the pain.

D: How have you been treated by the doctors since you've been in the hospital?

P: How have I been treated?

D: Yes.

P: Well, doctor, some have been nice, and some have been so-so. Everybody has done a lot.

D: What makes them nice, and what makes them so-so?

P: I don't know.

D: What do you want from your doctors?

P: All I want them to do is talk to me nice and treat me nice and ask me about my condition, so I can tell them the best I know how.

D: Like what for example?

P: Well, you see I never had to walk down the hall in my life. When I was first in the hospital, when I had my stroke, they didn't have me walk up and down the hall. They had me going in a wheelchair to take therapy. Now I have to walk down the hall.

D: Why do they make you do that?

P: I don't know. I'm going to find out who's the expert and try to ask him. I'll ask you.

D: I don't know why they want you to walk up and down the hall.

P: Well, I don't either.

D: Have you asked your doctors?

P: No.

D: How come?

P: I just go ahead with what they command me to do (*angrily*). I'll go ahead and do it.

D: Well, you don't sound too happy about it.

P: No, I'm not happy.

D: Well, I'm surprised you haven't asked them.

P: I don't know. When you're scared of everything . . . I guess I act like I'm with my mother. If she told me to do something, I told her I'd do it, because if I didn't do it I'd get a whipping. So I don't want no punishment, and I just go ahead and do it.

D: I see. Do you have this pain in your chest everyday?

P: Pretty much. Now you see last Sunday the doctor said to me, "Do you want to go home today?" I asked him if the pain was cured, and he said, "I don't know." I said, "OK, if you want me to go home I'll go home." He said he'd tell the nurse and discharge me. The nurse came in then and said, "Here's the slip. Now you can go home." I asked her what the slip was for, and she said it was my prescription. I said, "I don't use that type of medicine. I'm going to take nothing." She was a little insulted. Then I said, "I'll take what you say here, but I'm not going to take this paper (*prescription*) because it's wrong." So then my doctor came in, and he asked if I had my right prescription. I told him no, and he gave me another one. Then he said I was discharged. I asked him what he thought about my pain, I asked if he thought it was gone. He said, "I think you're much better," and I said, "OK." Then I called my daughter, and she came to pick me up. And then, as soon as I got in the house (*loudly enunciates each word slowly, while banging her fist into her hand*) the pain struck me again. And it stayed, so I came back to the hospital.

D: You came right back into the hospital?

P: No. I waited until the next day, but still I had the pain.

D: So you don't really think that he helped you that much.

P: No. He didn't give me any new pills. I can't say what helps me. He tried his best to help, but he wouldn't try anything else (*again slowly, loudly, and emphatically*). But this time he said, "I thought this medicine would work, but it hasn't worked so you've got to have something else." That's when they cut me. I don't know what they cut me for. I don't know what they took out, but they cut me last week. (*Patient is alluding to her recent cardiac catheterization.*)

D: When you had your stroke, how did things go after that? How did you get by?

P: A housekeeper came over every day. She fixed my breakfast, my dinner, she combed my hair, she gave me a bath and did my washing.

D: Did you feel you were doing OK even though you had a stroke?

P: Yes.

D: After the stroke did you still feel you could carry on day to day, that things would be all right?

P: No.

D: You didn't feel that?

P: I didn't really give it a thought that way.

D: Would you say the pain troubles you more than the problems you had since your stroke?

P: Yes. Definitely!

D: The main thing that troubles you now is the pain?

P: Right.

D: Do you think the doctors are ever going to get rid of the pain?

P: I don't know. I'm going to keep on trying. I'm carrying all my trouble to Jesus. I have taken medicine for high blood pressure. It has not done me any good that I know. So I'm looking up there (*points to the sky*). I'm going to fight Him from now on.

Janet R.'s initial response to the heart attack was denial, extreme in degree though temporally predictable with the onset of illness. Despite classic symptoms of myocardial ischemia—severe precordial pain, diaphoresis, and shortness of breath—she declined treatment in Chicago "because I didn't have my medicaid card." Almost immediately, however, anger displaced this denial. While describing the acute phase of a life-threatening event, she informed me of her annoyance with the ticket salesman at the bus depot, of struggles with a cabdriver, and of fury at her daughter for not meeting her at the bus station. She not only recalled these events, she described them as meticulously as she detailed her physical symptoms, a hint that her eventual illness response would be dominated by anger. In fact, Mrs. R. was an extremely angry woman; her hostility was intense and diffuse. She condemned her family for not supporting her, criticized physicians for not curing her, and even blasphemed God for abandoning her despite her deep religious convictions. Her basic position concerning the physical decline following her heart attack was simple: no one had successfully relieved her anginal pain, and for that she was unforgiving. The extent of these feelings initially surprised me, given her apparent adjustment to a stroke several years earlier. However, that condition reached a steady state which permitted a fair degree of autonomy despite residual paralysis. The heart attack, on the other hand, resulted in chronic unstable angina, a painful and unpredictable symptom. As a result her life was much less under her control, an important reason for her anger response but not the major determinant.

An appreciation of Janet R.'s psychodynamics, specifically concerning the relationship with her parents, provides the most precise understanding of her illness response. Her mother was described as "mean," someone "you had to obey." To defy her invited ostracism ("We had to do it or else we were out.") or physical harm, such as getting "a chair around your neck" or having "a knife land up in your heart." Even though these perceptions were exaggerated, they still shaped Mrs. R.'s basic feelings toward nurturing and authority: compliance is rewarded, disobedience severely punished. Imagine the impact of this philosophy on a child. Her early years conditioned her to respond to authority with terror—and subsequent fury. This response became a sort of conventional wisdom for her, and it prevailed throughout her life. She certainly interacted with physicians in accordance with these dynamics. She rarely questioned their authority, feeling comfortable with her passivity when treatment was successful. However, when the doctors were unable to relieve her symptoms, she felt cheated because they had failed to reward her compliance. This enraged her although she was too fearful to criticize openly. When asked why she acquiesced to "what they commanded" despite the fact that she was "not happy" with her treatment, she replied, "I guess I act like I'm with my mother. . . . I don't want no punishment, and I just go ahead and do it." Unfortunately, owing to this fear, her fury was expressed covertly, taking the form of a sustained, smoldering resentment evident throughout the interview. She frequently informed me of her doctors' failings, holding them responsible for persisting pain from a chronic bursitis, unremitting angina, and a prolonged convalescence following an appendectomy. She questioned their ethics when they informed her children of her medical conditions while allegedly withholding information from her, and she implied negligence in the anecdote about the incorrect prescription. She illustrated her doctor's clinical ignorance by recalling how she required rehospitalization the day after discharge despite being told she was "much better." She even snapped at me several times. The legacy of her domineering mother was powerful; resentments against control that smoldered during childhood were still being acted out in her adult life.

The effect that Mrs. R.'s relationship with her father had on her psychological functioning is another important determinant of her illness response. She obviously idealized her father. Describing him as the one person she used to love, she sums up the intense pain of his loss by her statement, "The day he died, I died." She attempted to diminish her grief by turning more toward religion, an action that, interestingly, was promoted by her physician. After her father's death, Jesus became "the only one I've got." In this manner she transferred to the Heavenly Father some feelings she held for her biologic father. And just as she looked to her father for support and protection from her mother, so she frequently turned to God for guidance, strength, and relief during periods of illness. Jesus was a caring and loving savior, "the only one who's going to hear you." She prayed constantly, asking Him to ease her anginal pain, thanking Him when relief came, calling on Him to "take me out of the hospital." It is therefore surprising that she ends the interview by implying her disappointment in God and announcing, "I'm going to fight with Him from now on." However, this too reflects unconscious feelings toward her father. Mrs. R.'s continued suffering was proof that despite her faithful worship, Jesus had abandoned her. She loved Him and he disappointed her, leaving her defenseless against her pain. This paralleled her feelings at the time of her father's death. Her sadness must have been accompanied by considerable anger, as his passing deprived Mrs. R. of her major ally against her mother's wrath. For years she was able to contain her rage under a veil of enhanced faith. It finally emerged when she concluded that the Heavenly Father, like her biologic father, had abandoned her.

Janet R.'s case demonstrates the overwhelming importance of understanding an individual's feelings vis-à-vis authority figures. These emotions insidiously define the patient's transference to physicians and can significantly affect the doctor-patient relationship. This is particularly true of the anger response to illness. Lacking an accurate psychological assessment of patients, physicians frequently find themselves embroiled in struggles they simply do not understand. This may cause them to view certain patients as unreasonable and stupid, if not irrational. Unless physicians realize that such patients are merely fighting old ghosts, they may respond with a comparable hostility and, thus, further undermine the therapeutic relationship.

A final point about the anger response concerns the various means of expressing the affect. As with other emotions, hostility is communicated through words or deeds, either overtly or covertly. Conscious awareness permits overt expression such as Nellie T.'s stated complaints or her acted out anger, which included sending me on numerous errands at the outset of the interview or merely ignoring me. Patients frequently express anger behaviorally; they may refuse necessary diagnostic tests, therapeutic procedures, or prescribed medications. In the extreme they can leave the hospital against medical advice or terminate the relationship with the treating physician. The passive expression of anger suggests that the affect is unconscious, out of the patient's awareness; however, it may also reflect a chosen style of aggression. Such covert expression is effected via characteristic behavior, including stubbornness, sullenness, forgetfulness, disinterest and withdrawal, or persistent negativism. Both of the patients described in this chapter demonstrate passive aggression, although it is considerably more evident in Janet R.'s behavior. This was reflected in a generalized negativism and sullenness, as well as specific interactions, such as her inability to provide me with a coherent medical history. All of this behavior is infuriating, but it should not distract the physician from the task of determining why the patient is angry. If he is able to discover the cause, he is equipped to help the individual work through the angry affect and, thus, to provide more comprehensive, effective treatment.

6

The Depressed Patient

DEPRESSION IS A WORD used excessively, perjoratively, and often incorrectly. It is naive to label as depressed any individual expressing the normal sadness that accompanies difficult, sometimes tragic, life circumstances. As already noted, the expression of sadness is an integral part of normal grief and is necessary for the individual to achieve the emotional growth required to cope adequately with losses. Depression, on the other hand, is pathologic; it is a disease. Like any other disease, depression has specific signs and symptoms which define a predictable clinical syndrome. It is primarily an emotional disorder; however, like any other disease, it affects the mind and the body. Its symptom complex can be broken down into four major categories.

First, depression is characterized by alterations of affect. The emotional pain of the depressed individual is usually reflected in a sustained lowering of mood. He is at best subdued; more pronounced depression brings gloom or a profound sadness. Intermittent tearfulness and crying are common. A growing sense of joylessness and despair contributes to the patient's acute loneliness. In the extreme, this feeling state may be so exquisitely painful that it provokes suicidal behavior. An alternate affective change that accompanies depression is an elevation of mood. Some individuals become chronically anxious or agitated, finding themselves incapable of relaxing, of feeling calm. In the extreme, manic feelings, even euphoria, predominate. The presence of such inappropriate feelings, supposedly antithetical to the depressed state, is felt to represent an unconscious defense that distracts the individual from the pain of his particular loss.

Second, depression induces definite changes in the body's physiologic functioning. Somatic symptoms are varied and diffuse, affecting many different organ systems. Appetite disturbances are common. The depressed patient often eats less, reporting that "food has lost its taste" or "I just don't feel like eating." This may result in varying degrees of weight loss. Conversely, some people find solace in eating, consume more, and gain weight. Other gastrointestinal symptoms, such as constipation, occur. Sleep disturbances are a cardinal symptom of depression, presenting either difficulty in falling asleep, waking frequently during the night, waking up in the morning hours incapable of returning to sleep, or sleeping excessively. Associated with this is a diminished energy level, often accompanied by lethargy, listlessness, and chronic fatigue. The affected individual may have difficulty concentrating, experiencing memory lapses or a more generalized forgetfulness. Libido is impaired, resulting in decreased interest in sexual activity or diminished enjoyment and pleasure. This can progress to total abstinence, produce impotence in men or anorgasmia in women. Often a woman's menstrual cycle becomes irregular or even ceases for several months. A myriad of bodily complaints, sometimes bordering on hypochondriasis, may occur. These may be nonspecific, such as diffuse vague musculoskeletal aches and pains, or more focused, such as headaches or the lower back pain frequently reported by depressed patients. In short, depression has a pervasive impact on the normal functioning of the body, and as Lindemann (1944) noted, it can affect any organ system.

Third, the depressed individual suffers from a progressive lowering of self-esteem. Reacting to his change in mood and impaired mental and physiologic functioning, and fearing he may never regain his former self, he becomes plagued with self-doubt. He views himself in a harshly negativistic, self-disparaging light, minimizing his accomplishments and maximizing his shortcomings. He feels weak, guilty, helpless, worthless, and ineffectual. Self-esteem may be so damaged that feelings of hopelessness surface and the depression deepens. Everyday thoughts become increasingly gloomy and despairing.

The fourth major aspect of depression is an alteration of the usual patterns of behavior, most probably the net effect of the above factors. The most universal change is a generalized withdrawal—both psychically and physically—from one's environment. The morbid self-preoccupation accompanying impaired self-esteem fosters feelings of inferiority, which enhance a sense of detachment from others. There is a loss of interest in daily activities (family relationships, work, recreation, and social functions) rendering the patient increasingly isolated. Interest in daily life wanes. The ability to perform everyday functions decreases. The world is perceived as boring, joyless, and threatening, and the depressed individual spends an increasing amount of time by himself. He may take long solitary walks, or retreat to his room, spending many hours reading. If poor concentration prevents him from finding pleasure in books, he may sit in front of the television for long periods. Some patients become so withdrawn that they spend the major portion of each day sleeping. Depression markedly constricts everyday behavior. Deriving little enjoyment from life and lacking hope that he ever will, the affected individual feels increasingly alienated from his world. He takes refuge in a much smaller world of his own making, separating himself from those he perceives as strong and more worthy.

Depression is diagnosed by the presence of these four interrelated components. It affects a person's body and emotional status, his perception of himself and his environment, and the conduct of his daily life, constituting a clinical syndrome similar to the grief process. What then differentiates normal grieving from the disease depression? This question was addressed by Freud in his monograph *Mourning and Melancholia* (Freud 1917); he responded in both pragmatic and theoretical terms. Practically, grief and depression are distinguished by degree and purpose. Grief is a dynamic growth process, as discussed in Chapter 2. When grieving, an individual reminisces about what he has lost, recalling the associated positive and negative emotions. In this manner he acknowledges and then analyzes his feelings related to the loss, establishes a new emotional equilibrium, and, consequently, is able to derive continued satisfaction and pleasure out of life. Depression, on the other hand, interferes with one's enjoyment of life. It brings stagnation instead of emotional growth. Depressive symptoms are generally more severe, persist longer, and interfere more profoundly with normal functioning.

The theoretical differentiation of these two entities, as set forth in *Mourning and Melancholia,* is based on the inability to assess accurately and honestly the feelings associated with loss. Using bereavement as a model, Freud argued that in melancholia (depression) the individual is unaware of a segment of his emotions—namely, hostile feelings—toward the deceased. The reason for this emotional block varies, but Freud believed that the effects are universal: because unacknowledged, unexpressed anger must be discharged somewhere, the bereaved ultimately directs it toward himself. This is the theory of internalized aggression. In Freud's view, the symptom complex of depression—the painful feeling state, withdrawal and isolation, decline in bodily functions, and self-recriminations resulting in lowered self-esteem—results from pronounced angry feelings that the bereaved unconsciously and unremittingly directs internally because of his unwillingness to view the deceased in a negative light.

In recent years the study of the brain's neurophysiologic functioning has brought into question the validity of Freud's theoretical explanation of depression. The catecholamine hypothesis first postulated that mood disorders derive from abnormalities in the balance or concentration of specific neurotransmitters. This has been demonstrated experimentally in animals by altering levels of cathecholamines and indolamines, findings that have been supported in humans via clinical studies of antidepressant medications. As reflected in the *DSM-III,* a connection most probably exists between various types of depressive illness, which suggests an interaction between psychological and biologic factors in the individual patient. This would explain why depleting stores of norepinephrine and serotonin in rats' brains with the use of reserepine, socially isolating infant monkeys (Harlow and Harlow 1971), or sensorily depriving human neonates (Spitz 1945, 1949) all produce the same clinical syndrome: depression. Unquestionably, there is a biologic component to depression, particularly severe depression; however, this does not negate the psychodynamic determinants of the illness. Many nonpsychotic depressive conditions, such as adjustment disorders, dysthymia, and characterologic states, derive from an individual's inability to acknowledge fully, to bear, and to put into perspective all of his emotions relating to a particular loss. This includes depression precipitated by loss of health. Such was the case with Eric (Chapter 1), who became depressed because of an inability to perceive all of his feelings related to diabetes, particularly his resentment toward peers and physicians. Once he acknowledged this hostility he became more concerned with his own well-being, began to comply with the medical regimen prescribed by his physician, and consequently, showed a marked and rapid improvement in his physical status.

The following case study offers a more detailed illustration of the depression response to illness. Carl N. is an elderly gentleman who was recuperating from a recent heart attack at the time of this interview. He was admitted to a hospital two and a half weeks earlier, following a syncopal episode which was accompanied by severe precordial and left shoulder pain. During the first twenty-four hours of hospitalization, he became markedly hypotensive, and there was concern that he was lapsing into cardiogenic shock. A sinus bradycardia necessitated the insertion of a temporary pacemaker, which rapidly stabilized his clinical status. His congestive heart failure remitted, and his ectopy was well controlled; and, except for concern about a mild pericarditis, the physicians were pleased with his progress. He showed remarkable physical resilience for a man of his age; however, his emotional adaptation to his illness was less successful. As the nursing notes reported as early as the second day of hospitalization, Mr. N. became "belligerent and aggravated . . . stating that he doesn't want to be here and he would rather die." Several days later a nurse reported "the patient feels fine physically but says he has felt for a while that his life has been long enough." Ironically, as he became stronger physically, surviving a complicated myocardial infarction at his advanced age, he became increasingly debilitated emotionally. He complained of lethargy, chronic fatigue, anorexia, and poor concentration, and he was frequently observed to be tearful or crying. Some aspects of his symptomatology, specifically his physical and mental energy levels, were partially attributable to his heart attack. Mr. N. was unquestionably depressed, and it became increasingly apparent that his clinical depression was a greater threat to his well-being than his cardiac status. As a result, approximately three weeks after his admission, he was transferred to an inpatient psychiatric unit for treatment.

As we talked in his room, Mr. N. looked to me like a beaten man. He was unkempt; his clothes, wrinkled and dirty, hung from his frame, indicating weight loss. He wore no socks, and his shoes were untied. He had not shaved for several days. He sat almost motionless, shoulders hunched over, head hung down, staring at the floor. When answering questions, he moved and spoke slowly, his voice very soft. He seemed distracted, periodically drifting and staring off into space. He seemed pathetic, and as we talked I wondered how he could have gotten to such a state in three short weeks. The following interview provides the answer.

D: Could we begin by you telling us the events that led up to your coming into the hospital?

P: When I got sick?

D: Uh huh.

P: Well, I got up, it was the 18th of October. I got up about 7:15. I felt fine; I felt good. Then I went to the door, to pick up the paper, the newspaper. So, it wasn't there, and I went to the kitchen to make some coffee. I remember that, I mixed some coffee. I decided to go back to the front door to pick up the newspaper, and the paper was still not there. So I turned around, and something happened that I will never forget as long as I live. It was just like a ton of bricks got on me, and I couldn't stand up anymore. Then my chest felt bad, it hurt. So I sat; I thought I'd shake it off, but I couldn't do it. I called my wife and my son, and they came down. Meanwhile, I was sweating, sweating a lot. (*Although obviously on the verge of tears, the patient was fighting hard not to cry.*) My son called the ambulance right away . . . you know . . . it seems to me . . . the rescue squad came so fast . . . in about ten seconds . . . seems to me they were just waiting for me, I guess. I don't know what to make of it. That would have been impossible, because the nearest place to my house was about a mile away, and it would take at least five minutes by the time they got started and got around to my house. But it was just about a minute or two later that they arrived inside my home. You know. That's about the end of it. They put something on my face and then they took me to the hospital. That's all I can tell you about this.

D: Have you ever had any pain in your chest before?

P: No. That's the strange thing about this. I was never in my life in any hospital. I've been in hospitals visiting friends and relatives. I never was a strong man, a strong-built man, but I was never sick. So going to the hospital for me was something new altogether. I've never been here before so. . . . (*The patient drifted off.*)

D: Did you ever feel any chest pains before?

P: No, I never had that . . . but I must say that about four months ago I did begin to feel tired. I think that's the mistake I made. I should have gone to the doctor right away, which I didn't do. I took it for granted that I was all right. I was working, driving my cab a lot, and making a very good life, you know, feeling good. To me, it still is a mystery how all of a sudden I'm in the hospital. To me, I still don't believe it fully. I don't say it was a shock because everybody gets sick, I guess, including me. I'm no different from the rest. But anyway it was a big surprise to me how I suddenly wound up in the hospital. . . . I've been driving a cab every day of the week, except of course I don't drive as much as I used to. I stopped driving as much six or seven years ago, when I got social security. I thought I did enough work in my life. I've been working since I was twelve years old, and I thought it was time that I take my time and not rush around as much as I did. So I've been driving my cab for a few hours, then go home and rest. I have a hobby. I play the organ. I go to classes sometimes . . . at least I did, and there hasn't been a lot I can do because . . . (*tears*) . . . I feel so weak. I'm not sure if I'll be able to drive again, because I'm not sure that I'll have the strength (*tears*).

D: You've been feeling weak and tired for four or five months now?

P: No, not quite. For the past four or five months I felt well. I would say maybe a week or two before I got sick I did feel . . . which I didn't think much of it before . . . a little bit weak. I remember one day going upstairs into the house. I did feel a little bit that I was beginning to get on, you know, getting older. Of course, I must say this: I've been smoking quite a bit, average about two packs a day, which I thought about then. You know the strange thing is that since I got sick I have no desire to smoke cigarettes. Since October when I came to the hospital I haven't smoked one, and I have no desire to smoke one. I don't know if that's helpful but . . .

D: You say you felt a little strange a couple of weeks before you got sick.

P: Well, I felt a little weak, let's put it that way, but no pains.

D: Did you feel dizzy at all?

P: No, I just felt that . . . well, I remember the last few days I drove a cab. I drove about three hours each day, and I went inside to go home, which I did, and I lay around and slept for a couple hours. And when I got up I played the organ for a couple of hours, you know. And during that time I felt a little sick during the day . . . you know, weak, sick. . . . But prior to that I didn't feel nothing. I had a small headache, and I didn't feel quite as strong, but I'm seventy-six years old. And I took it for granted that when you get old you haven't got the strength anymore, which you had before.

D: What do you think about your symptoms now?

P: Well, today I don't know what to think about all this, because something happened to my cousin, he had a heart attack some time ago. This goes back about ten or twelve years. It got worse this past summer. He works in his yard, he does pretty heavy work, and many times he comes to help me in my yard. Really I don't know, I couldn't understand the guts he's got doing all that work.

D: And do you expect you'll do that when you get over this?

P: Well I have to answer it this way. Really, I don't expect much at all. I would like to have my strength back and return back to my work.

D: Do you expect to do that?

P: Well what can I do? I mean, as I said a little while ago, you see, I was twelve years old . . . (tears).

D: You look very sad.

P: When I started to work I was twelve years old . . . (tears). Can I have a little water please? My throat is very dry (drinks a glass of water). What I was going to say is that the only thing I've ever known in my life is work. I was twelve years old when I started to work. I was an old man at twelve years of age. I came to this country when I was sixteen. I came by myself. It's not so easy for one of us to come to a country like this. It's because we don't speak the language. If I see you on the street, I might say hello to you, I might say good morning to you, but I don't know how to say that. I have no education. And it wasn't so simple, but in those days, I never worried about anything. I mean, I went through life. I've done all types of work, including shoveling snow, which I'm proud of. I've been cleaning garages and basements. I had a brother in Baltimore. At one time we never got along too good. His life was different from mine. But one day I went to see him, and we got to talking about work. I had a job in New York, where I was making twenty-five or thirty dollars a week, but at that time I was only making six or seven dollars a week, and even in those days that wouldn't even pay my board. So my brother said he had an idea. He said, "Why don't you stay in Baltimore. I'm a carpenter by trade, but I can't find any work, and I'm driving a cab." I told him I didn't know anything about Baltimore or driving a cab. But he said that if I really wanted to do something, to learn something, that I'd learn in a few weeks. The next Monday morning I applied for a license to drive a cab. In those days it wasn't like today. In those days the police asked you questions, and if you answered about four out of seven you'd get the license. But the truth is that I only answered one and that was a lie anyhow because he asked me how long I'd been in Baltimore. I said, "One year," but I had only been there one day. But he didn't say much. He asked me where a certain hotel was, where the emergency hospital was, and I didn't answer him. So the policeman—he was nice to me—he said, "Don't worry about it." He told me to get myself a little book about the city, which I did. So I went back two more times and I got the license. The policeman said, "I'm going to give you the license but you don't know anything about Baltimore." And he was right. I got the license and the little book which he told me to study. He said if I didn't study it I would find myself in jail. I didn't buy that, but sure enough, after driving a cab in Baltimore I found myself in jail. And that was the first and last time in my life that I went to jail. And if I had read the thing I wouldn't have gone to jail. You see, in those days they had regulations like on a certain street you could not cruise in an empty cab. You had to learn which streets you could not cruise in an empty cab, and I didn't know that.

D: Have you been driving a cab ever since then?

P: Yes sir.

D: So it's forty years since you've been driving a cab?

P: More than that.

D: Forty-eight years? I see. And you said before that you weren't sure that you'd be able to go back to work.

P: Well, yes. Before I got on this discussion, yes, I still believe it today. That's the way I feel. You know I've been gone over two weeks now, and I have no appetite. The only thing I drink is water, no juice. I sleep all the time. And I can't seem to get any strength back.

D: You look sad. You look like you feel sad.

P: Well, I guess all of us . . . *(tears)* . . . a little bit disappointed, I guess. Maybe I shouldn't be, because I've driven people in my cab—I get them every once in a while—young kids who are deformed. Young girls, young boys, which I feel so sorry for them . . . *(tears)* . . . you know. I say to myself, "God, thank you so much," because I'm to an age . . . and looking at these kids . . . just taking the fare. . . . One had to get the money from his coat. He finally had the money in his hand, but he couldn't even reach me to give me the money. I felt so sorry for him. And what I'm trying to say is that I shouldn't be sad because I had a long life, a good life. But, yes, the sadness I do feel but. . . .

D: Why do you think you do?

P: I don't know, I'm just sad.

D: Did you feel this way a few months ago?

P: No, no, no, no.

D: When did it start?

P: I would say it started the day that I got sick. That's right. Because the day before that was Sunday, and I went to see my son in Maryland. I went out there with my wife. We met the rest of the kids out there, and we had a fine time, all of us. We had dinner, all of us together. That was in October. And I was so happy to see my kids all right, and their children; I went to bed feeling fine, and I slept good. I got up, and it's after I got up, all of a sudden, I was struck out of nowhere. I felt good prior to that. As I mentioned to you, I did feel a little tired about a month ago. I took for granted I was not what I used to be. I said to myself, "After all you're seventy-six." I didn't expect to dance around every moment of the day. I'd sit down and take a rest, you know.

D: But you started to feel your sad feelings when you got sick?

P: Oh yes.

D: And what's the connection in your mind? Why do you think that is?

P: Well, I don't know. You know, I've been speaking to you people, and I guess I ought to tell you about another part of my life which is a different situation altogether. (*The patient goes into a lengthy, detailed reminiscence of his married life, rambling and becoming distracted frequently.*)

D: Let me interrupt, because I want to talk a little more about your physical problems. What did the doctor say about how you are now physically?

P: Well, I'm sorry to say that due to the fact that I've been sick since October I've never really had a long discussion with the doctor about what's wrong. Before I go home I will discuss things with him, and he can tell me a little more about what's wrong, about what to do. I didn't get to that because . . .

D: What did they say was wrong with you? Why were you admitted to the hospital?

P: They told me I had a heart attack.

D: So you were in the cardiac care unit for awhile?

P: Yeah.

D: How do you feel you are doing now physically? How do you feel your health is now?

P: You know, I'm going to be honest with you. It's a strange thing. For the past one or two weeks I just don't eat. Yesterday I had some ice cream and that was just about what I ate all day. This morning I had a glass of orange juice, and my wife—of course she knows what things I like—she brought some stuff from the house. But it didn't taste any better than the food here.

D: Why do you think that is?

P: Well, I wish I could answer that.

D: Do you have any thoughts about it at all? Any thoughts about why you are feeling that?

P: You know that's a good question. The possibility is that if I could answer that then I wouldn't be here in the hospital.

D: Do you think it's because of your heart that you feel the way you do?

P: I don't think so because . . . no doubt, my heart's not quite what it used to be. Of course things are better now. I have no pains I would say since about two or three days after I came to the hospital, but after that my heart has been in good shape. At least I think it is. I haven't really tried very much. The only walks I've done—it's been very little activity—was a little while ago on the ward. I didn't walk in the other place a lot, maybe a couple of times. Of course, it's been a couple of weeks since I've been sick. I'm not strong enough yet to pull myself together.

D: Have you been able to sleep well here?

P: Oh yes.

D: Do you find yourself at night dreaming?

P: No.

D: You have no dreams that you recall?

P: No.

D: When you wake up in the morning, do you feel rested or do you feel tired?

P: Feel tired.

D: As the day goes on do you feel more tired?

P: Well actually, I get up in the morning at 7:30 because the girl comes to take my blood pressure. But we were up dressed before she took my blood pressure . . .

D: You look now like you're on the verge of tears, like you feel like crying.

P: Yes . . . uh . . . I am not . . . I don't know how to put it. You know, there are some people who can go out and not shed a tear. In my case when I feel like I do, I start crying.

D: What kinds of thoughts do you have in your mind when you feel like crying?

P: Nothing. The only thought is always the thought that I keep to myself, whatever that is. As far as my family is concerned, the truth is that I'm proud that I did stick to the house. I raised my kids properly; my kids went to school. And they're healthy. Sometimes I think about that. As for my wife . . . if something were to happen to me today or yesterday or tomorrow, we're not millionaires, but we're not really down and out. We have the house paid for, we've got some other things, plus social security. So really I've got nothing to be sad about. Sometimes I feel that—and this is maybe like being crazy I guess—right now should be the best years of my life to enjoy my life more because my kids don't need me; my wife doesn't need me. But yet I feel that for myself of all the years I was out there working, to see that the family would get the proper food and clothing and try to get ahead . . . *(tears)*. But today I feel my job is done. I feel like "the hell with everything . . . what's the use?" You know?

D: Did you feel this way before you got sick?

P: I never felt much of it because my health was good. I kept myself busy, as I mentioned to you, since I was a boy. Since driving a cab is different . . . what's different about driving a cab is that you don't go to work at 7:30, and the boss says at 4:00 that you can go home. See, driving a cab is something else. In my time I felt nothing about getting out at 7:00 in the morning. You work when you want, as many hours as you want. So you feel more strong. I'd get out there day and night, and it was needed really. There was no other way to support my family, several of us. I worked my whole life, as long as I felt in good health. I never thought of these things at all. When I worked I'd never say, "Oh the heck with that" and then go home early. But of course, there's no question about it, in the past two weeks since I got sick . . . sometimes I'd really feel . . . but before I say these words I want you to know that I would never attempt anything on my life, because I like living very much: God made me and God is going to take me *(tears)*. You understand what I mean? *(Patient is sobbing)*.

D: Yes, I understand.

P: God made me and God is going to take me. I will never, never destroy myself because I believe to do that is a sin. I believe very much that it's a sin. *(Patient is very tearful.)*

At this point Mr. N. said that he was "tired" and requested that we end the interview. I spent a few more minutes with him, attempting to determine whether he was seriously considering suicide; he assured me he would never take his life. I tried to be encouraging, reiterating that the medical tests indicated that he was recovering rapidly and reminding him that many people (like his cousin) do resume normal lives after a heart attack. He made no comment. He seemed so preoccupied, so self-absorbed that I wondered if he even heard me. Mr. N.'s depression was obvious and it was deep. His affect was profoundly sad, punctuated by a good deal of crying. He spontaneously reported common somatic symptoms characteristic of depression: anorexia with weight loss, fatigue, lethargy, difficulty sleeping. His self-esteem was markedly impaired, reflected by statements as, "I feel like the hell with everything." This negativism was most apparent when he speculated on his future—he imagined he would be incapable of doing anything. As for the fourth aspect of clinical depression, changes in established behavior patterns, that could only be inferred as Mr. N. had yet to return to his usual environment. However, he was observed to become increasingly isolated from patients and staff on the ward. This behavior, coupled with his fears about being unable to carry out his daily activities upon leaving the hospital, suggested movement toward a more generalized withdrawal from his environment.

Mr. N.'s clinical depression was unmistakable, and it was severe. Talking with him, I found it difficult to imagine that a month earlier he was a vigorous, energetic man, a responsible provider for his family who had a joyful enthusiasm for work and play. His heart attack was the obvious precipitant of his depression; he dates the onset of his sadness to "the day I got sick." Why was Mr. N. so overwhelmed, so impaired by his illness that he required inpatient psychiatric treatment? The answer requires an understanding of his personal psychological makeup. His life has been that of a survivor. His independence, self-sufficiency, determination, and sense of adventure enabled him to provide for himself and his family for more than sixty years. Relating that "the only thing that I've ever known in my life is work," he describes himself as "an old man at twelve years of age" because that was when he began to work. Four years later he came to this country, alone, from Puerto Rico. Despite difficulties with English and his lack of an education, he made his way, doing "all types of work, including shoveling snow, which I'm proud of." He accepted challenges, using a combination of native intelligence, common sense, and daring to get what he needed. The quest for his taxi license well illustrates his life-style. And if he stumbled, as when he was arrested for violating the regulations for operating a cab, he learned from the experience. He became more vigilant and self-disciplined to insure that "that was the first and last time in my life that I went to jail." As a result of this philosophy, Mr. N. was a successful provider, keeping his family financially secure and enabling his children to receive the education he never had.

Mr. N.'s life-style is based largely on his strong belief in the fairness and rewards of the work ethic; namely, people advance because of a combination of hard work, intelligence, and perseverance. This belief, combined with a personality structure predominantly concerned with obtaining and maintaining control of his life circumstances, resulted in Mr. N.'s success and self-satisfaction. From early adolescence he had to search actively for work, and once he found it, he had to do the job accurately and responsibly in order to make a living. Food and shelter depended on his ability to produce. He had no one to fall back on; he was literally in complete command of his survival. He was too uncomfortable to rely on the unpredictable performance and whims of others, since their failures might also bring him down. This dominant theme in Mr. N.'s personal psychology was largely responsible for his ultimate choice of work. As a cab driver he was his own boss. If he needed more money, he worked longer hours. If he felt like taking off time to relax, he would go home for a few hours to rest or play the organ. Periodically he would take off extended periods of time to be with his family. He kept his life ordered and controlled in this manner for the forty-eight years that he drove a cab. Not to be in control of his life was anathema to Mr. N., stirring up feelings of bewilderment, helplessness, and fear. Tragically, his first heart attack had precisely this effect on him.

Mr. N.'s self-sufficiency was undone from the very start of his illness. He was literally struck down by his heart attack, and as he reveals in the interview, he still cannot comprehend this helplessness. As he states, "To me, it is still a mystery how all of a sudden I am in the hospital. To me, I still cannot believe it fully." During the acute and early recuperative stages, Mr. N.'s heart attack stripped him of all that was most dear to him: to be his own boss, whether at work or play. He tried to regain some semblance of control immediately after being hospitalized. An early nursing note reports "patient awake, belligerent . . . demanding to get out of bed and stating that he doesn't want to be here. . . ." Unfortunately that was the pathetic extent of protest from a man who is still fighting off death. But Mr. N.'s protest is eminently understandable; since all of his life roles were threatened, he perceived himself exclusively as a sick man, and he was terribly frightened. He tried to deal with the fear in his usual manner, via action, but his physical state prevented this. Furthermore, having never been ill before, he had not developed alternative coping skills to help him adjust to the sick role. It was this loss of control of his life, the loss of his pre-illness self, that Mr. N. could not accept. Unable to grieve that loss effectively, he focused solely on the negative aspect of his illness, and the depressive feelings of his grief reaction became so entrenched that pronounced clinical depression evolved. He was incapable of viewing his heart attack in any kind of perspective; he could not appreciate that he had progressed well physically, nor imagine that he, like his cousin, could recover significantly. Preoccupied with the thought "my time has come," he was convinced he would never return even to a semblance of his former self.

In an effort to prove to himself that he still ran his own life, Carl N. precipitately signed out of the hospital against medical advice.

Despite strong protests from the medical staff, which was concerned that his depression would become even more severe and might ultimately culminate in suicide, Mr. N. chose to leave "this place where they try to tell me how to live, what to eat, when to sleep, and what to do." Only by invoking such demands could he regain some control over his life and thereby attempt to return to his pre-illness self. In terms of the grief process, this was a regression to the first stage, denial, and a dramatic reflection of his inability to resolve the conflicting feelings concerning his loss of health. Consequently, when he left the hospital, he was physically stable but significantly impaired psychologically.

As Carl N.'s case dramatically illustrates, one serious result of the depressive response to illness is its interference with comprehensive medical care. Generally, patients plagued by depression do not cope with disease as well as nondepressed patients. Acute and chronic medical illness, as well as surgical interventions, result in statistically significant increases in morbidity and mortality in depressed individuals. These findings have been explained on both organic and psychological grounds. The physiologic explanation is supported by observations of a decreased immunologic response in the depressed individual. These include impeded mobility of T cells from lymphoid tissues (Amkraut and Solomon 1974), as well as distorted endocrinologic function, such as hypothyroidism (Stein et al. 1976). The psychological explanation focuses on the progressive negativism and impaired self-esteem of some medically ill patients. Illness can induce a sense of hopelessness and worthlessness in which the individual no longer cares whether he regains his health. The consequences of such an emotional withdrawal are reflected in self-neglect, such as rejection of a prescribed treatment regimen, which ultimately results in accelerated physical decline. For example, the patient recovering from a cerebrovascular accident may refuse or neglect his physical therapy, thereby aggravating the already present muscle atrophy. A patient's ability to rally against physical illness may be so seriously compromised that he essentially abandons the will to live and dies. This "giving-up/given-up" syndome is described by Engel (1968). It has been observed in prisoners of war and, as Spitz (1945) reports, in hospitalized infants whose psychological withdrawal precedes the onset of physical ailments and a generalized apathy that ultimately proceeds to unresponsiveness and death. Whether the impact of depression on the medically ill is mediated through physical or psychological pathways or, as is most likely, an interplay of the two, the net effect is certain: depression enhances complications and the risk of death in medical and surgical illness. Engel suggests that it may even precipitate sudden death (1970, 1971).

A further consequence of the depressive response to illness concerns accurate diagnosis. Depression causes alteration in the body's normal physiologic functioning, producing somatic complaints which can confuse the clinical picture. Unless the physician recognizes depression in his patient, he may incorrectly attribute these symptoms to organic pathology. Subsequent treatment will be misdirected, with varied consequences: at best, the patient's symptoms will not be relieved; at worst, his clinical status will be aggravated. A common example of this phenomenon is seen in the elderly patient who responds to illness with depression. Forgetfulness, impaired concentration, and poor self-care are too often interpreted as signs of dementia instead of symptoms of the pseudo-dementia of depression. Frequently the patient is then subjected to unnecessary diagnostic tests which expose him to the risks attending those procedures. Such treatment is as destructive as diagnosing the epigastric distress accompanying an inferior myocardial infarction as indigestion and treating it with antacids.

A final difficulty deriving from the depression response to illness is specifically demonstrated by Carl N.'s case. Depression can progress in severity to the degree that it becomes a greater threat to the patient than his physical illness. Regression and the uncaring, self-destructive behavior accompanying a deepening depression can progress to the extremes of psychosis and active suicidal ideation. At this juncture, psychiatric treatment takes priority over medical issues. It was precisely for this reason that Mr. N. was transferred from a cardiac care unit to an inpatient psychiatric facility instead of a general medical ward. Treating medical illness can be difficult enough. When it is compounded by a coexisting depression, it can become untenable. The physician's ability to help a patient regain his health is gravely limited when the patient's outlook on life is, as Carl N. expressed it, "What's the use?"

7

The Helpless Patient

REGRESSION IS THE REVERSION to more primitive patterns of behavior. When subjected to excessive stress, either from external threats or internal stimuli, individuals frequently respond with this common psychological maneuver in an attempt to combat fears of being overwhelmed. The retreat to behavior characteristic of earlier developmental stages may transiently render the individual more helpless; however, it permits an emotional retrenchment which immediately alleviates anxiety and can ultimately result in enhanced psychological strength and developmental strides. The process of learning to play an instrument well illustrates these characteristics of regression. The pupil abdicates some autonomy by willingly placing himself in a dependent position vis-à-vis the instructor. In return he is introduced to new techniques which he is expected to learn, but with the understanding that he will be forgiven many wrong notes during his quest for mastery. Hopefully, this process maximizes enjoyment, concentration, and achievement by minimizing anxiety.

Regression serves both an adaptive and a defensive purpose. Freud makes the analogy to a migrating population that deploys members at strategic points along the journey. When confronted

with setbacks, such as military defeat, it falls back to its strengthened positions, revitalizes its forces, and then proceeds with renewed vigor (Freud 1924). The regressed individual walks a similar
path. His return to previously known behavior provides the comfort
of familiarity, a welcome escape from the apprehension and uncertainty endemic to the more complicated adult existence. And by
behaving in an uncharacteristically immature manner, he usually
elicits attention and the required support from those close to him;
this recreates the dynamic of a needy child's behavioral request for
parental help. A similar reconstitution occurs during the grief
process. Preoccupied with the loss of a loved one, the bereaved
becomes relatively irresponsible in most aspects of his life, a neglect
that affords some relief. His self-absorption is actually regression,
which permits the sorting out of all emotions felt toward the
deceased. This facilitates ultimate acceptance of loss and, consequently, allows the bereaved to proceed with his life. Regression,
then, is a protective reaction; it provides an emotional time-out
when the ability to cope with current stressors becomes tenuous,
and it ultimately fosters emotional growth.

Regression is an integral part of illness. Disease forces a patient to
live a more dependent existence, a point that is obvious to any of us
who has wrestled with a bout of influenza. High fever, headaches,
and light-headedness, nausea, myalgia, and generalized malaise
require us to rest passively in bed while our bodies reconstitute.
When plagued with these uncomfortable symptoms, we feel like
doing little or nothing. We lie in bed, possibly reading or watching
television, often just sleeping intermittently throughout the day. We
enjoy being cared for and appreciate inquiries about our health. We
welcome having friends cook for us or run necessary errands, but we
try to avoid prolonged visits or phone conversations. We wish to be
tended to and then left alone. Essentially we just wait for our
discomfort to remit with the tincture of time. The enforced inactivity of this dependent state promotes a psychobiologic restitution,
and we gradually return to our premorbid level of physical and
mental well-being.

This process of regression is even more exaggerated when illness
requires admission to the hospital. Most inpatients experience
hospitalization as a benign form of incarceration. Although they
appreciate the therapeutic purpose of their confinement (relief of
pain and suffering), the abridgment of autonomy leaves many

feeling helpless and inadequate. The experience is reminiscent of a child's perception of the adult world. The hospitalized individual is almost completely taken over by his caretakers, who present him with a lengthy list of do's and don'ts. He is told what to eat, when to eat, when he may see visitors, what extent of physical activity is permissible, when he should retire in the evening and awake in the morning. He must wear a hospital johnnie, which leaves many feeling physically and psychically exposed, and he is then made to feel even more vulnerable by being continually observed in his uniform by innumerable health care personnel, fellow patients, and visitors. He is passively transported about in a wheelchair or on a stretcher and subjected to numerous diagnostic tests in a myriad of stark, imposing rooms. In many of these places he finds himself half naked in the presence of strangers who scan his body with strange machines, probe various orifices, stick him with needles for the purpose of extracting blood or injecting medications or diagnostic materials, and generally cause varying degrees of embarrassment and physical discomfort. In sum, the patient finds he has little or no control over himself. His self-perception is as a small, helpless individual; he invests his caretakers with omnipotence and, in contrast, underestimates his own skills and abilities.

The anticipated compensation for voluntarily placing oneself in the demoralizing, if not frightening, role of patient is expert attention from the medical community. The individual expects to receive a thorough work up and to be correctly diagnosed and intelligently apprised of his illness. He expects empathic treatment—tender and caring ministrations, as well as support and encouragement—from everyone involved in diagnosing and treating him. And he expects to get well. His unconscious mind-set is simple: modelling the conduct of an obedient child should yield the rewards of good health from people perceived as benign parental figures. Physicians conspire with patients, both implicitly and explicitly, to implement this equation. In the medical model, just as in the process of learning to play an instrument, regression is necessary. By virtue of his dependency the patient abdicates a degree of autonomy, which helps eliminate from the treatment process areas of potential struggle with his doctors. Within reason he essentially does what he is told, a stance that generally promotes more effective, efficient care. He will not refuse diagnostic tests, prescribed medications, or recommended therapies. At the same time his dependency invites reassurance and support, which helps defend against disturbing affects fostered by illness. Talcott Parsons addresses these points in detail in his discussion of the dynamics of the sick role (1951).

Parsons, a sociologist, conceptualizes illness within a biopsychosocial framework. He views health on a continuum, with wellness as the normative state. In addition to causing organic pathology, deviation from this condition affects social interactions and psychological functioning. Parsons delineates four distinct phases of the sick role, the first of which is "exemption from normal social role responsibilities." This societal permission to regress is relative to the nature and severity of the illness and requires legitimization of ill health, which is most often dispensed by the physician. The next aspect of the sick role is recognition by the ailing individual and members of the health care system that a patient cannot be expected to get well merely by willing it. This invites an individual's growing dependency vis-à-vis caretakers. Such mutual acknowledgment between the dispensers and the recipient of medical treatment condones the patient's regression and further justifies his abrogation of diverse responsibilities involving his occupational, family, and social lives. The last two elements of the sick role are the most relevant to the dependency response to illness. In the third phase the individual must recognize his state of health as undesirable; the attendant obligation of this perception is to strive for wellness. Consequently, in the final phase the ailing individual is expected to seek and obtain competent help and to cooperate with his trained healers throughout the process of getting well. At this point, medical treatment becomes a collaborative process between patient and doctor, what Parsons calls a "common task." This element of the sick role has extremely important implications concerning the role of dependency in illness.

As previously illustrated, by maintaining a proper balance between the adaptive and defensive aspects of regression, the patient maximizes opportunities for successful treatment. However, with progression toward wellness, regression becomes less desirable and may even present an impediment to reattaining premorbid functioning. This is because the shared work between physician and patient occurs not only in the state of illness but also during the patient's return to health. At this point in treatment, professional attention is less necessary, as it becomes increasingly important for the recovering patient to assume incrementally greater degrees of independence in preparation for his resumption of normal activities. Should he resist this evolution his regression becomes excessive, either in degree or duration, and the attendant dependency becomes maladaptive and counterproductive. Consider the patient recovering from a cerebrovascular accident. During the acute illness he does little more than passively wait to see if he will survive the acute catastrophe. However, when he is medically stable and fully cognizant of the extent of impairment, the major responsibility for further successful treatment falls on his shoulders. He is quickly relegated to rehabilitative personnel, who teach him how to live as effectively as possible given his impairment. Through this process he learns to maximize the ability to do for himself. Some patients aggressively pursue this task; in physical therapy they continually challenge themselves, seeing how many more unassisted steps are possible. Others bring into the recuperative phase the passivity characterizing an earlier stage of illness. They loudly declare their inability to exercise any control over a crippled extremity. They rely more and more on various therapists, a pattern that is both physically and emotionally harmful. By neglecting the efforts that are required to strengthen musculature, the patient aggravates existing atrophy and, consequently, enhances his debility. Instead of learning to walk unassisted, he may require the use of a cane; accelerated decline to a wheelchair or to bedridden invalidism can readily follow. Furthermore, by abdicating responsibility and repeated turning to others for help, this establishes a dangerous antitherapeutic pattern. This individual prefers rewards of the dependent position (alleviation of anxiety via external support) to the satisfaction of self-realized accomplishment and achievement. The collaborative aspect of the physician-patient relationship is seriously disrupted if the patient merely seeks the immediate gratification of dependency; the physician becomes frustrated, and the patient pays the insidious price of progressive helplessness.

Patients who choose the latter path of treatment only partially fulfill the criteria of the sick role as it is defined by Parsons. They gladly seek and accept the ministrations of caretakers who, by legitimizing their illness, grant exemptions from usual societal rules and responsibilities. However, these patients do not cooperate in their treatment because they do not wish to attain wellness. Their motivations may be conscious or unconscious, but the expression of such wishes takes a standard form: both overtly and covertly these patients resist and undermine efforts of their caretakers. Common examples of this type of patient include the diabetic who flagrantly disregards his diet or the stroke victim who refuses physical therapy. The analogous psychiatric patient is one whose basic motivation for seeking treatment is the wish for unending nurturance from the therapist, along with a sanctioned excuse from the responsibilities of adulthood. Rather than actively working toward emotional growth, such individuals simply luxuriate in the warmth of the therapeutic environment. This stance may provide symptomatic relief, but it is usually transient, rapidly dissipating when treatment is terminated and the patient no longer feels protected by the therapist.

All such patients, medical or psychiatric, impede their own progress while simultaneously frustrating health care providers. An intense struggle evolves between the patient committed to remaining ill and the physician bent on making him well. The patient usually wins the battle—and suffers the consequences. One common resolution of this conflict finds him functioning at a level considerably lower than anticipated given his particular pathology. A more devastating resolution occurs when the individual's illness becomes the catalyst for his transformation into a professional patient. Obsessed with his state of health, such an individual becomes hyperattuned to his physical status. Forever discovering new symptoms, or fearing the onset of new ailments, he submits to extensive diagnostic workups and therapeutic regimens in order to manage what is often an easily treatable—if not nonexistent—problem. His passivity, worry, and neediness cause him to neglect life's pleasures and excitement. The following interview illustrates this tragic scenario in an elderly woman who had had open heart surgery.

Mary Elizabeth W., a seventy-two-year-old housewife, was admitted to the mental health unit for evaluation of her progressively impaired functioning over the preceding five years. Numerous diagnostic tests failed to demonstrate any physical cause for her decline; consequently, her internist wanted to investigate the possibility of a psychopathologic etiology. At the time of admission she had been neglecting most activities of daily life beyond the essential tasks of preparing meals, feeding herself, and tending to her personal hygiene. She professed a strong desire to resume her previously responsible routine (making her husband "feel like a king in his castle" and entertaining her children and grandchildren); however, she felt it was "beyond hope to be the way I was before they operated on me." A relatively healthy woman until a heart attack eight years previously, she presently lacked the energy to do more than "merely exist." She attributed this to the effects of an open heart procedure she had undergone two years after her myocardial infarction. Yet she could not articulate how the surgery produced her prolonged debility, and in fact, she recognized symptomatic relief postoperatively. What she did communicate—repeatedly—was her inability to do anything beyond "reading and doing crossword puzzles."

Mrs. W. was neither depressed nor demented. Rather the overwhelming dependency that pervaded our meeting reflected her current, prevailing characterologic style. Her behavior of the past five years was the result of a determined crusade to secure attention and support from those around her. Unfortunately, the more she pursued that goal, the more her physical and emotional well-being suffered.

D: When did you come here?
P: I got here yesterday.
D: Why was that?
P: I didn't feel well and I was agitated.
D: That had been going on for awhile?
P: Yes.
D: How long?
P: I don't remember. I don't know how long.
D: Has it been days or weeks or months?
P: Years.
D: Years of feeling agitated?
P: Since my heart surgery.
D: Since your heart surgery.
P: I had been doing very well, but gradually I declined.
D: You mean you felt well physically?
P: Yes.
D: And what happened in this gradual slipping?
P: I did less and less. I had different hospitalizations, you see, but I can't remember all these things right now.
D: How old are you now?
P: Seventy-two.
D: And you had the heart surgery when you were sixty-seven?
P. Let's see. Five and a half years ago.
D: Sixty-six. . . .
P: I've been going downhill for a long time. And I'm worried about the family and what I've done to them. I worry about what I've done to my husband. He's got a back condition, and he's tied up with me twenty-four hours a day. That's too much for anyone. I have these sleepless nights and he's there with me. I'm unable to get out—we used to be with our friends—so he's always there with me.
D: When did you stop going out with your friends?

P: I don't know.

D: Well, were you sick for a period of time before you had the surgery?

P: No.

D: You felt well?

P: Yeah. Even after my heart attack.

D: When was that?

P: I had an attack and I didn't consider it an attack. I just went about my business.

D: That was before the surgery?

P: Yes.

D: Many years before? Shortly before?

P: About a year before the surgery.

D: I see. Prior to that you had been physically well?

P: Yes.

D: No major symptoms?

P: No. Well let's see. I had all kinds of tests. I had a brain scan (*pause*). I really cannot tell you things in chronological order. Recently I've had trouble in the genital area. It's uncomfortable. And they said it was an inguinal hernia, and I was operated on.

D: When was that?

P: Approximately two months ago.

D: And the brain scan?

P: I really can't recall.

D: Since the heart surgery?

P: Yes.

D: Why did you need a brain scan?

P: I really can't recall.

D: I see.

P: And I don't know why, but I was zonked out for a full week. They kept me under sedation so I really don't know anything that happened. Right now my stomach is distended, and they gave me an enema, but I'm still in agony.

D: So you've had physical symptoms that just won't go away.

P: Yes. My eyes are just burning all the time. Now I wish I could recall more in detail the different tests I had. I had a CAT scan of my abdomen, I had a brain scan. . . .

D: Let me go back to before the surgery. You were relatively physically well before that?

P: In a sense.

D: Had you been in the hospital overnight prior to the surgery?

P: Oh sure. I had an appendectomy and an ovarian cyst removed.

D: How did those go? Were those long-term affairs? Were you just in the hospital and out and healed fairly well, or did the symptoms persist for awhile?

P: No, I was all right. But I worry about everything recently. I get scared. Now I'm very upset because I wrecked the lives of those I love, my family. My children have their own families, the money is going, and my husband remains sick. I'm scared. I also had an accident three years ago. I fell and hurt my leg, and I can't drive without pain. So I have this handicap. . . .

D: What did you do to your leg?

P: I bruised it. And I have this handicap in that I'm tied down to the house. And my husband has to take me everywhere. My friends have gradually drifted away.

D: You're a different person now from the way you were before you had your heart surgery.

P: Yes. I was in the hospital for four months.

D: For the surgery?

P: Yes.

D: How come?

P: I had a bypass and a huge aneurysm on the left ventricle. And all the medications reacted very badly. And that's become a major problem. The medications did not sit right.

D: Did they know you had an aneurysm of the ventricle before they operated on you?

P: Well I had an angiogram.

D: Yes. Did you know what it showed?

P: That I don't know.

D: Were you surprised that they had to operate on your ventricle? Did you know they'd have to do it?

P: No, I didn't.

D: You didn't know that. What did the surgeon explain to you as to why that had to be done?

P: I don't think the aneurysm showed, because they never did say anything about it.

D: You learned about it after the surgery.

P: I think so.

D: And you were telling me that you were in the hospital for four months.

P: Yes. Because of the reaction to the medication. And, oh yes, I also . . . through the carelessness of some of the staff I developed a very bad infection where the veins were taken out of my leg.

D: I see. How did you feel when you went home from the hospital. Were you debilitated? Were you feeling vigorous?

P: Well I took it easy.

D: Yes. Did you change your usual routine, your daily routine when you came home?

P: I took it easy.

D: What had you done before the surgery? How would you spend your days?

P: Mostly housework and seeing friends.

D: Would they visit you or would you visit them?

P: Both.

D: Would you go out shopping?

P: Oh yes. You know my house is falling apart now. And I'm scared that my husband is falling apart. I suggested, after my heart attack, to sell the house and move into an apartment or a senior citizens' home. But he loves the house, he loves the work, he wanted to paint, and so on. Now he can't do anything. So I guess underneath it was my boiling point, my resentment of having to stay there. I wanted to get rid of the house.

D: You sound like you have a lot of underlying resentments.

P: Not really.

D: No? Well it sounds like you don't think the doctors treated you too well.

P: No, they did.

D: I thought you told me you were hospitalized for four months because they couldn't correct the medications, and that caused an infection in your vein.

P: Oh, that was one individual, one member of the treatment team. But I don't blame them. No, it was I, my body, that didn't respond.

D: Your body had been pretty vigorous before this surgery though.

P: Pretty good, pretty good. . . .

D: You and your husband have been married for how long?

P: Fifty-two years.

D: That's a lot of years.

P: But I've become so debilitated. I don't understand me. I've always taken care of everybody.

D: You did?

P: Yes.

D: In what way?

P: Family members. I nursed them. I took in family members if they needed it. . . .

D: What type of work does your husband do?

P: He used to be an architect for a large firm.

D: And did you work?

P: No.

D: You were too busy taking care of people?

P: And the children.

D: How many children do you have?

P: Three—two sons and a daughter. She has diabetes. She's had it for twelve years.

D: When was the last time you were in the hospital? Oh yes, you told me about the hernia two months ago.

P: Yes.

D: I'm interested when you say you've taken care of everyone. Has anyone taken care of you over the past few years? Or since you've been in and out of the hospital?

P: My husband.

D: Uh-huh.

P: Though it's been very rough on him.

D: It has been. You say he's changed his life accordingly over the past few years to help take care of you. Does anybody else help take care of you?

P: No.

D: But you've taken care of a lot of people. How come they haven't reciprocated?

P: What?

D: How come they haven't reciprocated?

P: What are they going to do? They can come over and say "hello" and "how are you?"

D: Where are your children?

P: In West Virginia—my daughter, that is. It's not easy for her to commute. My sons are here. We are a very close family, but of course what I've become doesn't endear me to them.

D: Do you feel you and your children have been drifting apart?

P: Oh yes.

D: Mutually? Or do you feel they have been putting more distance between themselves and you?

P: They're busy.

D: Do you think it's more their decision to drift away from you and your husband?

P: I can't speak for them.

D: Do you think that?

P: But I feel . . . they want to, but they can't give more. They can't stay with me. They have their own problems, and I mean problems.

D: Your husband can give more?

P: He's given too much, much too much. . . . Do you know Dr. A. (*a psychiatrist*)?

D: Sure.

P: We were seeing him. He tried different medications.

D: Was he the doctor who suggested you come into the hospital?

P: Yes.

D: How long had he been seeing you?

P: For over a year I think.

D: Has it helped or not?

P: No.

D: Not at all?

P: No.

D: How often do you see him?

P: I was seeing him once a week, twice a week, then back to once a week. And he kept trying different medications and none of them worked. I started to get zonked out. I haven't slept for weeks, for weeks.

D: What did you and Dr. A. figure could be done for you here in the hospital?

P: I don't know, my husband talked to him. My husband felt I was so bad and so agitated that he called Dr. A and said he couldn't handle me anymore. He just didn't know where to turn. Every time I spoke to my doctor about how bad I felt he told me to see a psychiatrist. So I felt I had no sympathetic doctor. . . .

D: Have you been satisfied with any doctors that you've had?

P: Some.

D: But not Dr. A.?

P: Well I like Dr. A., but he hasn't helped me. That's why I wound up here.

D: Who's your doctor here?

P: I can't recall his name.

D: When were you admitted? When did you come in?

P: Two days ago.

D: You haven't seen him yet?

P: No. He said he'd see me today. We only talked briefly yesterday.

D: Do you think this place is going to be helpful to you?

P: Frankly?

D: Yes.

P: I don't think so.

D: Why are you staying then?

P: My husband thinks it might be helpful.

D: And who's going to decide . . .

P: (Interrupts) That's what's bothering me.

D: What's bothering you?

P: Who's going to decide.

D: I didn't finish my question. Who's going to decide whether or not you stay?

P: That's the problem.

D: Do you want to leave?

P: I don't fit in. And I'm afraid to go into the room with some of these people.

D: Does that mean that you want to leave?

P: I can't take a shower. I don't know where to go.

D: It sounds like you haven't decided what you want to do.

P: If I go home . . . I went to a couple of the patients' meetings, and I don't seem to fit in. I can't do it.

D: Because?

P: I'm like a zombie, too tired.

D: Are you taking medication?

P: Just the Xanax, from Dr. A. He had me on it, then off it, then on it. . . .

D: What do you think is wrong with you?

P: I've flipped my lid.

D: You flipped your lid. What does that mean?

P: I can't function.

D: You told me you used to take care of everybody. You used to be a vigorous, strong woman.

P: Yes.

D: So what's happened that that's no longer the case?

P: I don't know. I'm staying home more and more.

D: It started with the heart surgery. What was it about the heart surgery?

P: No, the heart surgery went fine.

D: I understand that, but apparently everything started . . . this progressive decline started after the heart surgery, which is somewhat surprising considering you had previous surgical procedures, got over them, got back on your feet, and continued to be active.

P: I was never a very active person. I didn't join organizations, because I was raising three children. I really didn't have the time. Then when I finally had the time I was so tired, I wanted some time to myself, so I did part-time work, one or two days a week. I enjoyed it very much. Now I'm trying to think why I gave it up. I guess one of my illnesses caused that.

D: Let me ask you again. Where do you think your hospitalization is going? How do you think we could be helpful to you?

P: I don't know.

D: Do you think you're going to get better?

P: I don't know.

D: Do you worry about it?

P: I do.

D: What's your greatest concern when you worry?

P: My greatest concern is my husband's well-being. I don't drive. I used to, but I had an accident and I'm too agitated to drive now. The finances I know nothing about. So I don't know what will happen. If anything happens to him, I'm lost.

Throughout her life Mary Elizabeth W. was a vigorous, responsible woman who took great pride in her abilities and achievements as a wife and mother. She provided loving care for her immediate family as well as distant relatives who had fallen on hard times. She was sociable and extroverted, an active member of a large coterie of friends. Her life was not without difficulties—including a sickly daughter and some personal health problems—yet she had few complaints. She was philosophic about periodic adversity, regarding it as unavoidable, and seemed able to enjoy the good while tolerating the bad.

Mrs. W.'s gradual, but persistent, decline began shortly after the open heart procedure, necessitating several rehospitalizations to diagnose the cause of mounting somatic complaints. During the eighteen months prior to her current admission she had undergone a full neurologic workup because of headaches and "confusion"; extensive radiologic studies to evaluate diffuse abdominal pain; endoscopic examination of her stomach; and ear, nose, and throat testing because of tinnitus and dizziness. Apart from incidental findings, all test results were negative. She had also received a seven-month course of tricyclic antidepressants on the basis of an assumption that her somatization was a depressive equivalent. She showed no clear-cut response to the medication, raising doubts as to the accuracy of an affective diagnosis, yet her internist referred her for psychiatric treatment. Ongoing therapy, as well as trials of numerous psychoactive medications, failed to improve her functioning. Mrs. W. was bewildered by her current state, as was reflected in the pathetic admission, "I don't understand me."

Given her past medical history, it is unclear why Mary Elizabeth became so regressed following her cardiac surgery. Two previous operations went smoothly, including an emergency appendectomy. In each instance she recuperated rapidly, quickly resuming her normal routine. She had even tried to disregard the symptoms of her heart attack, a reaction that is difficult to imagine in light of her current preoccupation with bodily aches and pains, and after treatment she again returned to baseline functioning. One hypothesis about her prolonged regression concerns an identification with her parents, each of whom died in their seventies of cardiovascular disease. Her father had chronic congestive heart failure and required repeated hospitalization. This background could easily have sensitized her to the impact of heart disease late in life, a period in the life cycle when individuals are already preoccupied with thoughts of death and dying. Another reason Mrs. W. may have responded so negatively to this particular bout of illness concerns the surgical procedure itself. Anticipating routine angioplasty, she awoke from anesthesia to learn of an unplanned ventricular repair. This may have increased the uncertainty about her condition; subsequent concern could easily progress to a pathologic vigilance regarding her health, in a fantasied effort to prevent any future surprises. A third possible explanation of this patient's regression requires interpretation of her behavior as an unconscious expression of anger. Throughout her life Mary Elizabeth was the caretaker of the family, providing shelter and succor to those in need. Her persistent helplessness could represent a means of demanding attention and support she felt she was owed.

Though each of these formulations is speculative, the latter is the most probable given the data from the interview. Two themes predominate in Mrs. W.'s psyche: conflict over dependent wishes and conflict over aggressive impulses. They are crystallized in her worry about having "wrecked the lives of those I love, my family," reflecting both a fear and a wish. Unconscious dependency has prevented Mrs. W. from continuing her previous autonomous existence. She expresses concern about the detrimental effects of her current reliance on the family, recognizing that her husband has "given too much," and she understands that her children "have their own problems" and "can't give more." Despite these observations she has continued her demands for support by becoming increasingly helpless and isolated. Seemingly at the mercy of those around her, she effects control over them via passivity. Her inability to do for herself is a loud demand to be cared for, and her family, motivated by a combination of concern and guilt, assents to these wishes. Mrs. W.'s debility provides her with great strength. Additionally, it thrusts her mounting frustration onto those close to her— particularly her husband and inept physicians—who repeatedly fail in attempts to reverse her pathologic regression.

In response to my question, "What do you think is wrong with you?" Mary W. replied, "I've flipped my lid." In light of our discussion I interpreted this to mean, "I can no longer take care of myself like I used to." She is obviously ambivalent about such helplessness. Unable to comprehend that part of her no longer wants to function as she used to, she cannot request overt support from her loved ones because this would reverse established family roles. Yet her illness permits her silently and successfully to solicit the assistance she desires. This secondary gain is an integral part of the dependency response (although, technically, the individual's exploitation of a symptom to his own advantage applies only to psychoneurotic disorders). Unfortunately, the benefits realized through illness in this fashion are usually offset by their emotional cost. In Mrs. W.'s case this is overwhelmingly clear; the effects of her dependency response have been devastating. In addition to transforming her into a marginally functional woman isolated from friends, her response has alienated her children and physicians and has stressed her husband close to the breaking point. The luxury derived from maneuvering herself into a position of total dependence on her husband—alleviation of all responsibilities—is balanced by an everpresent terror. As she puts it, "If anything happens to him, I'm lost." Mary W.'s pathologic dependency makes her childlike and so pervasively helpless that it is difficult to imagine her functioning in a self-reliant fashion either premorbidly or in the future.

An individual's dependency response is not always so obvious. It may be disguised, hidden behind a false bravado of seeming understanding or equanimity. For various reasons, some individuals do not openly declare their extreme wishes for dependency. This may be an unconscious process, primarily designed to deceive themselves, or a more studied manipulative pattern. Regardless of the motivation, by hiding the need for excessive nurturing, these patients also deceive caretakers who initially respond to their progressive clinical regression with confusion. Ultimately, however, the therapeutic relationship is again disrupted by a struggle between the patient who wishes to remain ill and the physician who is committed to making him well. However, this is an insidious battle and, to the outside observer, completely different from the warfare between Mrs. W. and her physicians. Unfortunately, the consequences for the patient are identical: psychobiologic regression that limits autonomous functioning.

The following interview illustrates this presentation of the dependency response. Bruce Y. is a forty-two-year-old married carpenter, who was reportedly in good health until he was in an automobile accident eighteen months prior to admission. Although he was bruised and shaken, no significant injuries were initially obvious, and he returned to work that afternoon. Several days later he was awakened in the middle of the night by severe abdominal pain. Despite numerous medical interventions, the pain has persisted unabated since that time. According to Mr. Y., it has essentially ruined his life. He sets forth the details of his medical odyssey in a brash, flamboyant fashion, which belies an underlying dependency that declared itself as our meeting progressed. We pick up the interview at the point immediately following Bruce Y.'s meticulous description of his accident. He ended the narrative by stressing that at that time he was certain "nothing really serious happened to me."

P: Several days later I was awakened at 2:00 in the morning in bed, and there I was . . . pain was bad—very, very bad. Not just pain, it was sticking and jerking pain, like something running right up your chin and right out your mouth, and I went to the hospital by ambulance, and they plunged around for a day or so before they began to find out what was wrong. They x-rayed and x-rayed and x-rayed. So, they finally discovered . . . a gastroenterologist said it was probably traumatic pancreatitis, because I had no previous illness of the pancreas. In other words, it was something unusual. So they set me up for surgery, for exploratory surgery. And there it came. They saw nothing in there that would indicate that anything was bad. There was a bruised spleen, but other than that they really couldn't see anything. So they lingered on and lingered on, medicated it and medicated it, and finally it was . . . they said something had to happen surgically, so it did. They sent me to Stanford and there I was under the care of Dr. S., who was the man who was going to use the little tube (*gastroscope*). He observed that the pancreas walls inside were all scarred and livid. He recommended surgery. So I came back here and had surgery and did all right.

D: What sort of surgery? Did they take out part of the pancreas?

P: They took out the whole pancreas [*an inaccurate statement, either a misperception by the patient or a purposeful exaggeration*], the spleen, and the gallbladder. And I healed up and went home. I was home about a week or two when all of a sudden it started hurting like hell again in the same old-fashioned way.

D: The same pattern of pain?

P: Same pattern of pain. Always right under this left rib cage here, nowhere else. I went back to the surgeon, and I told him I'm in a helluva lot of pain here. Did you leave something in there? He said no, that everything had been taken out. He told me I looked perfect. I said it still hurts though. I can't understand that. So he says let's go back to the hospital and have Dr. S. look in there again and see what he says. I did that. And the next thing he says is "chronic pancreatitis." The pancreas was enlarged and inflamed, and he felt it would be a source of pain, probably for the rest of my life. There's no cure for it. So I went back to my surgeon and told him. He said, "I recommend you go back to see Dr. S. because he's a world special-ist." So I ventured forth back down to Stanford, and I stayed with Dr. S. for two weeks, and he did everything but turn me upside down and put me on a skateboard. So they finally wound up going in there again and looking at the pancreas, and he said, "Yes, it's definitely inflamed and enlarged. You'll have to try something else. We have a pain clinic here, where we have an electric stimulator, and we can attach it to your side with electrodes and hang it on your belly and put it in your pocket." He told me that would take care of it, or if that didn't work, there was a nerve block. Not the type of nerve block you probably know around here. This is where they inject an alcoholic solution with something else—fiber, I think—and they destroy the nerve instead of cutting it. And this is perfect; it destroys the nerve. The sensitivity is all gone. But he said, "If it's that bad, I don't like to do it." In the meantime, all I'm doing is taking narcotics for the pain and not getting anywhere. My business is standing still. I can't possibly function with narcotics. And I can't live without something to kill the pain. I'm in a spot. I went on using the narcotics for about six months, and finally I got to a point where I started building up a tolerance. They told me that I would definitely build up a tolerance, and that would cause me to eventu-ally withdraw. You could just take them, and they would pass through your system, and that's it. Unless you take higher and higher doses. And you can't do that. So here I am. I was referred by my internist to see Dr. K., to see if he had any ideas.

D: When did you stop seeing the people at Stanford?

P: Several months ago.

D: Why was that? Did you feel they had done everything for you?

P: I felt that way, that they had. And I felt also that the only obvious conclusion would be the nerve block. And from what they told me about the nerve block, I wasn't sure I wanted that either. But I knew I had to get something for it—what or who I didn't know. So I saw Dr. K., and he brought my enthusiasm up, really. He's a very precise individual, and he doesn't stop trying. And that's what I needed I guess. So now what I need is a replacement for a worn-out pan-creas—if you boys could come up with it, I'd appreciate it very much. So my plan now is if Dr. K. can't do this, then I will have to have the nerve block. I have no choice, no choice at all. Because I have a business laying there dormant without me. That's throwing my livelihood away. My family still has to be supported, and I can't just function with Demerol in my system all the time, and I can't function with the pain in me all the time. So I have to have the nerve block. It's the only sensible thing to do.

D: And what have you been told by Dr. K. about the nerve block? Does he feel that it's going to be the final straw?

P: Dr. K. said one day—he was clear about it—he said, "Well I don't know. I think the best thing for you to do is let's see what we can do for you this way. If not, we'll move towards the nerve block." The nerve block can be a very atrocious affair. Because if you contract any other difficulties or problems you'd never know it. In other words, I could be walking around like a time bomb, you know, so sick that I could die right here and never know it. Because the sensitivity of the nerve ending would be gone completely. You feel nothing. And I'm all for that right now. Really.

D: You're all for the nerve block?

P: Yes indeed. Because the medication . . . when I started taking it, they gave me 50 mg of Demerol. That would put me to sleep for three to four hours. No pain, no nothing. Now I need 100 mg just to ease off the pain a bit. And that's no good. You know you can only build something up so high, and then it flops down on you again. Can't live like that. I'm told that particular drug has some adverse effects on your system, on your respiratory system and everything else. And so you see that I do have to do something. I knew you'd agree.

D: Sounds like a nasty predicament. . . . What was your health like before the accident? Any problems?

P: No.

D: Did you ever have to see a doctor for anything?

P: Never. I made the varsity lacrosse team my freshman year at college. I played all four years there, and I wrestled. Then I went to Vietnam and had thirteen months of combat over there. I came back, and I was still healthy. But the pain's been too much; it takes too much away from you. You know what I mean?

D: So it sounds like the past three years you've been having to deal with pain, constant pain.

P: No. No. I only had to deal with pain constantly for the past year. Up to that time I would have a bunch of pain—it's one and a half years ago it started—and during that time I would get pain periodically. But now it's getting to a point where it's in there all the time. The steady pain I can live with; it isn't that horrible. It's the acute pain that kills me.

D: So you have episodes when the pain flares up worse than other times?

P: Yes.

At this point an intern came into the room, informing the patient he had to begin an intravenous drip because a liver biopsy was scheduled for later that afternoon. I asked the patient if he objected to continuing the interview, to which he replied, "I don't give a damn." Then he added, "I think it's time for a pain shot. Would you check with the nurse out there? Will you ask her to bring in my medication?" As the intern began inserting the intravenous needle, the patient began howling in pain. He stopped the interview for several minutes, composed himself, and then gave me permission to proceed.

D: Let me talk a little bit about your parents. Are they still living?

P: No.

D: Both of them passed away?

P: Yes.

D: When was that?

P: Oh, eight and eleven years ago, respectively. My father died first.

D: What did he die of?

P: He had a problem where he was a solid worker and he couldn't quit. He had four heart attacks. He worked himself into a bad heart, and then he had pneumonia and the last heart attack took him away.

D: And what about your mom?

P: She died of grief, I think. Over the loss of her husband.

D: They must have been very close.

P: Yes, they were. They were good parents; they were always there. . . . Do you think this fellow (*intern*) is adequately trained to do this (*put in the intravenous catheter*)?

D: I think he probably is.

P: I don't know. Look at the size of that needle. This couldn't be for me. (*The needle is inserted, and patient again screams in pain.*)

Intern: Relax, this is almost over.

P: Relax! That's bone you're hitting, man. Tell the nurse to hurry up with that pain shot before this guy kills me. (*Patient turns to one of the students.*) What year are you guys in?

Student: Fourth year.

D: Let me ask you some more questions about your family. How have they related to your problems? Have they been supportive?

P: My personal family? They've taken a beating. I've been in the hospital—six times in one hospital, twice in the other, twice here, and four times in Stanford. And in the meantime they're running from the house to the hospital. Naturally it's going to affect them adversely; it just has to. Shouldn't do them any good anyway. It affects me—it got me so screwed up mentally that I'm really . . . that before long I'll have to see a psychiatrist really, not just talking to you like this.

D: Why do you say that?

P: Oh man! Come on, man. Why do I say that? One and a half years of this. Can't you get that through your head that's unusual, unreasonable, and horrible.

D: Well, what do you think a psychiatrist will be able to give you?

P: He'll probably tell me what to do with myself. I don't know. (*The nurse with the patient's pain medication comes into the room.*) Let that girl in. She's more important now than anybody here. Give it to me in the shoulder, right, it's the only thing you got left. Put it in the back of the biceps. All right. (*Patient then tells the intern how to secure the new intravenous catheter.*) That will pull right off if you don't wrap it with tape twice. (*Turns to group of medical students.*) Boy, you really got to have a lot of guts to get well. (*Turns to nurse.*) Thank you. Thank you very much.

Nurse: You're welcome.

D: How do you see the future?

P: Hopeful. Well, a quitter never wins and a winner never quits. If you want to make something out of it you've got to go ahead.

D: So whichever way it goes, if you need the nerve block or something else . . .

P: He can't do anything other than that. I must have the nerve block. I will. Destroy it or not, I'll have the nerve block. I have a pancreas that's not operating now.

D: How long have you not been working?

P: One and a half years.

D: That long?

P: That's right.

D: That's a long time.

P: Well, during periods in between surgery I decided not to do any kind of work, so I supervised. Well, I'm not an egotist, but I'm more capable than anyone else.

D: Do you have pain every day?

P: Every day. Twenty-four hours.

D: Do you have it right now?

P: Yeah.

D: How would you grade it now? Mild, moderate, severe?

P: Right now it's hellish. (*Patient does not appear to be in pain.*)

D: When it's at its worst, how would you describe it?

P: Have you ever had like a slight toothache?

D: Yes.

P: Well, that's what the day by day is. And sometimes it will activate more. That's when I get it good, when it's hellish. That's miserable. I don't know what it does.

D: Does it stop you from sleeping at night?

P: Yes, it does.

D: Wakes you up in the middle of the night?

P: It sure does wake me up.

D: And has it gotten worse recently?

P: Oh yes. It's gotten worse in the last thirty days, progressively . . .

D: The only other thing I want to ask is this. Let's say the pain goes away and maybe you need some Demerol, but not a lot. Would you go back to work right away?

P: If my physician said all right, that I could and it wouldn't bother me, I would happily.

D: You'd go right away?

P: Happily. But I know one thing, all the time I've been laid up . . . it's going to take me a little while to work out effectively. You even get out of breath when you climb the steps and walk from the bed to the bathroom. That's a problem, too. And sometimes I get pain so bad I actually black out. Last night I flipped out here, just behind the medicine station.

D: What do you mean flipped out?

P: I passed out.

D: Really? That happened . . .

P: You don't realize how bad it is, do you?

D: Well I'm beginning to get an idea from what you're telling me.

P: It's indescribable.

D: So you feel your physical state is much worse than it used to be?

P: No, it's just that I'm out of shape. All of this lying in bed, taking medicine, eat, sleep, you deteriorate that way . . .

D: You don't know when you're going to be discharged?

P: I don't know. I'm just leaving it up to Dr. A. As soon as he says so I'll go. I've come to the conclusion now that I don't know anything about medicine, and I can't handle my own situation so I have to leave it up to a responsible physician. I used to think I could handle anything, but it's different now. When you're in pain, severe pain, you don't want to hear from anybody. You can call me chicken, a big sissy. I'll give anybody in this room $10,000 if you can take my pain away. Anybody!

D: Well, you're obviously hurting pretty much. We're going to have to stop in a minute.

Student: You just mentioned money. What kind of problems has this caused for you financially? How are you taking care of your medical bills?

P: Workman's compensation takes care of that. But my wife has also had to go to work, and she makes about $350.00 a week. You just can't live on that. No way.

Student: So has your life-style been affected?

P: In more ways than one. Because, first of all, we don't go out. I can't go out to a restaurant and feel good about eating. I may wind up . . . I take a bowl of soup. . . . When you start to hurt you can't eat.

Student: Do you find pleasure in anything you do when you're not in the hospital? Is there anything pleasurable you find that relaxes you?

P: You mean before this?

D: In the last year and a half?

P: I used to be very good at physical culture. I liked to play tennis, lacrosse, basketball, anything.

Student: Have you been doing that in the last year and a half?

P: No. If anybody dropped me down with a body check, I'd never get up, ever.

Following the incident with his intravenous line, Bruce Y.'s credibility was considerably weakened. Previous self-reports suggesting a determined response to adversity were questionable; his words could no longer dispel suspicions than an underlying dependency played a significant role in his chronic pain. Possibly in response to a growing sense of vulnerability, he began to reassert himself in the interview, predominantly through behavior. He effectively controlled the remainder of our meeting, fending off my attempts to address the underlying emotions concerning his illness. When I tried to elicit his family's medical history, he interrupted my questions and shifted discussion to the intern who was completing his work. Mr. Y. again complained about the pain of the needle, though to a lesser degree, and again requested analgesics. Next, he began a conversation with one of the medical students, ignoring me completely. I felt he was clearly communicating his ability to be assertive and strong, in charge of our conversation in spite of his distracting pain. He was more challenging, criticizing me for not understanding his "unusual, unreasonable, and horrible" suffering. He was condescending to the intern who, in his opinion, had inadequately secured the intravenous line. And he became more heady; he talked of requiring "guts to get well," espousing the philosophy that a "quitter never wins and a winner never quits." As proof of his desire to get well, he offered a $10,000 prize to "anybody in the room" who could relieve his pain. Yet his words and behavior failed to hide the dependency underlying this false bravado.

The basic psychological theme characterizing Bruce Y.'s illness response was an overriding reliance on others to make him well. He chose the role of passive participant in his treatment because of a self-acknowledged inability to "handle my own situation." This took the form of abdicating to a "responsible physician" complete control over decisions such as discharge from the hospital. It might involve letting a psychiatrist "tell me what to do with myself." Despite a professed desire to "happily" return to work, his opposition to independent functioning was overwhelmingly obvious. Mr. Y.'s statements about being "out of shape," which he feared could prevent him from working effectively "for a little while," reflected both a concern and a wish. Clearly he feared chronic debilitation; he worried, for example, that return to vigorous athletic competition would literally kill him. However, he also desired the helplessness in which he had luxuriated for eighteen months. His extreme regression had not only excused him from work, it prompted sympathy and nurturance from family, friends, and many, many physicians.

Because of his guardedness, the psychodynamics of Bruce Y.'s illness response are unknown, but an interesting hypothesis can be offered from the scraps of available data. A compulsive drive caused his father to "work himself into a bad heart" and finally a fatal myocardial infarction. His mother died grieving for her husband. In Mr. Y.'s mind, hard work and continued health may have been incompatible; not only did the patient suffer, but so did his loved ones. In reaction to his father's maladaptive illness response— excessive denial—Bruce Y. may have responded to ill health in just the opposite fashion. He became helpless and thereby contained his competitive urges, which might get out of control and drive him inexorably to debility and death. And Mr. Y. did have considerable competitive feelings in him. At one point I asked him his ambitions prior to the accident. He reported he had wanted to "take over the entire area in my business and run the other guys out," which "didn't turn out because I got hit in the belly." In order to suppress his competitiveness, and thereby remove the possibility of becoming a workaholic like his father, he became helpless. Paradoxically, in his effort to stay healthy he was actually contributing to his decline in health.

Bruce Y.'s case vividly illustrates the importance of recognizing a patient's disguised dependency as early in the treatment as possible. By misinterpreting false bravado as gutsy determination, the physician promotes even greater regression in his patient. Reading passivity as motivation, he may overestimate the patient's desire and willingness to work collaboratively in the therapeutic task. This can lead to unrealistic expectations, such as discharge of a postoperative patient ahead of the usual timetable. The secretly dependent patient feels overwhelmed by this aggressive treatment approach and regresses to an even greater degree. This is akin to the negative therapeutic reaction elicited by an appropriate psychotherapeutic intervention with a masochistic, self-defeating patient. In both instances a dangerous struggle between physician and patient ensues: the former becomes increasingly dedicated to making the latter better, despite his wishes to remain ill. The consequences of this battle harm everyone. Physicians view persisting symptoms as glaring statements of inadequacy, and they experience a gnawing helplessness and sense of frustration. Should these emotions fester, they can foster an angry countertransference toward the patient, which is often acted out. The physician may order questionable diagnostic tests, extensive therapeutic procedures, or unnecessary medications. All these interventions carry risks of morbidity and mortality; Mr. Y.'s drug dependence was certainly helped by his physicians' repeated attempts to silence complaints of pain by pharmacologic means. In this fashion, the angry component of a patient's dependency response—his demand to be made well—is matched by the angry caretakers' control over him. This dangerous competition frequently occurs when treating an individual who attempts to hide his extreme dependency.

8

Illness Dynamics

EACH CASE HISTORY set forth in the preceding chapters delineated particular factors that shaped the individual's singular reaction to disease. Viewed as a group, they demonstrate a fundamental concept concerning illness—namely, the impact that any disease has on a patient is a highly unique experience. During every phase of illness, a multitude of factors converge in his mind, causing him to perceive, evaluate, and defend against the loss of health in an extremely subjective manner. Diabetes mellitus is a different experience for a college freshman and a middle-aged executive approaching retirement, even if both patients require the same daily dose of insulin, similar restrictions on diet and limitations of activity, and identical prophylactic measures designed to abort potentially complicating conditions. Each individual has specific strengths and handicaps that characterize his response to diabetes and, consequently, influence the course of treatment. The interplay between a patient's physical pathology, his intrapsychic life, and the supports and stresses of his social matrix define his illness dynamics, an idiosyncratic standard by which he evaluates and responds to disease. An individual's illness dynamics represent a personalized assessment of the physical and emotional cost extracted by the loss of health, data as salient to a patient's care as laboratory findings, radiologic studies, and physical signs and symptoms.

Unfortunately, the prevailing model of health care, the biomedical model, is unconcerned with the psychosocial aspects of illness. Originally formulated as a research model, it is an antiquated standard based on the investigative premise that disease can be fully accounted for by deviations from the norm of measurable biologic variables and physiologic functions. By excluding the emotional and social factors from the process of diagnosis and treatment, the clinician completely ignores the interrelationship between mind and body and, consequently, does damage to his patient. This is alchemy in reverse, trivializing rich clinical data by neglecting their essential role in medical care.

Every patient lives within a distinctive context that may be beneficial or destructive to his general welfare, a reality obvious to the many physicians who understand the relevance of an individual's psychosocial environment to his physical status. For example, the reactions of the diabetic college student and the executive to identical treatment regimens—and to all the implications of the diagnosis—might be so diverse as to make the disease seem like two distinct illnesses to these patients and their physicians. Unfortunately, numerous clinicians are ignorant of this reality. They approach the practice of medicine as an intellectual exercise, a problem-solving endeavor which objectifies patients by defining them exclusively according to organic pathology. Although not universal, such parochialism continues to pervade the day-to-day practice of medicine. Fortunately, it has generated considerable controversy, such as Engel's double-barreled criticism that the biomedical model "embraces both reductionism, the philosophic view that complex phenomena are ultimately derived from a single primary principle, and mind-body dualism, the doctrine that separates the mental from the somatic" (1977).

He sums up its "crippling flaw" as follows:

> [I]t does not include the patient and his attitude as a person, a human being. Yet in everyday work of the physician the prime object of study is a person, and many of the data necessary for hypothesis development and testing are gathered within the framework of an ongoing human relationship and appear in behavioral and psychological forms, namely, how the patient behaves and what he reports about himself and his life. (Engel 1980)

The exclusion of psychosocial factors as significant elements in the pathogenesis and course of an illness invalidates this model as a standard for clinical care.

Because of this unequivocal truth, Engel has consistently advocated abandoning the biomedical model for the more realistic and pragmatic biopsychosocial model. In a paper concerning the clinical application of this comprehensive treatment approach, he underscores its correctness through a discussion of a middle-aged man with coronary artery disease (1980). A theoretical explanation of the biopsychosocial model, utilizing general systems theory as a framework, precedes the case history. The treatment approach is conceptualized by interposing the patient between two hierarchies that combine to form an overall hierarchy of natural systems. The person is at the same time at the highest level of an organismic hierarchy, which ranges from subatomic particles through the nervous system, and the lowest stratum of a social hierarchy, which ranges from a two-person system to the biosphere (Figure 1). These two hierarachies are in a dynamic equilibrium, since every system (such as tissue or family) within each hierarchy is a distinctive whole that is simultaneously interrelated with every other system. Consequently, disturbances at any system level can alter any other system level; through feedback controls, these may modify or aggravate the system originally affected. The practical implication of this model is that the impact of illness on a human being can no longer be defined exclusively by pathophysiologic changes but must additionally be evaluated in terms of the inputs from the individual's life and his external environment.

Reiser, another vocal advocate of the biopsychosocial model, discusses it from the standpoint of understanding the ways in which psychological and environmental forces are involved in the etiology and pathogenesis of illness. Synthesizing neurobiologic and psychological data from laboratory work and the clinical setting, he discusses the three phases of disease: the period preceding development of manifest illness, the phase of activation, and the period of established illness. Of the final stage he says:

> [W]ith time, perception of the disease and its meaning becomes increasingly elaborated within the individual's self-image and increasingly incorporated into ongoing mental life . . . [consequently] idiosyncratic symbolic meanings connected with the disease would, with increasing frequency, become enmeshed in important issues in the patient's psychosocial field, and in ongoing intrapsychic conflicts as well. (Reiser 1975)

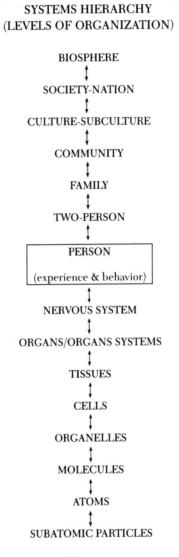

SYSTEMS HIERARCHY
(LEVELS OF ORGANIZATION)

BIOSPHERE
↕
SOCIETY-NATION
↕
CULTURE-SUBCULTURE
↕
COMMUNITY
↕
FAMILY
↕
TWO-PERSON
↕

PERSON

(experience & behavior)

↕
NERVOUS SYSTEM
↕
ORGANS/ORGANS SYSTEMS
↕
TISSUES
↕
CELLS
↕
ORGANELLES
↕
MOLECULES
↕
ATOMS
↕
SUBATOMIC PARTICLES

Figure 1

Hierarchy of Natural Systems

(Reprinted by permission from the *American Journal of Psychiatry* 137:535–544, 1980)

He postulates that this psychological reaction becomes increasingly associated with periods of activated or aggravated pathophysiologic responses.

Reiser's theoretical investigation of the biopsychosocial model places great emphasis on the brain as a clearinghouse for varied emotional and physiologic events, all of which have widespread effects on the total organism. In his words, the brain "orchestrates, integrates, and at points transduces across the biologic, psychologic, and the social realms," resulting in the disease state or the maintenance of homeostasis (1975). He describes the clinical implications of this intricate interaction between mind and body as follows:

> [The brain translates] nonphysical immaterial aspects of the social field (that is, symbolic meanings) into physical-physiological events within the CNS, and these in turn initiate physiologic changes throughout the body. At the same time brain function itself is, in turn, influenced by physiological changes occurring in the periphery of the body. These two-way interchanges of information and energy between the central nervous system (brain) and the periphery (body) are negotiated by the central and autonomic nervous systems and the neuroendocrine systems. This transactional continuity extending from subcellular metabolic processes throughout the body via the brain to the social environment makes it understandable that major life experiences, such as bereavement, can influence even the capacity to sustain the life process itself. (Reiser 1975)

This conception of the biopsychosocial model provides an interface between the two predominant orientations of contemporary psychiatry, the psychodynamic and psychobiologic schools. Like Engel, Reiser emphasizes the importance of understanding a patient's idiosyncratic perceptions concerning his disease state, because of the impact such symbolic thinking can have on the patient's overall response to illness. His work provides a theoretical link between pioneering demonstrations of the effects of neurohumoral mechanisms on emotional and physiologic bodily functions (Cannon 1920, 1932) and current sophisticated investigations of neurobiologic functions involved in such processes as immunologic response (Amkraut and Solomon 1974; Stein et al. 1976), or endocrinologic (Whybrow and Silberfarb 1974; Kiely 1974) and cardiovascular (Henry 1975) functioning.

Engel's work, which focuses extensively on clinical implications of the biopsychosocial model, and Reiser's theoretical exploration of those diverse factors associated with the states of health and disease share a basic common denominator: appreciation of the importance of the meaning of illness to an individual. That perception, determined by the patient's illness dynamics, influences his ability to wrestle with the varied effects of a given disease. The confluence of each individual's biologic, emotional, and social forces produces a subjective cognitive and affective understanding of the illness state, which ultimately determines whether the individual will effectively grieve his loss of health or experience some pathologic illness response.

Lipowski, who has written extensively about the meaning of illness, discusses how individuals appraise illness-related information in light of personal needs, values, beliefs, hopes, and fears. He states:

> This process of evaluation, resulting in meaning, continues unabated throughout the course of every illness. It influences the patient's perceptions and mood as well as the content and form of what he communicates concerning his illness, how, to whom, and when. It affects his decision to seek or delay medical consultation, his degree of compliance with medical advice and management, as well as his relationship with his family, employers, health professionals and other concerned people. (Lipowski 1975a)

As a result of this process,

> [A]ny illness or injury, serious or even trivial, may disrupt psychological equilibrium if it means threat or loss for the person and cuts off a major source of gratification, or enhances intrapsychic conflicts by facilitating emergence of repudiated wishes, weakening ego mechanisms of defense or signifying punishment for realistic or neurotic guilt. (Lipowski 1975a)

In this fashion, medical illness can profoundly influence an individual's emotional state and result in an abnormal illness response, which may additionally compromise his physical status via intricate psychophysiologic feedback mechanisms. Consequently, if the clinician is to provide optimal—or, in many instances, even adequate—health care, he must tend to the patient's mind as well as to his body.

The necessary first step in the biopsychosocial approach is a thorough appreciation of the individual's illness dynamics. This is an invaluable blueprint that allows some prediction of behavior in the face of illness, and it can only be derived from a careful exploration and evaluation of all the factors affecting and affected by the individual's disease. The manner in which they converge in the patient's mind defines his illness dynamics; this is portrayed schematically in Figure 2, which uses three circles to represent the relevant components of the patient's biologic, psychological, and social existence. The area of overlap by these circles defines his idiosyncratic perception of illness.

A practical illustration of this schema is provided by referring to our two hypothetical diabetics, supplying a single factor to each of the areas that coalesce into each patient's particular illness dynamics. Both patients share the biologic fact of recently diagnosed diabetes mellitus. In the psychological sphere, the college freshman is preoccupied with emerging independence from his nuclear family, whereas the executive ambivalently contemplates the enhanced dependency that accompanies retirement. In the social sphere, the young adult is concerned with career development and eventual marriage. His counterpart is more focused on family issues, such as enjoying the achievements of grown children and sharing his golden years with a beloved spouse (Figure 3). The biopsychosocial issues of these individuals can easily shape illness responses quite different

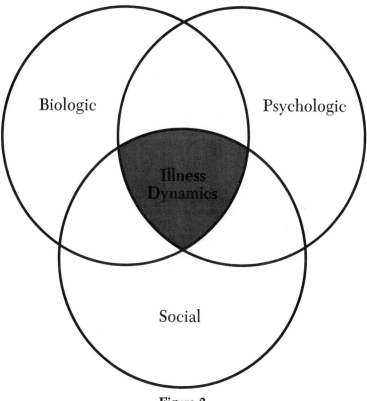

Figure 2

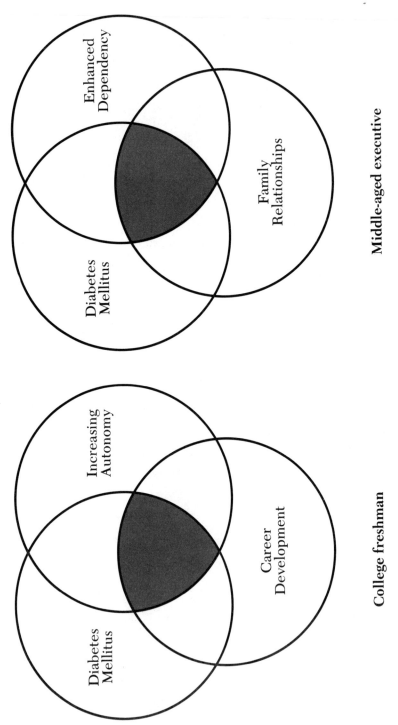

Figure 3

from one another. For example, it is anticipated that limitations placed on a young man by diabetes would stir considerable conflict between developing autonomy and a longing for the prevailing dependency of earlier life stages. He might respond with more anxiety, anger, or depression than an individual who has discharged most parental responsibilities during the course of a long marriage. The latter patient may also resent his bad luck, as it occurs at a time of life primarily reserved for relaxation and recreation; however, these feelings may be tempered by the knowledge that a loving spouse will provide reassurance and additional support if needed.

By programming a solitary factor into the three areas which determine one's illness dynamics, the immediate biopsychosocial profile of each of these men is observed to be quite distinctive. Consider, then, the uniqueness of any patient's illness dynamics, given the breadth of psychosocial factors influencing any organic pathology. This reality of the experience of being sick has been repeatedly highlighted in the preceding case histories, which have also demonstrated the interrelationship between illness dynamics, illness response, and overall medical treatment. The remainder of this chapter will review fundamental biopsychosocial factors which influence a patient's reaction to his disease. Although these items will first be presented in a list format, I emphasize that Figure 4 is more of an outline than a checklist. To scan the columns and then address each issue with the patient the same way one surveys by questionnaire is to defeat the purpose of this book. Practicing biopsychosocial medicine requires careful interactive discussion between physician and patient, guided by the latter's affective, behavioral, cognitive, and associative cues. Only by building a therapeutic alliance and objectively exploring with the patient the intrapsychic and interpersonal aspects of his life can the physician accurately determine that individual's illness dynamics.

BIOLOGIC COMPONENTS OF ILLNESS DYNAMICS

Nature and Severity of the Disease Process

An individual's illness response depends greatly on the specific disease affecting him. Generally, the more benign and self-limited the pathologic process the more readily an individual can grieve his loss of health because of the accurate recognition that his condition will be short-lived and will minimally affect overall functioning.

Biologic

- Nature and severity of the disease process
- Physical integrity of the patient
- Genetic endowment
- Affected organ system or body part
- Response to pharmacotherapy

Psychological

- Personality type
- Ego mechanisms
- Stages in the life cycle
- Past medical history
- Past psychiatric history
- The physician-patient relationship

Social

- Family relationships
- Personal history
- Family medical history
- Cultural factors

Figure 4

Components of Illness Dynamics

Conversely, catastrophic illness is more likely to produce an abnormal illness response, as acceptance of permanent debility is a considerable emotional task for anyone. The issue of acuteness versus chronicity also has an impact on the individual's reaction. Some patients contend much better with an acute disease process, comforted by the knowledge that the illness state will soon be over regardless of the outcome. Others are more capable of adjusting to chronic illness. The familiarity of symptoms, even if they are uncomfortable and enervating, is peculiarly reassuring. Such individuals experience the sudden onset of sickness as too anxiety provoking. Whether an illness is congenital or acquired must also be considered. The ramifications of being born deaf are far more extensive than loss of hearing that develops after an individual has learned to speak. Similarly, congenital hypothyroidism can produce permanent retardation, whereas that same endocrinologic disturbance later in life is readily treatable and rarely has lasting sequelae.

Physical Integrity of the Patient

Individuals vary greatly in their vulnerability to organic pathology. The reasons for this variation range from simple factors, such as age, to progressively more complex issues, such as allergic reactions to necessary medications or idiosyncratic deficiencies in the immune response. The physical threat that pneumonitis poses to a twenty-year-old is considerably less than the potentially life-threatening impact of pulmonary infection in an eighty-year-old. Similarly, an abscessed tooth is a painful annoyance to a healthy, young adult, a potential source of serious infection to a diabetic, and a grave threat to an immunosuppressed cancer patient. Previous episodes of ill health also have an impact on an individual's selective vulnerability to subsequent illness. For example, rheumatic heart disease can predispose to subacute bacterial endocarditis, necessitating prophylactic measures in certain situations, such as administration of antibiotics before dental procedures. Similarly, prior abdominal surgery places an individual at greater risk for intestinal obstruction secondary to adhesions, and major surgical procedures increase the probability of thrombophlebitis or urinary tract infection, common postoperative complications. Patients are quite aware of their particular constitutional strengths and vulnerabilities. Their attempts to measure such variables may be fundamentally objective or strikingly unrealistic, with consequent effects on their illness response.

Genetic Endowment

An individual's genetic heritage can have considerable effect on his illness dynamics. A patient who is genetically loaded for a particular disease frequently has a heightened emotional reaction when suggestive signs and symptoms appear. Excessive affect, such as anxiety or depression, and cognitive distortions about the facts of his illness may ensue. One such example involved a young woman recovering from a brain abscess which resulted from a bacteremia caused by an osteomyelitis of her toe. Thoroughly knowledgeable about her medical condition, she became progressively anxious during her convalescence; she was increasingly preoccupied with the thought that her abscess marked the onset of Huntington's chorea, the horrible neurologic disorder which claimed her father. Considerable denial is an alternative reaction to one's hereditary predisposition to an illness. The following chapter explores this response in a middle-aged man whose entire family succumbed to heart disease. He denied obvious symptoms of a myocardial infarction before seeking emergency medical attention. Prior to this acute episode he had lived a type A life-style, unconcerned that his behavior might activate a presumed predisposition to heart disease. How a patient interprets his medical heritage when he becomes ill is unpredictable and can only be determined by careful attention to his stated and unstated cues.

Affected Organ System or Body Part

Obviously a patient's particular physical pathology can have tremendously significant psychological and social effects. A narcissistic individual may never be able to resolve feelings about disfiguring surgery; a young childless woman may have equal difficulty adjusting to a needed hysterectomy for carcinoma in situ of the cervix. Certain diseases, by virtue of their pathophysiology, interfere with the patient's ability to grieve his loss of health effectively. Central nervous system pathology is the prime example of this phenomenon. The delirium produced by meningitis or the aphasia resulting from a cerebrovascular accident can prevent an individual from realistically assessing the impact of illness on his life, let alone resolving the varied emotions about his plight. Endocrinopathies and toxic metabolic disorders can have similar effects. Recovery from such ailments is complicated in those patients whose feelings about their transient loss of control, due to impaired cerebral functioning, surpasses concerns about the organic process that caused the change in mental status.

Response to Pharmacotherapy

The pharmacologic treatment of disease, in and of itself, can be an important component of an individual's illness dynamics. Most patients respond therapeutically to medications; however, many drugs have numerous side effects, ranging from the gastrointestinal distress produced by antibiotics to impotence caused by anticholinergic agents. Drugs may also induce distinctly adverse responses, some potentially lethal, and they can cause allergic responses, which may be relatively mild or have serious systemic impact. Certain medications, such as narcotic analgesics or anxiolytics, have an addictive potential. In addition to providing symptomatic relief, then, medications can also cause discomfort, alter mood, and sensitize patients to the potential dangers of medical treatment in general. For all these reasons, pharmacotherapy may play a significant role in shaping an individual's illness dynamics.

PSYCHOLOGICAL COMPONENTS OF ILLNESS DYNAMICS

Personality Type

Character style, or personality, is a term that basically refers to an individual's predictable response pattern to pleasurable or noxious stimuli, which may derive internally or from the environment. Much has been written about the correlation between personality type and the reaction to sickness (Kahana and Bibring 1964), as well as its role in the management of patients (Reichard 1964; Groves 1978). In general, an individual's characteristic behavior becomes that much more pronounced when he is forced to contend with strong, diverse emotions such as those precipitated by illness. An obsessional individual tends to become more rigidly controlled, a histrionic patient, increasingly dramatic and attention seeking. Although reversion to familiar patterns can be an adaptive response to stress, it can also quickly evolve into self-defeating conduct. Rigid characterologic behavior may retard the necessary collaborative work between physician and patient, as when an obsessional individual isolates his affect or disguises his true emotions by means of reaction formation. It can complicate accurate diagnostic assessment, as when a histrionic personality type becomes increasingly hypochondriacal. It may also interfere with effective grief work, as when a dependent individiual becomes pathologically regressed and helpless, abdicating responsibility for his welfare to others and never attempting to gain an emotional perspective on his illness. In this manner, the patient's personality is an enormously significant determinant of his illness dynamics.

Ego Mechanisms

The level of ego functioning, integrally linked to personality type, is another important component of illness dynamics. In general, the greater the degree of ego maturity the greater the ability to assess the impact of illness accurately. Mature mechanisms, such as anticipation, humor, and sublimation, facilitate the grieving process associated with loss of health. An individual who relies heavily on psychotic mechanisms, such as denial, distortion, and delusional projection, is obviously handicapped in this regard. Such a patient defines his own reality by opting to see only what he desires, particularly when stressed. Under these circumstances, it becomes impossible to acknowledge and gain perspective on the emotions accompanying an episode of illness.

Stages in the Life Cycle

Intrapsychic issues that characterize specific phases of the life cycle also have a bearing on the individual's illness dynamics. The omnipotence of adolescence, for example, predisposes teenagers toward denial of illness. An unfortunate consequence is noncompliance with required medical treatment, such as the dietary indiscretions or inconsistent use of insulin by a juvenile diabetic. Excessive narcissism compels the adolescent to reject most advice and controls of adults, including necessary proscriptions by physicians. The child in early latency and the geriatric patient also contend with distinctive issues that affect their medical treatment. The former, who has yet to evolve a mature understanding of death, is not adequately equipped psychologically to comprehend terminal illness. The latter, already faced with accelerated physical decline, is often quite despairing about additional burdens brought on by sickness. This complicates overall care and interferes with what Erikson describes as a more adaptive response to aging, the state of ego integrity (1963). Throughout the life cycle developmental events affect the illness response and are also affected by the impact of disease.

Past Medical History

Previous encounters with sickness can shape the illness dynamics attending subsequent episodes of ill health. A young man who unexpectedly discovers that he must temporarily curtail his sexual activity because of the pain accompanying his first flare-up of prostatitis will undoubtedly have strong feelings about suggestive urinary symptoms occurring at a later date. In addition, unanticipated complications endemic to medical care, such as postoperative pneumonitis or an allergic reaction to radiologic dye, can develop into powerful determinants of future reactions to illness. The onset of any symptom may revitalize unpleasant memories of previous treatment and thereby precipitate considerable anxiety, anger, or depression. Alternatively, the individual may deny any new abnormality in an effort to avoid again placing himself in the patient role, a condition he associates with discomfort and danger. Even if the physician is unaware of specific determinants of his patient's illness dynamics, the past medical history may provide a reasonably accurate prediction of that individual's reaction to his current ill health. For example, a three-week hospitalization for an uncomplicated appendectomy may highlight excessive dependency, a behavior that can readily recur during rehospitalization.

Past Psychiatric History

Individuals who develop demonstrable psychiatric disorders in response to life crises, such as divorce or termination from a job, are at greater risk of reacting to illness in a similar fashion. Loss of health can produce characteristic psychopathology, such as clinical depression, an anxiety disorder, addictive behavior, or even psychosis. Mood swings also affect the individual's illness dynamics. The phase of cyclothymia can heighten or diminish the individual's perception of illness, the trust he invests in his physician, and his motivation to get well. Physical illness can also aggravate an organically based psychiatric disturbance. A common example is the elderly patient with some degree of multi-infarct dementia. Infection, dehydration, or the effects of general anesthesia can disrupt tenuous central nervous system functioning and induce a delirium. Obviously, that patient's illness response is completely distorted by such underlying psychopathology.

The Physician-Patient Relationship

Transference to the treating physician can be a crucially significant element of a patient's illness dynamics. Several of the reported cases illustrate this point, perhaps most notably, Nellie T. and Janet R. in Chapter 5. An equally important determinant—and one that is entirely beyond the patient's control—is the countertransference he elicits from health care providers. Patients are perennial targets for the unconscious prejudices, favorable and critical, of those ministering to them. Some physicians, for example, prefer to treat young patients; others are more cathected to the geriatric population. Some physicians respond to a patient's seductiveness by investing more time and attention; others are made to feel anxious or angry by such conduct and may distance themselves or engage in a struggle designed to force the patient's compliance to the doctor's desired norms of behavior. Some patients are esteemed, others ignored, because of the physician's regard for such arbitrary factors as intelligence, physical appearance, cultural background, and personality traits. Whereas such preferences are idiosyncratic to the physician, determined by his particular psychodynamic forces, they can have considerable impact on the patient's attempt to accommodate to his loss of health.

SOCIAL COMPONENTS OF ILLNESS DYNAMICS

Family Relationships

Established patterns within a family or a marriage, and the effect an illness has on those patterns, contribute to the individual's illness dynamics. If relationships are based on a healthy interdependence, characterized by shared responsibilities, the partners can accommodate to life's varied stresses. If, however, a rigid equilibrium prevails, in which defined roles must be maintained in order to preserve a marriage or family unit, illness can have an extensive, sometimes devastating impact on that particular system. A common example involves debilitating sickness in the primary wage earner of a family. Forced into a dependent position, the patient may experience varying degrees of discomfort, resentment, or depression concerning the role reversal, and these feelings are often mirrored by family members who must also assume different positions of responsibility. A new, predominantly negative equilibrium can evolve, which may impede the patient's progress toward recognizing and resolving all the emotions associated with his illness.

Similarly, significant illness in a child can place great demands on the parents' time, energy, and finances, sometimes becoming an all-consuming preoccupation that stresses every area of the family's existence. Compromises must be made, including material sacrifices, prohibitions on recreational time, or changes in job-related decisions. Despite such adversity, an understanding family can maintain a supportive, helpful stance vis-à-vis the child and can assist him with the task of accommodating to his disease. A less empathic family may compound the difficulties brought on by sickness, enhancing the possibility of an abnormal illness response. Similar circumstances prevail in the case of a sick, elderly relative or a spouse whose declining years are marred by protracted illness.

The individual's position in the nuclear family can also affect his illness dynamics. Although there is a risk of overgeneralizing, it is true that some lifelong patterns prevail as a consequence of the birth order. Older siblings tend to be more autonomous, and younger ones tend to be more dependent, characteristics that can become increasingly conspicuous during periods of stress. I once treated a man who was the tenth child in a fifteen-member sibship. During his hospitalization, a definitive diagnostic procedure was postponed four times, an occurrence that would infuriate most patients but that failed to shake his calm. When I asked how he had maintained his composure, he informed me that his early years had taught him to "wait my turn." His philosophic reply was quite understandable given the tenacious persistence of childhood patterns.

Personal History

Although it is a reflection of intrapsychic issues, an individual's interpersonal functioning (his educational and occupational experiences, as well as the status of personal friendships or a marriage) can have a separate bearing on his illness dynamics. A serious heart attack in the young aggressive executive struggling his way up the corporate ladder provides an illustration of this component to illness dynamics. In addition to the psychological conflict caused by the physical constraints imposed on this obsessional man, his diseased myocardium also forces him to contend with crucial reality issues. His career is threatened if work-related activities are deemed too strenuous, compelling him to consider a change of employment at a time in life when most people attempt to consolidate professional gains. Not only does he have the difficult task (given his personality type) of dealing with diminished autonomy brought on by heart disease, he must also adjust to a potential loss of income and authority.

The quality of social relationships is another important determinant of an individual's illness dynamics. A characteristic loner style may limit that individual's friendships and camaraderie with professional colleagues. This can translate into minimal support during stressful periods, assistance that might be desirable and helpful during episodes of sickness. Even intimate friendships can falter under the impact of illness. The social stigma attached to certain diseases—tuberculosis, cancer, or alcoholism in the past; acquired immune deficiency syndrome currently—may drive associates away from an ailing friend. Feeling abandoned and resentful of the arbitrary judgment by people he cares for, the individual is at greater risk of developing an illness response predominated by anger or depression.

Family Medical History

In addition to any genetic predisposition to disease passed on through generations of ancestors, individuals also inherit a system of beliefs concerning illness and illness behavior from their families. Having witnessed a parent's longstanding struggle with a chronic debilitating disease, an individual can come to view all illness in a stridently pessimistic light. Consciously or unconsciously, illness represents an existence marked by repeated contacts with physicians, frequent hospitalizations, and inexorable physical decline despite the prescription of a multitude of medications and the implementation of numerous therapeutic regimens. In short, sickness becomes synonymous with suffering, invalidism, and death. Reared in such an environment, an individual may be seriously handicapped in his efforts to make a positive accommodation to illness. A more specific example of this scenario occurs when the patient, afflicted with the same disease as his parent, concludes that he will experience an identical course and prognosis. In the case of diabetes, he may define his disease exclusively in terms of multiple amputations or blindness or repeated heart attacks, depending on his parent's fate. Such conclusions may be irrationally based and unsupported by medical data; nevertheless, the patient is guided by these beliefs and inclined toward a pathologic illness response.

In a similar vein, the attitudes toward sickness that prevailed in an individual's family as he was growing up can greatly influence his illness dynamics. Some families, hyperattuned to the appearance of any symptom, whether major or minor, are in constant contact with numerous physicians. Their investment of time, energy, and money is considerable but is regarded as an acceptable price for frequent reassurances of good health. Children can readily become conditioned to such an illness behavior and may maintain it throughout later stages of their lives. Conversely, some families are intolerant of sickness, viewing it more as a stigma than a pathophysiologic response indicating the need for medical attention. Denial of illness then becomes an institutionalized norm within the family; violation of that standard invites criticism or abuse, a powerful incentive to suffer stoically and silently. One such patient, a young farmer from the West Virginia hills, was brought by a friend to the emergency room in a disoriented, semistuporous state. Examinations revealed a blood urea nitrogen concentration of approximately 200 mg/100 ml, the consequence of a previously undiagnosed congenital renal abnormality. When his parents were contacted they acknowledged that their son had been generally less vigorous and productive, but they minimized the significance of this behavior because "he kept on working." Obviously, the family's standards for illness were pathologically stringent, but they were never questioned by the unfortunate young man who adhered to these unrealistic beliefs. Folk medicine remedies and holistic cures, or the myth of a family's invincibility due to generations of superb health, can have equally detrimental effects on any individual attempting a reasonable accommodation to the impact of illness.

Cultural Factors

An individual's cultural background can have considerable bearing on his illness dynamics. Characteristic patterns of thinking and behavior concerning numerous aspects of diagnosis and treatment have been delineated in specific ethnic groups. Zola studied distinctive illness responses in Italian, Irish, and Anglo-Saxon patients, especially their motivation for seeking medical attention, their perception of illness, and their interaction with the treating physician. Irish patients were generally found to be stoic and accepting as compared with the demonstrably more emotional and flamboyant behavior of Italians (1963). Attention to an individual's ethnocultural heritage can help identify the effects that long-standing, broad-based social mores have on his recognition of illness and the adjustment to impairments brought on by disease. Such knowledge also helps the physician to appreciate that deviations from an anticipated illness response may be normal behavior in a given cultural group.

The precise definition of the individual's illness dynamics requires consideration of a multitude of factors. Some patients readily reveal many of these issues to health care providers during the course of treatment; others offer little more than a superficial view of the biologic, emotional, and social forces that shape their particular illness response, thus placing greater responsibility on their caretakers to elicit these data. Although the preceding list is admittedly incomplete, investigation of the enumerated areas should provide a broad understanding of the patient's personalized perception of illness. Comprehensive treatment is not possible without this information.

9

Treating Mind and Body

T HE PRECEDING CHAPTERS have focused on the recognition and understanding of the common illness responses. Case histories demonstrated the presence of these psychological reactions in medically ill patients, illustrating the degree to which emotional and social factors vary in individuals, with the consequence that the same disease can take markedly divergent courses in different patients. The physician's appreciation of this fact is crucial: optimal medical treatment requires a thorough understanding of each individual's illness dynamics. This knowledge provides the physician with a comprehensive psychobiologic assessment of his patient, permitting accurate diagnosis of his illness, as well as his illness response. The physician can then treat the physical ailment while simultaneously contending with any counterproductive emotional issues accompanying the illness state. This is the essence of the biopsychosocial approach.

The management of an abnormal illness response is addressed in the following pages, which detail the therapeutic interventions required of the physician and illustrate their implementation. The overall task involves application of short-term psychotherapeutic techniques to the management of medical patients. This first requires assessment of the patient's psychological maturity, to determine whether he is a candidate for introspective investigation of the emotions precipitated by his illness or more in need of reassurance and support. These two approaches respectively parallel anxiety-provoking and anxiety-suppressing psychotherapy, distinctive treatment modalities for different populations of psychiatric patients. This is not to suggest that the practice of biopsychosocial medicine is synonymous with psychotherapy. Rather, it requires incorporation of fundamental psychotherapeutic principles into the treatment of medical patients, thereby allowing the physician to simultaneously attend to his patient's mind and body.

THE CLINICAL INTERVIEW

The first step in this comprehensive treatment approach is the same first step required in the assessment of any patient, namely, obtaining a thorough, accurate medical anamnesis. History taking is the physician's most valuable diagnostic tool, a lesson I first learned from a professor of medicine whose repertoire of instructional epithets included the following: "Don't just do something, stand there!" He fervently believed clinicians should be able to justify all diagnostic procedures—from routine blood work to sophisticated radiologic studies—on the basis of information obtained in the clinical interview. Hence his admonition for aggressive, thoughtful investigation, instead of useless frenetic activity. Forced adherence to his somewhat oppressive dictates led to the reluctant discovery that my evaluation of patients became broader and more precise.

Careful, active history taking should uncover essential data concerning a specific disease process, as well as valuable insights into a patient's emotional status. Such an interview must be carefully focused and analyzed in terms of its content, the factual material offered, as well as process, the interaction between physician and patient. An interviewing style perfectly suited to this task, the associative anamnesis, was developed by Deutsch and Murphy, who worked extensively with patients suffering from psychosomatic ailments. This data-gathering technique requires the therapist to respond to key words, affects, and behaviors by persistently reflecting them back to the patient via echoing and repetition. The authors argue that such an approach, in addition to eliciting necessary clinical information, also benefits the patient emotionally by directly addressing unconscious issues and conflicts, thereby stimulating realignment of those psychic forces. Additionally, it strengthens the therapeutic alliance by repeatedly reminding the patient of the therapist's understanding and concern for his physical pain and emotional turmoil. The utility of this interviewing method to the practice of biopsychosocial medicine is immeasurable. The point is best demonstrated by a lengthy quote of the authors, describing the process and underlying theory of the associative anamnesis.

The method called "associative anamnesis" consists in recording not only what the patient said, but also how he gave the information. It is of consequence not only that the patient tells his complaints, but also in what phase of the interview, and in which connection he introduces his ideas, complaints and recollections of his somatic and emotional disturbances. If one asks the patient to give not only all his ideas, but also all accompanying somatic sensations, it is possible to observe the somatic and the psychic components more nearly simultaneously. One will soon find that somatic sensations which otherwise remain unnoticed slide in between associations, precede and accompany them. These seemingly irrelevant somatic manifestations will be found to be full of meaning and to constitute an inherent part of the existing psychic situation.

Being alerted to these manifestations, one finds that scarcely anything occurs in the body which is not understandable in terms of the psychic picture. . . . In organic diseases we are not so much interested in obtaining as many facts as possible as in getting information that has not been prepared for the occasion. If the associative kind of history-taking is properly elicited, one learns how the symptoms developed and what they meant to the patient from early childhood. The patient is stimulated to give the needed information when asked to describe his symptoms without being made aware of a psychological background in his illness. If the examiner allows him to talk without asking leading questions or answering his questions, the patient will usually give a detailed account of his complaints and ideas about his illness. Having exhausted his ideas and recollections regarding his organic disturbances, he will stop and want to be asked a question. The examiner waits until he feels that the patient will not continue spontaneously, and he then repeats one of the points in the patient's last sentence in an interrogative form. Usually the therapist repeats one of the somatic complaints last mentioned, being careful to use the same wording as the patient. The patient then as a rule gives new information centering around his symptoms and is stimulated to further associations. He drifts into a communication in which he inattentively mixes emotional and symptom material. (Deutsch and Murphy 1955)

That Deutsch and Murphy stressed the inseparable bond between mind and body, and recognized the impossibility of treating "organic disease" and "emotional disorders" as separate entities, is obvious. They also understood the importance of an active interaction between physician and patient during the clinical interview, echoing Sullivan's psychotherapeutic technique of participant observation. Sullivan argued that "the processes and the changes in processes that make up the data which can be subjected to scientific study" by a psychiatrist occur "not in the subject person nor in the observer, but in the situation which is created between observer and his subject" (1954). In large measure, the same can be said of the physician's interaction with a medical patient when psychological and social forces in the individual's life are being investigated. Certainly, impersonal observation of the patient will yield data concerning existing pathologic emotional states, such as excessive anxiety or depression. Psychopathologic conditions have objective signs and symptoms which can be discerned solely by observation, the analogue of inspection during a physical examination. However, the clinician can expand on these findings by involving himself more actively with the patient and observing the process of that interaction. In this manner he may highlight the patient's personality strengths and weaknesses, transference distortions, or prevailing psychodynamic issues. Supplementing his knowledge of the patient's physical pathology with this type of information, the physician acquires all the data necessary to treat his patient's mind and body. Utilizing the general technique of associative anamnesis, he is rewarded with a cornucopia of relevant clinical data that includes the following: 1) a complete medical history; 2) an assessment of the patient's general psychological functioning; 3) an understanding of the patient's positive and negative interactions with his environment and of how his illness affects relationships with family members, friends, and professional colleagues; and 4) the status of the alliance between physician and patient.

First, the clinical interview provides the physician with a comprehensive understanding of the particular disease process. He learns of his patient's baseline physiologic status and of deviations from that norm which have produced the prevailing signs and symptoms of illness. Precipitating and aggravating stressors—physical, psychosocial, or both—are identified. The historical course of the illness is defined; the family medical history is reviewed along with the patient's past medical history. The latter includes a discussion of prior flare-ups of the current illness, along with an assessment of previous diagnostic procedures and therapeutic interventions. Medications are reviewed, both in terms of their efficacy and adverse effects. Additionally, the physician evaluates to what degree his patient's daily functioning is affected by his illness. When the interview is properly conducted, the medical history provides the clinician with a panoramic yet precise view of the patient's physiologic integrity and resilience.

Second, data obtained in the clinical interview permit a sophisticated psychological assessment of the patient. The data afford a view of the patient's basic personality type, his prevailing ego mechanisms, the presence or absence of demonstrable psychopathology in the past or present, and tentative formulation of prevailing psychodynamic and psychogenetic issues. Each of these areas will later be discussed in detail, but some general illustrative comments can be made at this point. Thomas H. (Chapter 3), for example, demonstrated denial from the very inception of our meeting. His recounting of the signs and symptoms of thrombophlebitis permitted the diagnosis of an obsessional personality type, characterized by intellectualization, rationalization, reaction formation, and isolation of affect. Had his physicians been cognizant of his individual psychology, they would have paid scrupulous attention to *any* medical complaint he reported, and prompt hospitalization would have reduced the risk of a potentially fatal embolus. Similarly, Laura L.'s (Chapter 4) overdetermined anxiety was patently obvious as she related her symptoms. Her pathologic identification with her mother's misdiagnosed illness, as well as her general distrust of the medical profession, pervaded the recounting of her family history. Had her physicians recognized these psychodynamics, her eventual anxiety-ridden regression might have been minimized or prevented.

Third, the clinical interview provides important insights into an individual's social existence, including family connections, friendships, and academic or occupational performance. The physician learns of supportive relationships within the family—individuals he may have to call upon should the therapeutic alliance require external strengthening—as well as negative patterns of relating between the patient and those with whom he is most intimate. The physician obtains a general sense of how supportive or destructive the family will be as the patient attempts to cope with his illness. Inquiries concerning the family medical history can reveal prevailing attitudes toward illness when the patient was growing up, beliefs that frequently persist into the present, as well as important anniversary dates that may have relevance either as stressors in a disease process or clues to conversion phenomena that masquerade as organic illness. Evaluation of work or school performance offers data about the strengths of the patient's personality in terms of the capacity to adjust to particular demands of life. His ability to work consistently, reliably, and productively is measured. Discussion of friendships provides a general appraisal of the patient's object relationships. The physician may discern a pattern of schizoid withdrawal, excessive dependency, or a pervasive wish for autonomy and control. The presence of any such pattern should alert him to additional difficulties in the establishment and maintenance of a therapeutic alliance.

That these data are useful in an evaluation of a patient's psychobiologic balance is demonstrated in several of the case histories, perhaps most strikingly by the patient with tuberculosis discussed in the preface. His primary motivation for seeking treatment was the grim realization that his environment was devoid of external support, an absolute necessity given his declining state of health. His sense of isolation not only brought him to the hospital, it caused him to feel excessively dependent on a treatment team that was ignorant of the fact that he literally had no one else to care for him. Unresponsiveness to his special needs prompted an escalating anger toward his caretakers. As these facts emerged during his interview with the consultant the patient felt increasingly comfortable about ventilating suppressed feelings. He experienced immediate relief from his emotional tension, and ultimately the alliance with his physicians was strengthened.

Fourth, attention to the process of the interaction during the clinical interview provides the physician with important insights into the status of the therapeutic alliance. The quality of relatedness and flexibility between doctor and patient has an enormous impact on the overall treatment. As a rule, the ability of the physician and patient to work well together is directly proportional to the rapport they enjoy. If the therapeutic interaction is adversarial, the net result is usually antitherapeutic, as when two rigidly obsessional people seriously impede effective treatment by devoting their energies exclusively toward struggle for control of the relationship. The responsibility for a destructive alliance may reside with the physician, as countertransference issues can easily interfere with objectivity. More often, personality deficits or transference distortions can motivate a patient toward intransigence in the sick role. Identifying adverse behaviors of the patient that prevail during the interview provides clear signals as to their probable presence during treatment. For example, confusing, circumspect responses to questioning may suggest a patient's obsessionalism, paranoia, or passive-aggression. Conversely, excessively verbose, dramatic, or disjointed replies may indicate an anxiety-laden hysterical personality type. Alerted to these situations, the physician can anticipate specific difficulties in the treatment and plan his approach to the patient accordingly.

A properly conducted clinical interview provides a broad biopsycho social appreciation of the patient, a necessary perspective if the patient is to receive optimal care. Bibring and Kahana correctly observe that "within the usual framework of a thorough medical examination, . . . a psychologically meaningful history can be taken." They further believe that while following a "regular plan of history taking and examinations, . . . the knowledgeable doctor can listen sympathetically and use his understanding to help the patient with emotional distress" (1968). This is the second point to be made about the medical anamnesis: despite the contention that there is a sharp distinction between the therapeutic and diagnostic interview, the division is more imagined than real. Viederman (1984) emphasizes this in his description of the "active dynamic interview," a history-taking technique that strongly echoes the associative anamnesis. He discusses how "active, supportive engagement of the patient with primary attention to the dynamics of the immediate situation" enhances communication between physician and patient. This strengthens the working alliance in the present and future. Empathically listening to a patient, while simultaneously learning about his physical distress and communicating back an understanding of his fears, needs, and wishes concerning that illness, is the necessary first step in the practice of biopsychosocial medicine.

Two Types of Medical Psychotherapy

After acquiring all the relevant data from the clinical interview, the treating physician must expeditiously interpret it and make a crucial decision concerning the psychological management of his patient: Will he commend and encourage the individual's fundamental emotional equilibrium, hoping to create an atmosphere of support and reassurance, or will he pursue a more analytic path, in an attempt to help the patient work through conflicting feelings precipitated by illness? While attending to physical pathology, the physician must either court the patient's emotional dependency or help facilitate grief work. The latter course may result in transient emotional distress, but should ultimately yield psychological functioning at a healthier and more stable level. The choice is between a supportive, anxiety-suppressing approach and an introspective, anxiety-provoking one. These are diametrically diverse psychotherapeutic techniques, appropriate for specific types of mental disorders. Their modified use in the practice of biopsychosocial medicine transforms them into two types of medical psychotherapy, distinct methods for dealing with the emotional distress precipitated by physical illness.

As indicated by their names, these therapies are concerned with an individual's ability to cope with anxiety. In the treatment of mental illness, this determination is often made on the basis of the prevailing psychopathology. That issue is rarely so clear-cut with medical patients, barring obvious circumstances such as postoperative psychosis. Anxiety, as previously described, serves an adaptive and defensive function. It is adaptive when alerting us to danger—present or future—helping to mobilize mechanisms necessary to cope with the threat. However, excessive anxiety can overwhelm an individual, paralyzing him instead of preparing him for action. The crux of successfully dealing with a medical patient's emotions is correctly assessing the positive and negative impact of anxiety on that individual. Anxiety may be a liability, a potential hindrance to effective treatment, or it may be channeled productively and used as a stimulus to help cope with an illness state. The choice between these two treatment approaches basically depends on a patient's ability to grieve his loss of health.

The earlier discussion concerning the relationship between the grief process and one's reaction to illness described the staged emotional adjustment to loss. Under normal circumstances these are identical processes. Many patients attain considerable acceptance of their loss of health unassisted by family, friends, or medical personnel. Others, like Emily B. (Chapter 2), have great difficulty accomplishing this task. Not only do they suffer, but their torment often infects cherished relationships. These individuals essentially get stuck in a particular phase of the grief process, experiencing one affective state to the relative exclusion of other feelings. Unable to achieve perspective on all the emotions precipitated by illness, they are prevented from resolving conflicting feelings; as a consequence, acceptance of ill health is not realized. The treating physician must either help his patient overcome this emotional impasse or, if the pathologic illness response is static and ingrained, provide emotional support and reassurance throughout the course of illness. This requires a so-called medical psychotherapy, which is the essence of biopsychosocial treatment. Like most therapeutic interventions—from prescribing medication to performing standard surgical procedures—these forms of psychotherapy cannot be applied by rigid formulas. They require ongoing assessment of the patient, analogous to constant monitoring of his reaction to medication, with scrupulous attention to the therapeutic and adverse effects of the treatment process. Medical psychotherapy is one of the many crafts of the art of medicine.

The physician must first recognize what not to do when treating a patient in the throes of a pathologic illness response. He must never force the patient to fit the treatment. An individual who continually fends off enquiries concerning his emotional reaction to illness may be declaring his current inability to contemplate his loss. The physician accomplishes nothing by demanding that the patient stop procrastinating and get down to the business of grieving. His expert knowledge concerning the substantive and temporal course of a grief reaction becomes counterproductive if it is used as a weapon to assault his patient's psychological integrity. Relentless confrontation of those defenses (denial in this hypothetical case) is purposeless and can easily alienate or harm the patient. There is always some adaptive component to an individual's emotional state, even if he is rigidly defended. (The delusions of a schizophrenic, for example, permit temporary escape from overwhelming emotional pain and may prevent dangerous acting-out of those feelings.) Prolonged denial may be a patient's only means of accommodating to his particular loss. If this defensive posture is taken from him, he may become emotionally overwhelmed and, lacking additional psychological reserves, experience considerable emotional and physical regression. Alternatively, he may counter the physician's aggressive demand that he face the reality of his illness by simply leaving treatment. Obviously, either course is antitherapeutic. Such a patient requires anxiety-suppressing therapy.

Even if the patient is capable of effective grief work, tension between his psychological defenses and a physician's attempt to work with those mental mechanisms exists throughout the course of an illness, because grieving is a dynamic process. Although ultimate progression of grief work is toward a resolution stage, the path toward that end is rarely a direct one. The constant variation of emotional forces produces a dynamic equilibrium such that patients often experience minor regressions while they generally move forward through the various stages of grief. In practical terms this means that individuals rarely experience pure feelings of denial, anger, depression, or even acceptance. For example, some degree of denial may linger during later stages of grief. In the case of a spouse's death, the bereaved may be well into the anger stage yet still feel that the deceased will shortly be returning home for dinner—a clear remnant of denial in a later phase of grieving. Feelings of anger often persist into the depression phase, and in fact, some aspects of denial, anger, and depression may be present in the acceptance stage. The completeness of grief work varies with the individual. That variation must be respected by the treating physician, especially if he utilizes the anxiety-provoking approach in the psychological management of his patient. Didactic understanding of the substantive and temporal course of a grief reaction is meaningless if the physician attempts to impose that knowledge ↗ niformly on all patients. The practice of any medical specialty by direct application of didactic knowledge is a self-defeating endeavor. How often does the practitioner see a "textbook case" of an illness? Variations from this standard in the clinical presentation is the norm; appreciation of such nuances separates the superior clinician from mediocre colleagues. And recognition of variations from anticipated emotional reactions in patients is just as important as recognition of an atypical presentation of cholecystitis. At best, unreasoned psychological assessments of patients are meaningless; at worst, they are as malignant as making the diagnosis of "indigestion" for the epigastric discomfort produced by an inferior myocardial infarction. So a physician's cognitive knowledge of the interrelationship between grief work and the emotional response to illness benefits his patient only to the extent that he understands and respects the psychology of that individual. This is analogous to the intellectual and emotional "knowing" that the patient experiences in psychotherapy; the former is helpful, but it rarely results in lasting symptomatic or characterologic changes unless complemented by the latter.

Anxiety-suppressing medical psychotherapy requires active supportive efforts by the clinician to help contain his patient's anxiety within the limits that were acceptable premorbidly. The treatment is geared toward symptomatic relief, not psychodynamic change, an approach that requires the physician to be concrete and directive, sometimes heavily controlling. Appropriate patients are not guided toward discovery of unconscious motivations and conflicts that crystallized into their abnormal illness responses. Rather, the physician's energies are directed toward dissipation of their anger or anxiety or depression in order to minimize the negative impact of those emotions on medical treatment. Offering reasonable, consistent encouragement, the physician persistently solicits his patient's trust; this solidifies his influence, enhancing the patient's cooperation and acceptance of treatment suggestions which span the spectrum from use of psychoactive medications to environmental manipulation or even hospitalization. Such interventions, alterations of factors external to the patient, are specifically implemented to help him cope with any emotional dysfunction brought on by his disease. For example, psychopharmacologic agents can be used to treat excessive anxiety or depression when their effects produce a detrimental illness response that may threaten the patient's medical status. Carl N. (Chapter 6) and Laura L. (Chapter 4) are candidates for such treatment. And neuroleptics can be used when a patient's denial reaches psychotic proportions. For individuals too immature or inflexible to grapple successfully with the emotions accompanying the stress of illness, anxiety-suppressing medical psychotherapy is an extremely useful treatment modality. Shoring up existing defenses minimizes emotional as well as physical regression.

The anxiety-provoking approach, on the other hand, seeks to exploit emotional crisis. It is based on the belief that successful negotiation of stressful situations, such as physical illness, promotes emotional maturation. An outgrowth of psychoanalytic treatment, this approach applies traditional concepts to a more time-limited model. Many disciples of the analytic school (for example, Alexander, Malan, Sifneos, Davanloo, and Mann) have devised their own particular type of anxiety-provoking therapy. Despite conceptual and technical differences, all these approaches share two characteristics: persistent pursuit of unconscious material (instinctual drives, as well as ego defenses) and active, confronting interventions by the therapist. The goal of such treatment is working through. According to Greenson (1967), this therapeutic process guides the patient toward psychological insight and insures the effectiveness of such self-understanding so as to effect significant and lasting behavioral change. The fundamental therapeutic task is to help the patient acknowledge, bear, and put into perspective the painful feelings that adversely affect his life. This is a paraphrasing of Semrad's (1969) often quoted definition—eloquent in its simplicity—of psychodynamic psychotherapy. It views anxiety-provoking therapy primarily as a grieving process in which the physician and patient work collaboratively to help the latter achieve an emotional equilibrium that he has been unable to attain on his own. First, the patient must be made aware of unrecognized emotions, feelings kept out of consciousness by a variety of defensive maneuvers. He must then feel those affects within the therapeutic environment, as well as in the context of important relationships. Hopefully, this allows him to experience enhanced intimacy, reflected in a growing comfort in sharing his feelings. Finally, the patient must achieve some perspective on his newly discovered emotions, which basically involves appreciating the ambivalence of his feelings. Few things in life are all good or all bad—although we may tend to use all-or-nothing tunnel vision—and it is a major task of therapy to instruct the patient regarding a normal, prevailing level of conflict in his emotional life.

A common clinical example involves the highly successful professional who experiences repeated, unsatisfying personal relationships. Often this derives from unconscious discomfort with aggressive instincts which are automatically minimized or disguised through such mechanisms as denial, reaction formation, intellectualization, and sublimation. Although aggression is successfully channeled into productive occupational accomplishments, smouldering resentments frequently infect personal relationships and drive people away. The therapeutic task is to help this individual recognize and feel his aggression in both its guises: as an adaptive competitiveness in his professional world and as a destructive force in his personal life. Successful accomplishment of this task affords a greater emotional self-awareness; that is, the patient recognizes his own aggression, sees its positive and negative aspects, and understands that it is a feeling he finds both pleasurable and hurtful. Achieving this balanced view of one's feelings is what Semrad means by putting one's affective life into perspective. And again, grief work is the basis of anxiety-provoking psychotherapy. Once denial of affect is overcome, the individual experiences a gamut of conflicting, often disturbing, emotions and ultimately some resolution of these diverse feelings.

This process can be seen in microcosm during an individual psychotherapy hour. After being offered an accurate interpretation, the patient often responds with an initial denial that gives way to an angry repudiation of the therapist's observation. Subsequent sullenness evolves into a more subdued withdrawal, at which time the patient recognizes—affectively as well as intellectually—the veracity of the interpretation. Now more accepting of the pathologic aspect of some long-standing behavior, he becomes transiently depressed. He is saddened by the recognition of the self-defeating nature of his actions as well as by the realization that he will have to give up a familiar behavior pattern. This feeling state eventually passes as the patient becomes accepting of the interpretation and reaches a resolution of his underlying emotions. In the hypothetical case mentioned above, this would involve an acceptance of previously denied aggressive feelings, which are eventually seen as helpful, not merely hurtful, and which rarely seem as dangerous as previously imagined.

The decision concerning a patient's appropriateness for the anxiety-provoking type of therapy or the more supportive treatment model is partially based on the intuition that comes with clinical experience. However, there are abundant objective data that serve as reliable and convincing indicators in directing the treating physician toward the appropriate therapeutic path. Evaluation of an individual's ego functioning and object relationships—information readily available from the medical history—provides rich insights into his relative psychological health and, consequently, his ability or inability to tolerate the anxiety of emotional introspection. General measures of the patient's ego strength include the level of sexual development and adjustment, the level of educational and occupational achievement, intellectual skill, and the degree of autonomy and ability to assume responsibility. These criteria permit an assessment of inner psychological strengths and weakness, measures of an ability to pursue self-selected goals while simultaneously contending with both the usual and the extraordinary stresses of life. For example, the middle-aged bachelor still residing in his parent's home, limited in his social relationships and sexual attachments, and incapable of retaining steady employment for a period longer than several months at a time, would generally be a poor candidate for anxiety-provoking therapy. His presumed dependency and difficulty with intimacy argue against a desire to be introspective and a capacity to work collaboratively with his physician. His entire lifestyle suggests an overdetermined quest for protection, a goal he has attempted to realize by isolating himself from any relationship that might threaten his emotional equilibrium. Processing information from the clinical interview in this fashion—assessing the patient's ability to work and to love, the two central life tasks according to Freud—permits a general determination of the patient's ego strength.

A more detailed evaluation of ego functioning can be determined by observing the predominant ego mechanism used by an individual. Vaillant's (1977) volume on basic styles of adaptation is an excellent study of the topic. The prevalence of psychotic mechanisms (denial, delusional projection, or distortion) or immature mechanisms (schizoid withdrawal, projection, passive-dependent and passive-aggressive behavior, acting out, or hypochondriasis) during the clinical interview suggests a psychological immaturity which is generally a counterindication for the anxiety-provoking approach. Conversely, the presence of neurotic mechanisms (intellectualization, repression, displacement, reaction formation, and dissociation) or even more sophisticated mechanisms (suppression, humor, anticipation, or sublimation), implies flexibility and resilience of ego functioning sufficient to tolerate the heightened anxiety of emotional self-scrutiny.

Evaluation of object relationships, another barometer of an individual's psychological health, helps determine the appropriate type of psychotherapy for a particular patient. Object relationships offer a general measure of an individual's interpersonal functioning, including his ability to interact with medical personnel. While taking a medical history, the physician should be able to discern a pattern in his patient's relationships with family, friends, and work colleagues. A picture may emerge of marked dependency, in which the individual consistently assumes a passive stance vis-à-vis people in his life. Alternatively the physician may determine that his patient places a premium on autonomy but is able to abdicate a degree of independent functioning when he recognizes the need to rely on others. The physician looks for historical evidence of at least one meaningful relationship, characterized by trust and genuine emotional involvement. Maladaptive modes of relating are noted, such as approach-avoidance or fight-flight patterns, or a series of short-lived superficial encounters characterized by fluctuating idealization and unreasonable denigration of the partner. These data help define an understanding of the patient's motivation and ability to involve himself in a productive and gratifying manner with other human beings. An individual who has such an ability can tolerate the anxiety that accompanies the sharing and mutual exploration of feelings, such as those precipitated by physical illness, and this should protect against a pathologic illness response. Furthermore, a patient with a high degree of psychological strength would probably respond adversely to an anxiety-suppressive stance. Sensing that his physician was judging him to be too weak to wrestle with the powerful emotions precipitated by his debility, he might feel infantilized, demeaned, and ultimately resentful, with consequent adverse effects on the physician-patient relationship.

Certain specific measurements of a patient's psychological health should supplement the general assessment provided by attention to his ego functioning and object relationships. Some of these criteria are also specific indicators for anxiety-provoking short-term psychotherapy. These include a willingness for introspection and self-scrutiny and a motivation for emotional change. Both are predicated on a requisite degree of intelligence and psychological-mindedness, which may be evidenced in the clinical interview by the patient's expression of particular insights concerning his illness. The following illustrates such painfully accurate observations by a patient. Florence N. has had progressive rheumatoid arthritis for more than twenty years. Despite repeated clinical setbacks, she has been cooperative in her treatment, an attitude that is attributable in large measure to her philosophical attitude toward her plight. She expressed this attitude as follows:

> A chronic illness is like grieving forever. You never get over a kind of a grief feeling. It's affected our whole family. In a terminal illness you know there's going to be an end to it. Some place along the line the family knows it and the patient knows it. As hard as that may be to deal with, there is going to be a cessation of whatever you're going through. It's going to stop. Whereas a disease like this—especially associated with the kind of pain you deal with—not only involves me as a person with the pain that I suffer, but my family suffers it along with me. Seeing me hurt and not being able to do very much except support me as best they can in other ways, there's no rest from it. And that sometimes gets very, very difficult to deal with. You can't say it will be over within six months or two years . . . but there is always the hope that maybe they will come up with the answer to this so that it isn't a completely hopeless thing. But it's very difficult to deal with sometimes.

Mrs. N. later reported the immense guilt she experienced whenever her family anguished in helplessness during her many flare-ups.

She lamented that her physical state interfered with her ability to be a responsible mother—she was particularly distressed over her inability to dress her children for school each morning—reporting periodic surges of anger over and above a chronic sense of frustration. Yet through it all she had adjusted as well as could be expected given her particular illness, and she functioned to the limits permitted by her impairment. Her realistic appreciation of her physical state and her acceptance of her debility were derived in large measure from a thorough emotional self-awareness. Introspection and psychological-mindedness had greatly facilitated her ability to cope with her disease emotionally, an approach that her internist consistently promoted while attempting to arrest the arthritic process that was decaying her body. Contrast this with the patients discussed in Chapter 3. Their dedicated refusal to cope with the realities of illness produced an emotional dysynchrony that greatly interfered with treatment.

The physician's scrupulous attention to the therapeutic relationship supplies other indicators of his patient's psychological health. These include the patient's realistic expectations concerning the physician's abilities and the projected goals of treatment, the patient's ability to be actively involved—both intellectually and affectively—in his treatment, and the patient's ability to relate flexibly with his physician throughout encouraging and disheartening phases of illness. These criteria measure the degree to which an individual can experience a mature relationship with his physician. Nellie T. and Janet R. (Chapter 5) lacked this psychological development. The influence of past relationships, aggravated by excessive dependency on physicians and childlike expectations of treatment, greatly interfered with their care. The following patient, Anne S., on the other hand, had a much more realistic understanding of the interactional process with her physician.

> D: When your son got sick many years ago, you felt his doctors didn't help you with the problem. How have your feelings been in terms of your illness, and how helpful or cooperative have your doctors been?
> P: They've been very helpful.
> D: Why the difference?
> P: I think years ago they treated the illness, not the patient, psychologically, or the family. They didn't help the family cope, learn to cope with the problem. They were left to sort of drift on an ocean. And if you learned to swim you could save yourself, but if you weren't a good swimmer there was no one to help you.

D: And you feel that's changed now?

P: To some degree. I've been very fortunate. My doctor is a very compassionate man, and he helps me to cope. I've noticed that with some doctors you go to their office and they're busy. And when you're talking with them you don't really have their attention; their mind is elsewhere and you feel the lack of attention. They'll shuffle papers or accept personal calls and things like that. But I've been fortunate when I go to the doctor. He sits and listens, even if I make a foolish remark. He's not interfered with telephone calls unless there are emergencies. When you're with him you're his prime interest. I think that's what gives a patient confidence.

Mrs. S. well understands the importance of the relationship with her physician. She expresses the wish to discuss with him psychological issues associated with her long-standing essential hypertension and is able to differentiate between physicians who do and do not assist their patients in this regard. She wants to attend to the emotions precipitated by her illness, particularly since that task was neglected by her son's physician years ago to the detriment of the entire family. For these reasons she is suited to emotional introspection and is capable of tolerating the transient, heightened anxiety caused by that process.

A final measure of psychological maturity, also determined by attention to the physician-patient interaction, concerns the individual's response to psychotherapeutic interventions by the treating physician. If the patient repeatedly ignores or rejects observations concerning his emotional status, that is a strong sign of his desire for support and reassurance as opposed to working through his feelings. Mary Elizabeth W. (Chapter 7) well illustrates this. Each time I attempted to clarify the significance of her cardiac surgery (the beginning of a five-year regression to a state of semihelplessness), she responded by delineating additional physical complaints and discontents. She simply refused to ascribe any psychological import to that event and instead attempted to convince me even more of her needs. Eric (Chapter 1) responded very differently. Although he initially refused to comply with his treatment—an unconscious demand for attention and support—he subsequently cooperated with efforts to explore his psychological state; his change of heart was initiated by a physician's observations concerning the intense emotions he seemed to be experiencing. Physical improvement and return to normal functioning paralleled this introspection. Testing a patient's emotional responsiveness by judging his reaction to observations concerning his psyche is akin to using trial interpretations to evaluate an individual's suitability for brief psychodynamic psychotherapy. Malan, Sifneos, and Davanloo rely heavily on this procedure to assess an individual's potential for connection with the therapist. Such testing measures the patient's ability to relate cognitive and affective experiences honestly and to view his difficulties in psychological terms. In addition to its prognostic value, a successful trial interpretation also solidifies the therapeutic relationship; when the patient feels understood he becomes more trusting and, consequently, more actively involved in psychotherapy. As Eric demonstrated, the same is true for medical patients when the physician communicates to them his accurate assessment of their emotional state.

The final two cases illustrate the use of anxiety-suppressing and anxiety-provoking techniques for the psychological management of the medical patient. Investigations of each individual's illness dynamics is supplemented by discussion of those factors that indicate the appropriateness for the particular type of medical psychotherapy.

ANXIETY-SUPPRESSING MEDICAL PSYCHOTHERAPY

Stan S., a forty-year-old twice-divorced professional musician, was recuperating from a heart attack that occurred two weeks previously. He had been awakened in the middle of the night with severe precordial pain, diaphoresis, and nausea—classic symptoms of myocardial ischemia about which he was knowledgeable owing to the prevalence of heart disease in his family. However, he resisted seeking medical attention for approximately twelve hours, attributing his distress to a hiatal hernia that had been asymptomatic for several years. Only after he developed dizziness and light-headedness did he call the rescue squad. The interview picks up with my first attempt at probing his feelings about this life-threatening event. His response suggested the need for a supportive, anxiety-suppressing approach, a hypothesis increasingly validated as the interview progressed.

D: What did you think at that point when they decided to take you to the hospital?

P: I was surprisingly (pause) uh, the fear that I thought should be there definitely was not at all. I was upset with the fact that this was

upsetting a normal routine because there are a lot of plans that I
have and a lot of things that I have coming up which are important
to me and I thought, "What a hassle this is going to be." I thought
I'd probably come to the emergency room, and they'd say I had a
severe case of indigestion and that would be that. So I got to the
hospital, and when I arrived they gave me morphine, nitroglycerin
tablets, et cetera, and ran the usual tests.

D: Did it help?

P: Not for quite a long while. I did not notice significant reduction in
the intensity of the pain for a while. Then they came out and said
they were going to admit me to the hospital. Of course, they wheeled
me up into the CCU.

D: Did you have the impression at that time, before you got into the
unit, that you had, in fact, had a heart attack?

P: Not at all. As a matter of fact it was not until the following morning,
after blood tests had been run—I had pretty much told myself that I
did not have a heart attack—and after blood tests had been run, Dr.
F. came in and he said—early in the morning he came in and
informed me of the fact that I had had a mild to moderate routine
MI. That was a considerable shock.

D: You've never had any problems with your heart in the past?

P: Never any problems with the heart; however, a long, long time ago
the original problems that I had with a hiatal hernia were one time
diagnosed by a doctor as a heart attack. This was way back, going
back maybe fifteen years. . . . That's why I was so convinced this
particular time that I was not having heart disease problems at all.

D: Had you ever had any problems with high blood pressure?

P: No.

D: Diabetes?

P: No.

D: Gout?

P: No.

D: Do you smoke?

P: Heavily. Three to three and a half packs per day. I had cut down
from nonfilter cigarettes which I started smoking when I was
seventeen, and then I came down to filtered cigarettes and then to
low-tar cigarettes. But on the other hand, with nonfilter cigarettes
you increase the intake of cigarettes. Of course the usual excuses are
there. You think, "Well, I can smoke a whole pack of these, and it
equals in nicotine and in tar content what one unfiltered cigarette
used to."

D: Does anyone in your family have a history of heart disease?

P: Both parents died of heart disease; however, one of those, in a sense,
I discount. My father had four heart attacks, two of which were

diagnosed as a gallbladder problem. Now this is going back to the time I was nineteen or twenty.

P: How old was he?

D: He was, let's see, he was sixty when he died. Now, my mother died of—I don't know in your terms what it is, but she had pulmonary problems—well, she died of a heart attack.

D: Anyone else? Uncles? Cousins? Anyone else with a problem like high blood pressure or heart attacks?

P: No, not to my knowledge. No.

D: Do you have siblings?

P: I have a younger brother, three years younger than I am.

D: And how is his health?

P: As far as I know he's in excellent health.

D: Have you ever been hospitalized before?

P: Never.

D: This is your first hospitalization?

P: Right.

D: What do you think about being in a specialized care unit like the CCU?

P: I have had occasion to visit a great many hospitals. One of my wives had had two operations in which they ultimately removed her uterus and both ovaries. And I have known a lot of other people whom I had visited in hospitals, and the thought of hospitals has driven me about half crazy because of the nonchalant care of the . . . the lack of any real personal care outside of the kind of a phony, surface, almost patronizing thing that would come from nurses, et cetera. I have just hands-off defense mechanisms against even the thought of hospitals. The smell of ether, the whole situation, that I'm sure calls up all the childhood memories of getting those shots at the doctor's office, etcetera. I must say my entire opinion of that has changed one hundred percent here. This was a vacation. It was almost like being in a luxury hotel; you push a button and they're there and you get what you want. In short, I'm not now patronizing this hotel (*slip*)in any way, shape, or form. I'm deeply impressed with the care that I've had here.

D: Did you have any complications after you were admitted?

P: Yeah. I can't remember now if it was the Monday or Tuesday—I'm sure the medical record will bear it out—after I was admitted Sunday. I had the same sort of thing, which I believe was angina, and/or possibly even some of the genuine hiatal hernia or reflux esophagitis. It disappeared fairly rapidly. I did have a couple of nitroglycerin tablets that morning and also a little bit more later, and it disappeared. From that time forward, my chest has not talked to me in any way, shape, or form. By that I also mean that I have not even felt the usual heartburn that I normally would feel after a breakfast—let's say for example—that I have been feeling for years. I'm quite sure that among other things that was due to the heavy smoking.

D: Have you stopped smoking?

P: Not completely, but I intend to. Let's see, I've gone from three and a half packs to having to slip out here in the hallway looking extremely nonchalant and melting into the background and lighting up one of the low-tar cigarettes once or twice a day. But I have decided that it's fool's play, it's crazy, and that I should get rid of it all.

D: Were you taking medications before you came into the hospital?

P: None.

D: Are you going to take any medications when you leave the hospital?

P: If the problem occurs, so far as the hiatal hernia, I will be taking antacids. In the meantime I'm on 10 mg of Isordil and, at the present, in order to slow the heartbeat down, 100 mg of Inderal every six hours.

D: How do you feel about taking the medications?

P: I feel that as long as I'm instructed to do so, I will do so. . . . I feel that whatever program that my follow-up program is with the cardiologist that I will be seeing when I leave here, I plan to do exactly what I'm told to do. Only because, being forty, I have a great many things I want to do, and I have looked upon my particular attack as a blessing in disguise in some ways. I know that sounds like a pretty stiff sort of blessing, but I've looked at it that way because there have been a great many things that I have intended to accomplish, but I have lacked structure in my life to do so. This has caught my attention most assuredly. As a result it will force me onto a structured program, which I need to do.

The degree of Stan S.'s denial during the first twenty-four hours following his heart attack was certainly within acceptable limits. However, as he related more of his clinical history, the denial took on a more malignant flavor suggestive of an abnormal illness response. Although both parents died of myocardial disease he "discounted" his father's death with a rationalization about "a gallbladder problem" and was vague about his mother's illness. He provided scant information about each, in an attempt, I felt, to move the discussion quickly away from a too threatening consideration of his genetic heritage. He went on to equate his hospitalization with a vacation, despite an admitted aversion to the medical environment and even made the slip of calling the hospital a "hotel." He also minimized an episode of postinfarction angina—a poor prognostic sign—attributing it to his old hiatal hernia despite the remission of pain with nitroglycerin.

Again endeavoring to measure his affective response to illness, I asked how he felt about taking cardiac medications. His response was intellectualized and almost Pollyannaish in its "blessing-in-disguise" optimism. He was either unwilling or unable to acknowledge and bear the emotions precipitated by his heart attack, let alone gain a perspective on those feelings. Consequently, he basically ignored my question. Of equal significance was his declaration to do "whatever I'm instructed to do," which I interpreted as a covert request for additional support from his caretakers. In my opinion, Mr. S. was terrified by the early onset of a disease process that had killed both his parents. I felt he was communicating an open-ended willingness to do whatever the doctors ordered, reasoning that his only chance for survival was nurturing from his physicians. He seemed to be struggling between two stances toward his illness, and neither option was healthy. On the one hand, he attempted to deny the reality of his myocardial infarction; on the other, he presented himself as a passively compliant patient who sensed the seriousness of his condition and completely abdicated responsibility for his welfare to his physicians. Noting the tension created by this internal struggle, I elected to conduct the remainder of the interview with an eye toward minimizing his anxiety. I chose to encourage his dependence on his doctors—at least in the short run—while gently challenging his denial.

D: Do you think this will change your life-style?

P: I think for the better. I do believe it will, because I've a tendency to burn the candle at both ends. I'll have to cut back some.

D: So you think you'll have to restrict your activities?

P: I believe that I will have to, but only in a very practical sense, in so far as not doing the kind of work I was doing throughout the day. I run a music school and play cello professionally. I can't take on so many of these things and at the same time think I can go out and blast it up and raise hell all night long.

D: You came in on the thirteenth, and today is the twenty-fifth. That's only a twelve-day stay. Have the doctors told you when you'll be discharged?

P: No. I've been informed that I have one tremendous good attitude about this, which is, I think, important. Secondly, I had a stress test yesterday, which they normally take up to four and that registered zero. They couldn't get anything out of me on that, so they increased it up to a six with a couple of minutes rest in between, before they could even get me to panting a little bit. Apparently I'm in excellent physical condition outside of the current and immediate problem. I have felt fantastic ever since the stress test, and I perhaps feel this may be a contributing factor to my leaving the hospital early. I've talked with patients who have had three or four MIs before, myself, and they have told me that they've been in hospitals where they've been tossed out of the door after the third day. But here they really keep an eye on you, and they don't let you go until they think that everything is going to go right. I carried around one of the little battery packs (*Holter monitor*). People made all kinds of jokes about it. But nevertheless, I was told this morning that it showed to be a perfectly normal one without any extra heartbeats anywhere on the twenty-four hour recorder. I don't feel that I'm being released too soon. The prognosis in my particular case seems to be excellent. . . .

D: I'd like to return to the night of your attack. You said it was the next day that it sank in, that you realized you had had a heart attack.

P: Correct.

D: What happened then? What was different at that point that it registered in your mind that what you had might be more serious?

P: Well, first of all, the doctor having come in and informed me that this was indeed a heart attack, as indicated by the level of enzymes in the bloodstream. He had caught me fairly early in the morning when I was just a little bit fuzzy, so I (*pause*) but as the day went on (*pause*) as it sank in I felt (*pause*) of course, I very quickly went through the thing that perhaps they had mixed my blood sample up with someone else's. That feeling subsided, because they had been taking so much blood I felt they couldn't possibly have mixed up all that blood (*laughs*). So I accepted it, and I therefore put myself on a positive mental attitude about it, and I decided, fine—this does not mean I have one foot in the grave. It means that I have to change considerably. I have not yet—and I don't think that I'm due for any shock about this because I've had long enough here—I don't think that I have experienced any genuine fear about it, so far as I'm going to die or I've only got five years to live, or maybe I'm going to die tomorrow type thing. I think that I have philosophized about it considerably. . . .

D: What do you plan on doing when you leave here?

P: When I leave here?

D: Yes.

P: I plan to sit down and figure out how to accomplish all the things that I intend to accomplish and yet do them with proper rest periods and with a degree of foresight and planning so that I have enough time to do this without burning myself out by the end of each week. I will go back to my music, teaching, and running my school. I do intend to resume a full life-style, but on a more structured basis, as I had said. However, I've been talking a long time about getting myself into physical shape and getting myself fit. I do plan to go through the rehabilitation program here at the hospital, at least as far as I feel to a point where I feel I can take it over on my own. I'm going to play that by ear. I'm not quite sure how far I'm going to go along with the situation.

D: Do you know when you're going to start working again?

P: I'm going to resume my classes the first week of February.

D: That's a week from now.

P: Yeah. That's the cello classes. I'm going to start those then.

D: Your cardiologist has advised you about going back to music classes?

P: Yes. There is a misconception about that, and I have labored furiously to try to get everybody to understand that teaching cello is not getting up on a stage myself personally and playing for hours on end, with induced emotional and physical trauma et cetera. My approach is different and extremely effective. I put artists on the stage, and I just simply sit at a desk and listen to what goes on, take notes, and when it's over sit them down and discuss it with them. So far as my energy output, it's no more than my conversation with you here. This is approximately the level of energy that I need to put out in a music class.

D: Is your cardiologist for or against that?

P: He's for it, but he was a little bit later down the road. However, it has been suggested . . . I think he may be coming around to a different way of thinking now, because there's apparently no one who's come up against this particular type of work that one might be returning to after going through the attack that I had gone through.

D: It seems to me that your doctors have taken good care of you so far. They've alleviated most of your symptoms—though you still get some chest pain and have some skipped heart beats—so maybe you should continue to listen to them and take it easy for awhile.

P: I plan to do that and follow the rehabilitation plan.

D: That sounds sensible to me. It will probably mean giving up cigarettes completely. Do you think you'll stop sneaking into the hall for an occasional smoke?

P: Maybe. No, I really should.

D: I agree with you. Did your father smoke?

P: Till the day he died.

D: Maybe you're more interested in preserving your health than he was. You sound like two different people.

P: We had our similarities.

D: Well I don't know how he lived his life, but his smoking alone must have contributed to repeated heart attacks. You sound more sensible—you say you're going to stop burning the candle at both ends. I guess if you're serious in paying attention to your health you won't have to worry about having four heart attacks. As you said, you're not the type who thinks, "I've only got five years to live." And of course, we know much more about treating heart disease now than we did twenty-five years ago. I think it would serve you well to listen to your cardiologist's advice.

P: Well, yes. I have put myself on a positive mental attitude.

D: And I know that doctors usually work better with patients who have a good, cooperative attitude.

P: Of course. They know their business, like I know mine. We're all professionals.

As evidenced in the interview, attempts to help Stan S. work through his feelings concerning heart disease were futile. He was unwilling to expose those emotions, even to himself. He accomplished this self-deception by utilizing the ego mechanisms of denial, distortion, and passive-dependent behavior and then congratulated himself on a "positive mental attitude." It is true that enhanced denial is associated with a better prognosis during the acute phase of a heart attack; however, Mr. S. was well onto the recuperative path and continued to be pathologically blocked on his emotions. He broadcasted overwhelmingly clear signals that anxiety-provoking introspection was contraindicated. He relied heavily on primitive ego mechanisms and was unwilling to be self-observing of his emotions. Additionally, his ability to sustain meaningful relationships was questionable, given two divorces. This can have negative implications for the ongoing doctor-patient relationship, which was already stressed by his wished-for dependent stance. Furthermore, his treatment goals were somewhat unrealistic; he anticipated an excellent prognosis despite his intention to return to a full work schedule shortly after discharge (and probably to continue smoking).

Mr. S. definitely required auxilliary support in order to cope effectively with the emotions produced by his illness. My remarks, particularly at the end of the interview, were focused on that goal. I elected to exploit the positive transference he held toward the "hospital/hotel" and the physicians caring for him, and to reenforce his "positive mental attitude." At the same time I indirectly challenged his denial; instead of harshly confronting him with the reality of his physical status, I consistently suggested steps he should pursue to insure his return to normal, healthy functioning. For example, after he ignored my questions concerning his feeling about taking medications, I tried to avoid further inquiries about underlying emotions. My next question was more open-ended, followed by the statement, "So you think you'll have to restrict your activities," instead of the question, "How do you feel about having to restrict your activities?" I opted to tell him what he had to do (often by rephrasing his own words and repeating them back), rather than helping him to work through his emotions, in an attempt to arrive at the same conclusion regarding a restricted schedule.

Utilizing this technique for the remainder of the interview, I concluded our meeting by communicating to Stan S. what I thought he needed to hear most. First, I tried to diminish concerns that because of his family history he was fated to die young of progressive cardiac disease. I wanted to help him differentiate himself from his father, and the issue of cigarettes was a potential wedge. Second, I wanted to support the positive regard he held for his caretakers. This was certainly at the cost of promoting the denial of negative feelings toward his doctors and, consequently, fostering enhanced dependency. However, I judged that course to be the most therapeutic, hoping it would allow him to be more receptive to the prescribed treatment regimen. Suggestions from a positively regarded physician might successfully guide Mr. S. toward gradual return to a full work load, an alternative to his planned immediate resumption of full activities, which was a potentially fatal gambit.

The anxiety-suppressing approach to Stan S. relied heavily on the therapeutic maneuvers of suggestion and manipulation. Bibring (1954), in his comparison of psychoanalysis with the dynamic psychotherapies, explores therapeutic principles and procedures "considered to be applicable to all methods of psychotherapy independent of their respective ideologies." He delineates and discusses five "technical" and "curative" principles employed in the various psychotherapies; these include abreaction, clarification, and interpretation, in addition to suggestion and manipulation. The application of all five principles is required to achieve the working through of emotional issues, the central task of insight-oriented psychotherapy. However, as Bibring states, "suggestion, emotional relief (abreaction) and manipulation per se do not furnish self-understanding on the part of the patient." It is for precisely this reason that these maneuvers are heavily employed in anxiety-suppressing work.

Bibring defines *suggestion* as "the induction of ideas, impulses, emotions, actions, etc., in brief, various mental processes by the therapist (an individual in authoritative position) in the patient (an individual in dependent position) independent of, or to the exclusion of, the latter's rational or critical (realistic) thinking." Bibring is describing a process of change effected by direct inculcation of beliefs, attitudes, or behavior. Manipulation is more broadly defined than its so-called "crude forms," which include "advice, guidance, and similar ways of running a patient's life." Bibring discusses manipulation in terms of the use of words or attitudes to "neutralize certain emotional systems in the patient, mobilize others and utilize them for technical purposes or curative aims." Technical manipulation can be employed either in a negative or positive form "to produce favorable attitudes towards the treatment situation or to remove obstructive trends." He illustrates with a discussion of transference issues. Curative manipulation involves redirecting emotional systems in a patient toward adjustive change, such as fostering more autonomous functioning in a given relationship. If the patient is induced to pursue this course, he learns he can take more responsibility; he profits from the new behavior and, additionally, from an increased sense of mastery and achievement. Bibring's discussion of these therapeutic maneuvers focuses solely on the practice of psychotherapy. However, the applicability of these techniques to anxiety-suppressing medical psychotherapy is ideal. They help a patient focus on one side of his ambivalence, thereby minimizing emotional conflict and its consequent anxiety, which can be an extremely therapeutic alternative to pressing the patient toward the working through of emotions. I used suggestions and manipulation with Stan S. (when discussing his smoking and vigorous life-style, his father's medical history, and his attitude towards physicians) in an effort to redirect prevailing emotional attitudes for the purpose of promoting more favorable behaviors regarding his health. With patients like him, insight is considerably less important than compliance.

The anxiety-suppressing approach requires the physician to take a relatively authoritative stance vis-à-vis his patient. This enhances the impact of his guidance, and consequently, his suggestions and manipulations exert greater influence. Certainly all forms of psychotherapy require the physician to exploit the power inherent in his role. This can occur implicitly or in a more calculated fashion, such as Alexander's studied manipulation of the transference (1946).

Anxiety-suppressing therapy relies more heavily on this direct influence of the physician, which derives from a combination of prevailing mores and the transference relationship. In *Persuasion and Healing*, Frank defines one of the three features common to the various psychotherapies as follows: "A trained, socially sanctioned healer, whose healing powers are accepted by the sufferer and his social group or an important segment of it." Because of this, "the administration of an inert medicine by a doctor to a patient is also a form of psychotherapy, since its effectiveness depends on its symbolization of the physician's healing function, which produces favorable changes in the patient's feelings and attitudes" (1961). If physicians feel comfortable exerting some influence over individuals—influence that Frank likens to "methods of primitive healing, religious conversion, and even so-called brain-washing"—they can utilize contacts with patients to reduce anxiety and positively influence behavior. Certainly this was the indicated course with Stan S.

ANXIETY-PROVOKING MEDICAL PSYCHOTHERAPY

Short-term psychodynamic psychotherapy seeks to help patients work through core conflicts during a relatively brief treatment period. The intended goal is ambitious: to effect characterologic change, which is subsequently reflected in behavioral change, within a period of months. The work requires a high degree of motivation on the part of the patient and vigorous activity by the therapist. They collaborate in a relentless probing of unconscious material, but because the probing remains focused on the central conflict, clinical regression is minimized. The therapeutic task requires studied attention to the interrelationship between two general areas of the patient's life: first, his libidinal impulses, the anxiety they provoke, and the defenses utilized to contain them; and second, his lifelong pattern of object relationships which characterize his historical past, current existence, and the transference relationship. Elucidating the dynamic interaction between these two triads provides the patient with meaningful insight which helps liberate him from long-standing maladaptive patterns. The active give-and-take between patient and therapist promotes a high level of therapeutic tension. This, plus the relatively rapid uncovering of previously well-defended powerful affects, earns the treatment its title of anxiety-provoking therapy.

How can such a sophisticated psychotherapeutic technique, which requires a delicate match between the motivated patient and highly skilled therapist, be applied to the treatment of medical patients? Obviously, in its pure form it cannot. The practice of biopsychosocial medicine does not seek to transform the treating physician into a psychiatrist or to diagnose the patient primarily in psychopathologic terms. It intends to help patients accommodate psychologically to illness; that is, to grieve their loss of health. The anxiety-provoking model is utilized to help those patients deemed appropriate to acknowledge, bear, and put into perspective the painful affects that are precipitated by illness and that adversely affect their lives. This limited application of short-term psychodynamic psychotherapy requires the physician to keep his goals clearly defined. His task is to help the patient adjust emotionally to illness, not to resolve long-standing emotional conflicts. He guides the patient toward discovery of underlying affects, which permits working through of previously unrecognized feelings. The patient thereby attains perspective on all emotions associated with his illness, which allows him to achieve the optimal psychological functioning permitted by his particular disease.

A general illustration of this treatment approach has already been presented in Chapter 2. Although I guided the interview with Gary L. more along diagnostic lines, the general tone of the interaction, particularly toward the end, demonstrates the principles of anxiety-provoking therapy with the medical patient. Suffering from progressive renal failure, Gary L. had an arduous, debilitating medical course which included multiple kidney infections, a myocardial infarction, and advancing azotemia. Through it all he remained remarkably philosophic, largely because of his ability to grieve effectively his loss of health, and he continued to work, maintain social ties, and remain a loving, responsible husband and father. The interview clearly depicts the different stages of the grief process occurring during his various episodes of ill health.

At the time of our meeting, Gary L. was hospitalized for evaluation of his declining renal status, a hospitalization that had been prolonged because of difficulties in regulating his markedly elevated blood pressure. His predominant affect was anger, somewhat muted in its expression. He was irritated by the minimal contact he had had with his nephrologist and was frustrated by the medical staff's inability to control his hypertension. He was overtly angry with his former physician who had withheld test results from him, data that indicated how grave his condition was. Hemodialysis currently loomed large as the next step in his medical management, a development one would anticipate would cause depression in the patient. Cognizant of his previously demonstrated tolerance for introspection, I proceeded to probe his feelings concerning his illness. It was not a difficult therapeutic task. After clarifying with him his current situation (being confined to a hospital bed because of an uncontrollable pathologic condition and being kept in ignorance of what his doctors had learned diagnostically or planned therapeutically), I simply asked how he felt about it. He replied, "I get annoyed and then that passes and I'm depressed." With very little prodding he acknowledged an emerging depression, signalling normal evolution of the grief process.

Gary L. had repeatedly demonstrated the ability to achieve a healthy perspective on the emotions precipitated by his illness. This is the ultimate goal of anxiety-provoking therapy. It requires introspective analysis of unconscious material, which according to Greenson (1967), is a four-stage process beginning with confrontation, followed by clarification and interpretation, and culminating in working through. Recall that clarification and interpretation, as discussed by Bibring, are two of the therapeutic maneuvers required to attain psychological insight. Working through is the final therapeutic step; it seeks to remove persisting resistances to insight, in order to insure its permanence and thereby effect lasting change.

Confrontation is a therapeutic maneuver that defines a particular thought, feeling, or behavior as an object of study. A common example occurs when a tearfully sad patient reports "feeling nothing" about a particular event. By informing the patient that his tears belie his words (challenging denial of emotion) the therapist focuses their combined attention on the patient's crying for the purpose of better understanding it.

Clarification is similar to confrontation, but it seeks to bring the awareness of certain phenomena into even sharper focus. It is a technique in which the therapist restates the patient's observations, thereby helping the latter see those particular issues more clearly. In Bibring's words:

> Many, if not all, patients are often rather vague about certain feelings, attitudes, thoughts, impulses, behavior or reaction patterns, perceptions, etc. They cannot recognize or differentiate adequately what troubles them, they relate matters which are unrelated, or fail to relate what belongs together, or they do not perceive of or evaluate reality properly but in a distorted fashion under the influence of their

emotions or neurotic patterns. . . . Clarification . . . refers to those techniques and therapeutic processes which assist the patient to reach a higher degree of self-awareness, clarity and differentiation of self-observation which makes adequate verbalization possible.

He offers some clinical examples.

We clarify the patient's feelings, e.g., when we show him that what he describes as fatigue a feeling of being tired is actually an expression of depression. It is clarification when we elaborate his patterns of conduct, demonstrating to him that he reacts in typical ways to typical situations; or that certain of his attitudes which appear to him unrelated are in fact related to each other, representing various manifestations of the same attitude or that certain reaction patterns form a characteristic sequence, etc.

This was demonstrated in my interaction with Gary L. when discussing the transitory depression that accompanied enforced inactivity periodically required in his treatment.

Interpretation, the third step in guiding a patient toward meaningful insight, attempts to bring to consciousness material that has previously been unconscious. This requires preparatory therapeutic steps, such as manipulation or clarification. Then, at a time deemed appropriate, the therapist offers an observation which, in Greenson's words, "make conscious the unconscious meaning, source, history, mode or course of a given psychic event." This "assigns meaning and causality to a psychological phenomenon," that is, it provides insight. Offering the patient an understanding of the forces that motivate a specific behavior affords him the option to alter it.

Insight is not, in itself, the desired end of the therapeutic work. In order for it to be meaningful, to have real impact on a patient's life, all psychic phenomena that impede its implementation must be neutralized. This, the final step in anxiety-provoking psychotherapy, is the process of working through. According to Greenson it requires "analysis of those resistances and other factors which prevent insight from leading to significant and lasting changes in the patient." The therapeutic task involves "repetitive, progressive and elaborate explorations of those resistances," which ultimately culminate in insight that the patient can readily apply to his daily existence.

The techniques of confrontation, clarification, interpretation, and working through—in concert with suggestion, manipulation, and abreaction—constitute the foundation of psychoanalytic treatment.

(In fact, the descriptions of these techniques by Bibring and Greenson appear in their writings about traditional psychoanalysis.) I have discussed these therapeutic interventions in some detail in order to provide a theoretical framework for their application to the medical patient. However, let me again stress that the practice of biopsychosocial medicine does not seek to transform the treating physician into a psychiatrist. Only limited application of the anxiety-provoking model is called for in order to help patients accommodate psychologically to illness. The final case illustrates this form of medical psychotherapy.

Alan P. is a thirty-two-year-old single professor of business administration. For fourteen years he has suffered from severe ulcerative colitis, with an unpredictable, intermittently debilitating course. He has generally adapted well to his illness, although episodes of physical regression have been accompanied by periods of depression which have transiently interfered with his functioning. Aware of the emotional component of these regressions he has repeatedly been able to overcome them, utilizing a combination of supportive encouragement from family, friends, and physicians and a self-determined effort to proceed with his life. He talked openly of his fears about the progression of his colitis and of his self-disgust when immobilized by depression. What he did not recognize was his significant anger concerning his illness. Mr. P. was an obsessional man who was exceptionally plagued by the issue of control, particularly as it applied to his own aggression. He was chronically concerned with being too assertive, fearing his inability to control that feeling, as well as the devastating retaliation the overt expression of anger might provoke. Consequently, he used intellectualization, rationalization, and reaction formation to minimize or deny aggression. A generally maladaptive behavior, this had particular relevance to his illness, with consequent effects on its overall course. First, it was one factor that contributed to clinical flare-ups. As the following shows, Alan P. was unaware of this, perceiving "stress" as the major culprit in his regressions.

D: You said when you get hassled your symptoms get worse. Could you tell me some about that?

P: My colitis began when I was a senior in high school. It was the beginning of thinking about college, SATs, a lot of pressure. You know. It was a lot of tension getting ready to go, and at that time I developed diarrhea with spotty blood. Right away I wondered what was going on. I thought it had something to do with the pressure I was under, so I went to get checked out. . . . In college, there would be a week of exams, and that would really be a hassling time. I'd be uptight, staying up all night studying and getting ready for the exams. Then I'd have a real flare-up. I'd literally turn red inside. Those were bad times at school. . . . It would be a real pressure situation. Studying for exams, wondering what was going to be on the exams, getting ready, that type of thing. My symptoms would get much worse. . . . But I've come to deal with my illness. It used to be depressing with my peer group in college and all. It was a hassle to live with it. But I more or less accepted it, and I lived with it. It doesn't hassle me anymore.

D: How was it a hassle with them?

P: In college you'd have a lot of beer parties, wild times, stuff like that. You just can't participate in that, you've got to put the brakes on and say, "No, I can't go." When I was in college a lot of guys would watch out for me and tell me I shouldn't be drinking all this beer, etc.

D: They'd be trying to take care of you.

P: Right.

D: After that, were there any so-called "hassling situations" that would affect you?

P: Well, I was in business for myself. In a business situation, if I had hassles at the office or hassles with my contractors or something, then I would have to . . . (*pause*) most of the time I could handle the situation as it was happening. But the next day I'd be all destroyed inside.

D: What kind of situations?

P: Well, you might have a discrepancy in the contract, or they may want extra work done. Each individual person would have their own opinion of what you should be doing. You'd have to go to bat. You'd have to argue with these people. You'd have to hassle over the contract, renegotiate certain things that needed to be done. So you'd be up against things on a daily basis. After that was over I would pay for it, because of the hassling.

P: It must be pretty aggravating in business.

P: Well the stresses are there.

D: I mean in addition to the stresses. Someone says he'll do some work and then he changes his mind, things like that. Sometimes you must get pretty irritated dealing with people.

P: Well I don't know if that's true . . . but I sure don't like the hassles of having to go over contracts once they're signed, things like that.

D: It sounds to me like you get irritated in business. Also in school. I'm sure there was a lot of stress with exams, but didn't you also get annoyed that you had to spend all your time studying, with no time left for having fun?

P: Sometimes.

D: You know you strike me as someone who really doesn't like to admit it when he feels annoyed or frustrated. It's like you minimize those feelings when they come up.

P: I don't know. I think I have to get angry in business, not like teaching. But it is true I come from an easygoing family. We rarely fought.

D: You say you have to get angry in business, but again, it sounds to me like you get more annoyed by what you call hassles than you get angry at the people causing those hassles.

P: I don't know about that.

D: Well, that's the way it sounds to me.

In this part of the interview I relied heavily on confrontation and clarification, attempting to guide Mr. P. toward the notion that feelings of anger played a role in his physical illness. He was not particularly receptive to the idea. As the discussion began to degenerate into a debate I shifted back to his medical history, exploring the health of family members. After establishing their general good health, I pursued the patient's comment about his "easygoing" family. He informed me of his exceptionally good-natured parents who never lost their tempers and always responded to adversity and turmoil with equanimity. Two of his three younger siblings had similar temperaments; the youngest was rebellious, which the patient attributed to his "adolescent stage." Alan P. then returned to the debate about anger versus stress as a factor in his illness. He persisted in trying to prove his point that "hassles" were the cause of his various decompensations, and he described to me his good health during a recent vacation.

P: I spent the last summer in North Carolina, the Outer Banks. It was a very relaxed time for me.

D: Yes. How did you feel? How were you doing in general?

P: Good. Really good. I don't know if it was just my state of mind, but that sure helped. Three months on the beach. We had a lot of boating, water activities, ate a lot of lobster, drank a lot of beer, and it had no effect on me.

D: None?

P: No. I even took a reduced amount of prednisone—20 mg every other day—so it was a good quiet time when I didn't need as much medicine and I felt well.

D: You reduced the medicine?

P: Yes.

D: By yourself?

P: Yes.

D: You knew how you were feeling so you adjusted the medication accordingly.

P: Yes.

D: How did your gastroenterologist feel about it?

P: Well, when I first told him, he didn't think it was possible. He thought I had a serious case, and the reduced medications just wouldn't work. Certainly, once I got back to the city it wasn't enough. I had to go back to 20 mg a day. But while I was in North Carolina it was enough, sufficient to take the 20 mg every other day. It was a real relaxed time, strictly vacation time all the time.

I agreed with Mr. P. that his vacation had been therapeutic because it had removed him from the stresses of his business and teaching responsibilities. However, I suggested his trip had also afforded him respite from the frustrations and irritations of everyday life, alleviating the need for having to wrestle with any feelings of anger. He basically ignored my comment and reported the significant relapse that followed his vacation.

P: My health got so bad last year, really for the past year and a half it's been bad. Over the recent months it's built back up. I'm feeling better, working better. But it has been so hard I could hardly walk. I was immobilized.

D: From what? From pain? Weakness?

P: Mostly weakness. I was anemic, my blood counts were bad. I was really down and out. . . . I had seen a general practitioner for a cold that winter, and he looked at me and said, "Someday you're just not going to get up. You're going to go to sleep and just not get up. You need professional care right away." His immediate recommendation was to go into surgery and have my colon removed, to have a colostomy.

D: You were that sick.

P: Yes. But it got to a point where I got sick and tired of being sick. I wanted to get up and get going. I had been getting out, but I just couldn't get around because I was too weak. I'd try to go out, like trying to change a tire on a car, but I couldn't do it. That made me mad. I wanted to do it. So I went to see another gastroenterologist who told me he would get me on my feet, that he would get me going. I believed him. I just knew he could do it.

When I asked why he had not continued with his previous gastroenterologist he was somewhat vague. With prodding he admitted his disappointment in him. Mr. P. felt so well on his vacation and then fell so far so quickly. He could not comprehend his physician's inability to stem his physical decline, and he elected not to see him anymore. In his words, "If I don't have any confidence in a doctor, I usually don't hang around." In fact, he avoided all physicians for several months, vegetating at home in a precarious state of health. This behavior recapitulated his behavior with the general practitioner who cared for him at the outset of his illness. At that time the prescribed treatment alternated between advising Mr. P. to "take it easy" and hospitalizing him for several weeks to "quiet down my bowel," despite the fact that his symptoms were relatively stable. After a short while Alan P. left the general practitioner's care because "I didn't feel he really knew what was going on." His judgment may have been correct; however, it began a prolonged period when he avoided any medical care despite his progressive physical deterioration. He had a long-standing pattern of sullen withdrawal when angry. He was unaware of this pattern and, consequently, was unable to express appropriately the anger he felt toward his treating physicians.

I questioned Mr. P. about those physicians he had found helpful over the years. He began by telling me of his first gastroentrologist, a physician at his college health service.

> P: Dr. Q. had started a gastroenterology clinic. He was an excellent GI man who knew exactly what I was talking about . . . the symptoms, the medications, everything that I needed. I could mention to him my feeling, my problem, what it was. He medicated me—no steroids at that time, I hadn't had any prednisone yet—he used lomotil and a low-fiber diet. And no spicy foods. And it worked pretty well while I was in college. He was terrific.

Alan P. described his present physician in equally glowing terms, perceiving him as a "doer," someone to be "trusted implicitly." He welcomed this physician's reassurances, such as a guarantee to "get me back on my feet and going again." This positive transference had definite therapeutic benefits. However, Mr. P.'s inability to acknowledge negative feelings in the physician-patient relationship was also a source of potential dissension; in the past it prompted him to precipitately leave a physician's care. His reaction formation against the hostility felt toward his current gastroenterologist was exemplified in the following description of what Mr. P. termed "a recent setback."

P: Last week Dr. Q. did a liver biopsy. About three or four hours later I developed a fever, trembling; so blood cultures were taken. I had an infection in my blood. So I was treated with intravenous antibiotics, and I've been having trouble with that infection ever since.

D: The infection is in the liver?

P: It's believed to be.

D: Was it caused by the biopsy?

P: No. They believe the liver was already infected and that by biopsying the liver that triggered the infection and kicked it back into my system.

D: I see. What was recommended to treat the infection?

P: I have to take intravenous antibiotics, which means I have to stay ten days in the hospital.

D: How do you feel about that?

P: Well, so far this year and last year—spending Christmas in the hospital and a total of twenty-six days—I'm getting pretty sick and tired of this hospital. It's a nice place to visit, but I'd rather be out on the street.

D: Do you have any specific feelings about being in the hospital? Could you identify one type of feeling you might have?

P: A hospital is a good place if you're sick. It's a bad place to be if you're not that sick, sort of in between. Because for me it's very depressing to see the people that are really sick. It makes me want to get up and get going. It's a good initiative to get going.

D: Just being in the hospital gets you down. Looking around and seeing the people. Is that a fair statement?

P: Especially the people who are immobile and need total care.

Because of specific changes in his clinical status, Alan P. had required a liver biopsy. Like all medical interventions, it carried certain risks—unfortunately, he developed a serious complication of the procedure. He quickly excused his revered physician from any responsibility, a singular accomplishment as he had performed the biopsy. Mr. P. discharged whatever anger he felt by displacing it onto the hospital as a whole. His sense of being "sick and tired of this hospital" was perfectly understandable; however, confining his anger to the institution conveniently protected his physician from any of his wrath. As previously mentioned, this was a potentially antitherapeutic situation, and it warranted a psychotherapeutic intervention. At this point in our meeting I felt a strong enough alliance prevailed to permit a challenge to Mr. P.'s defensive stance. I had already gathered enough data to identify his consistent pattern of avoiding angry affect and to define psychodynamic origins of that behavior. Consequently, I proceeded to confront and clarify his behavior and to interpret its origins.

D: You know you have a hard time being angry with people.

P: Hassles really affect me.

D: I didn't say "hassles," I said "angry." You don't even like the word.

P: Uh.

D: You have a pretty good sense of the way you feel about a lot of things. You know when you're down. You know when you're mad at yourself, like when you couldn't change the tire on the car. But when it comes to being angry with people, you seem to lose that good sense.

P: I'm really just pretty easygoing.

D: I think you try to be easygoing—that is, not angry—even when it's not possible. I hear it in your work. You hassle over contracts and then feel it the next day. I suspect you moderate a lot of feelings when you're hassling, and feel anger the next day in the form of symptoms. There's some connection there. And although you try to deny it, you do get angry at doctors. You just don't admit it to yourself. If you're disappointed in a doctor you ignore his advice or just stop seeing him. You even do a form of that with me. Two or three times I've tried to point out when I thought you were angry at some people, and you just changed the subject. For some reason you think there's something wrong with being openly angry. Maybe it frightens you? I don't really know.

P: I don't know (*pause*).

D: What don't you know?

P: I . . . I really don't know if there's any truth to what you're saying.

D: What do you think?

P: I don't know.

D: Well, at least that's a start. I mean disagreeing with me some. I can take it, and I'm sure you can too.

P: Uh-huh.

D: Do you think I'm hassling you? Do you feel the way you do when you're hassled?

P: Maybe a little.

D: Maybe you're a little angry, then. What do you think?

P: I don't know.

D: I think you come from a family that just doesn't like to show anger, and I think you learned the lesson well. I don't know what the concern is. Usually when people keep it to themselves they are either afraid of getting too angry—getting out of control somehow—or they are afraid someone will retaliate back. Or both. I don't know which it is with you. I think it's the former. You have this pattern, with doctors at least, of taking off when you're angry. You respond to anger by withdrawing or avoiding. I think—I may be wrong—but I think it's because you're afraid you'll get too angry with them because of their incompetence. What do you think?

P: I think . . . I'll have to think about it. I do know I tend to stay away from people I'm mad at. I just don't want the hassle. I'll think about it.

D: That's really all I'm asking you to do. After all, I've only met you once, and I don't propose that I'm preaching gospel. But I do think you have trouble getting openly angry and that you'd feel better if you were a little less of a saint.

P: What's wrong with being a saint?

D: Nothing—as long as you're a healthy one.

P: (*laughs*)

Alan P. was an intelligent, reasonable man, quite knowledgeable about his illness. He understood the general course and prognosis of colitis, as well as recommended medical regimens and indicated surgical interventions. In this regard he was an ideal patient. His impressive body of information alerted him to significant signs and symptoms, enhanced his understanding of, and compliance with, prescribed treatment, and motivated him to seek out competent, experienced physicians. Unfortunately, he was plagued by a glaring blind spot. He had great difficulty recognizing and subsequently dealing with angry affect; the ramifications for his health and general welfare were considerable. Unacknowledged hostility precipitated clinical regressions and interfered with the physician-patient relationship, causing periods of sullen withdrawal and self-neglect. This obvious pattern was quickly identified while obtaining his medical history, which revealed the psychological and social factors affecting and affected by his illness. The clinical interview also demonstrated that Mr. P. had ego strengths sufficient to tolerate and utilize introspective confrontation, indicating his appropriateness for anxiety-provoking medical psychotherapy as a means of dealing with his self-defeating anger. The therapeutic task required exploration and explication of the interrelationship between the impulse-anxiety-defense triad (the impulse being represented in this case by anger) and the configuration of object relationships in his past and present. Proceeding in this fashion, I offered some observations and judged his response to be favorable, as he agreed to "think about" what had been discussed. To expect immediate, enthusiastic

acceptance of my remarks—a rare occurrence in ongoing psychotherapy even with a motivated patient—would be naive. However,
Mr. P.'s willingness to consider statements about his difficulties with
anger suggested a favorable outcome to introspective work, which
was further indicated by his closing remarks.

P: We've gotten to a level where we're on a maintenance program. The
ulcerative colitis is being handled by steroids, watching the diet, or
monitoring for any abnormal growths in the colon. I found this time
that maybe he's (Dr. Q.) finally limited. He's to the point where he
can maintain a good healthy feeling, but I don't know about the
future. In the future I think I'll need some kind of surgery, and he
hasn't talked about that at all. His opinion is that as long as you're
doing well, let's continue to do well and keep it that way. . . .

D: Well what do you see in the future for you?

P: Well, I've done relatively well for the fourteen years with ulcerative
colitis. Usually you can go ten years, and surgery has to happen. Now
since I'm on a regular steroid program, and I've turned thirty, the
statistics are against me. Most thirty- [or] thirty-one-year-olds, the
numbers start going against them. So what we have to watch out for
is cancer, any type of growth in there. Of course, if that should show
up, it would mean immediate surgery. It's inconceivable I can spend
twenty years on steroids, so something will have to be done in the
future in the way of surgery.

D: How far into the future do you see that?

P: I think within three to five years. . . .

D: How do you think you'll tolerate the surgery?

P: I don't think I'll have any trouble because I'm an adaptor. I can get
along in any situation. . . . I don't think I'll have any problem with
the surgery. Hopefully, I'll be able to live normally with a good
energy level. That's the main thing. I have to keep that level up so I
can function day-to-day.

D: You're basically optimistic about the future?

P: Yes, definitely. Though it's too bad we're not into *Star Trek* medicine
yet. But we're doing pretty well, I think.

D: *Star Trek* medicine would make life easier for patients and doctors.

P: Definitely. But a lot more so for patients.

Suggestion, confrontation, clarification, and interpretation—
fundamental psychotherapeutic techniques—were successfully utilized in the context of obtaining a medical history to help this
patient accommodate to all of the emotions concerned with his
illness.

Psychiatry has long recognized the inseparable association between disorders of the mind and body. Breuer and Freud underscored the connection between symptoms defined as either physical or emotional in *Studies on Hysteria* (1893). Freud subsequently discussed therapeutic implications of this interrelationship in lengthy case histories, such as Dora (1905) and the Wolfman (1918). Adolf Meyer's theory of psychobiology emphasized the positive and adverse effects of environmental phenomena on individuals. His painstaking review of everyday details in an individual's life, organized into expansive life charts, demonstrated how that social matrix interfaced with intrapsychic and biologic forces to define the unique disease state in a given individual. The Holmes-Rahe life stress scale can be viewed as an abbreviated, standardized version of these life charts. Both Dunbar and Alexander studied the relationship between personality types and traditional psychosomatic illnesses—bronchial asthma, peptic ulcer disease, ulcerative colitis, essential hypertension, rheumatoid arthritis, thyrotoxicosis, and migraine headaches. Deutsch and Murphy treated the same patient population with sector therapy, a form of psychotherapy that was based on classic analytic theory but that greatly modified the technique of psychoanalysis.

Recent years have witnessed a broader based investigation of mind-body relationships, conducted primarily by internists and psychiatrists. Sophisticated neurophysiologic and neuroendocrinologic research—including studies of stress (Selye 1950; Cannon 1932; and Wolff et al. 1950), immunologic response (Amkraut and Solomon 1974; Stein et al. 1976), and endocrinologic function (Whybrow and Silberfarb 1974; Kiely 1974)—and the work of Engel and the Rochester group are representative of this course. These endeavors have produced a more accurate appreciation of the connection between psychological and biologic events, such as an understanding of the link between exposure to excessive stress and the heightened susceptibility to cardiovascular disease in animals (Henry 1975) and humans (Cobb and Rose 1973). The development of more effective and diversified treatment modalities has paralleled such research.

Since World War II there has also been a growing interest in the role of the physician-patient relationship in the treatment of medical illness. Balint, one of the more active workers in this field, repeatedly demonstrated the importance of the physician's impact on patient care. In *The Doctor, His Patient and the Illness* (1957), he characterizes the physician as "the most frequently used drug in general practice." His survey of British general practitioners led him to the following conclusion concerning medical treatment: "It was not only the bottle of medicine or the box of pills that mattered, but the way the doctor gave them to the patient—in fact, the whole atmosphere in which the drug was given and taken."

Despite these historical precedents, much of the day-to-day practice of medicine continues to minimize the importance of psychosocial forces that positively and negatively influence patients' responses to disease. Widespread acceptance and persistence of the biomedical model highlights this shortcoming of the profession. Certainly there are many physicians responsive to the emotional needs of patients, as is reflected in the emergence of specialty areas such as adolescent medicine and family practice. However, such physicians are in the minority, and recent years have also witnessed the rapid evolution of a highly specialized technological medical world which has had a dehumanizing impact on the individual. Computerized axial tomography and treatment with monoclonal antibodies are significant diagnostic and therapeutic advances, but they have also focused the physician's attention on smaller, more compartmentalized aspects of the patient. An inverse relationship generally exists between this level of technological sophistication and the perception of the patient as a total person. And, as the preceding pages have repeatedly demonstrated, treating a patient's specific organic pathology is not synonymous with treating the patient.

Hopefully, having demonstrated the theoretical and practical legitimacy of the biopsychosocial model, this volume will prompt health care personnel to consider carefully the patient's mind while ministering to his diseased body. This is not a difficult task. It requires respectful, empathic, and active communication with the patient, which permits recognition of abnormal illness responses and determination of the illness dynamics contributing to those reactions. A knowledge of basic psychiatric principles then allows implementation of the appropriate type of medical psychotherapy, to deal with the detrimental effects of unacknowledged emotions accompanying the illness state. That this approach is necessary for optimal medical treatment is unquestionable. It also benefits health care personnel, who experience a more intimate relationship with patients when they appreciate them as unique individuals. Indeed, sharing emotions in this intense manner makes life generally more meaningful and gratifying.

References

Alexander F: Psychosomatic Medicine: Its Principles and Applications. New York, W. W. Norton, 1950

Alexander F, French T: Psychoanalytic Therapy. New York, Ronald Press, 1946

American Psychiatric Association: Diagnostic and Statistical Manual of Mental Disorders, 3rd ed. Washington, DC, American Psychiatric Association, 1980

Amkraut A, Solomon G: From the symbolic stimulus to the pathophysiologic response: immune mechanisms. Int J Psychiatry Med 5: 541–563, 1974

Balint M: The Doctor, His Patient and the Illness. New York, International Universities Press, 1957

Bibring E: Psychoanalysis and the dynamic psychotherapies. J Am Psychoanal Assoc 2:745–770, 1954

Bibring G, Kahana R: Lectures in Medical Psycotherapy. New York, International Universities Press, 1968

Breuer J, Freud S (1893): Studies in Hysteria, in The Standard Edition of the Complete Psychological Works of Sigmund Freud, vol 2. Translated and edited by Strachey J. London, Hogarth Press, 1955

Cannon W: Bodily Changes in Pain, Hunger, Fear and Rage. New York, Appleton-Century-Crofts, 1920

Cannon W: The Wisdom of the Body. New York, W. W. Norton, 1932

Cobb S, Rose R: Hypertension, peptic ulcer and diabetes in air traffic controllers. JAMA 224:489–492, 1973

Davanloo H (ed): Short Term Dynamic Psychotherapy. New York, Aronson, 1980

Deutsch F, Murphy W: The Clinical Interview, vol 1: Diagnosis. New York, International Universities Press, 1955

Deutsch F, Murphy W: The Clinical Interview, vol 2: Therapy. New York, International Universities Press, 1955

Dunbar F: Emotions and Bodily Changes. New York, Columbia University Press, 1935

Engel G: Psychological Development in Health and Disease. Philadelphia, W. B. Saunders Co, 1962

Engel G: A life-setting conducive to illness: the giving-up-given-up complex. Ann Intern Med 69:293, 1968

Engel G: Sudden death and the "medical model" in psychiatry. Canadian Psychiatric Association Journal 15:527–537, 1970

Engel G: Sudden and rapid death during psychological stress. Ann Intern Med 74:771–782, 1971

Engel G: The need for a new medical model: a challenge for biomedicine. Science 196:129–136, 1977

Engel G: The clinical application of the biopsychosocial model. Am J Psychiatry 137:535–544, 1980

Erikson E: Eight ages of man, in Childhood and Society. New York, W. W. Norton, 1963, pp 247–274

Frank J: Persuasion and Healing. Baltimore, Johns Hopkins University Press, 1961

Freud S (1905): Fragment of an analysis of a case of hysteria, in The Standard Edition of the Complete Psychological Works of Sigmund Freud, vol 7. Translated and edited by Strachey J. London, Hogarth Press, 1955, p 7

Freud S (1917): Mourning and Melancholia, in The Standard Edition of the Complete Psychological Works of Sigmund Freud, vol 14. Translated and edited by Strachey J. London, Hogarth Press, 1955, p 237

Freud S (1918): From the history of an infantile neurosis, in The Standard Edition of the Complete Psychological Works of Sigmund Freud, vol 17. Translated and edited by Strachey J. London, Hogarth Press, 1955, p 3

Freud S: Aspects of development and regression: etiology, in A General Introduction to Psychoanalysis. Edited by Riviere J. New York, Boni and Liveright, 1924

Greenson R: The Technique and Practice of Psychoanalysis, vol 1. New York, International Universities Press, 1967

Groves J: Taking care of the hateful patient. N Engl J Med 298:883–887, 1978

Harlow H, Harlow M: Psychopathology in monkeys, in Experimental Psychopathology: Recent Research and Theory. Edited by Kimmel H. New York, Academic Press, 1971

Henry J: The induction of acute and chronic cardiovascular disease in animals by psychosocial stimulation. Int J Psychiatry Med 6:147–158, 1975

Holmes T, Rahe R: The social readjustment rating scale. J Psychosom Res 11:213, 1967

Kahana R, Bibring G: Personality types in medical management, in Psychiatry and Medical Practice in a General Hospital. Edited by Zinberg N. New York, International Universities Press, 1964

Kiely W: From the symbolic stimulus to the pathophysiological response: neurophysiological mechanisms. Int J Psychiatry Med 5:517–529, 1974

Kübler-Ross E: On Death and Dying. New York, Macmillan, 1969

Lindemann E: Symptomatology and management of acute grief. Am J Psychiatry 101:141, 1944

Lipkowski Z: Psychiatry of somatic disease: epidemiology, pathogenesis, classification. Compr Psychiatry 16:105–124, 1975a

Lipkowski Z: Physical illness, the patient and his environment: psychosocial foundations of medicine, in American Handbook of Psychiatry, vol 4. Edited by Reiser M. New York, Basic Books, 1975b

Malan D: The Frontier of Brief Psychiatry. New York, Plenum, 1976

Mann J: Time-Limited Psychotherapy. Cambridge, Harvard University Press, 1973

Mann J, Goldman R: A Casebook in Time-Limited Psychotherapy. New York, McGraw-Hill, 1982

Mendelson M, Meyer E: Countertransference problems of the liaison psychiatrist. Psychosom Med 23:115–122, 1961

Meyer A: The Collected Papers of Adolf Meyer. Baltimore, Johns Hopkins University Press, 1950

Parsons T: The Social System. Glencoe, Ill, The Free Press, 1951

Rahe R: Subjects' recent life changes and their near future illness reports. Ann Clin Res 4:1–16, 1973

Rahe R: Epidemiological studies of life changes and illness. Int J Psychiatry Med 6:133–146, 1975

Reichard J: Teaching principles of medical psychology to medical house officers: methods and problems, in Psychiatry and Medical Practice in a General Hospital. Edited by Zinberg N. New York, International Universities Press, 1964

Reiser M: Changing theoretical concepts in psychosomatic medicine, in American Handbook of Psychiatry, vol 4. Edited by Reiser M. New York, Basic Books, 1975

Selye H: The general adaption syndrome and the diseases of adaptation. J Clin Endocrinol Metab 6:117–230, 1946

Selye H: Physiology and Pathology of Exposure to Stress. Montreal, Acta Press, 1950

Semrad E: Teaching Psychotherapy of Psychotic Patients. New York, Grune & Stratton, 1969

Sheehan D, Hackett T: Psychosomatic disorders, in The Harvard Guide to Modern Psychiatry. Edited by Nicholi A. Cambridge, Harvard University Press, 1978

Sifneos P: Short-Term Psychotherapy and Emotional Crisis. Cambridge, Harvard University Press, 1972

Sifneos P: Short-Term Dynamic Psychotherapy. New York, Plenum, 1979

Spitz R: Hospitalism: an inquiry into the genesis of psychiatric conditions in early childhood. Psychoanal Study Child 1:53–74, 1945

Spitz R: Anaclitic depression. Psychoanal Study Child 2:313–341, 1946

Stein M, Schiavi R, Camerino M: Influence of brain and behavior on the immune system. Science 191:435–440, 1976

Sullivan HS: The Psychiatric Interview. New York, W. W. Norton, 1954

Thomas L: The Youngest Science: Notes of a Medicine-Watcher. New York, Viking Press, 1983

Vaillant G: Adaptation to Life. Boston, Little, Brown and Co, 1977

Viederman M: The active dynamic interview and the supportive relationship. Compr Psychiatry 25:147–157, 1984

Whybrow P, Silberfarb P: Neuroendocrine mediating mechanisms: from the symbolic stimulus to the physiological response. Int J Psychiatry Med 5:531–539, 1974

Whittkower E: Historical perspective of contemporary psychosomatic medicine. Int J Psychiatry Med 5:309–319, 1974

Wolff H, Wolf S, Hare S (eds): Life Stress and Bodily Disease. Baltimore, Williams & Wilkins Co, 1950

Zola I: Socio-cultural factors in the seeking of medical aid: a progress report. Transcultural Psychiatric Research 14:62–65, 1963

Index